FREE VIDEO

HESI A² Essential Test Tips Video from Trivium Test Prep!

Dear Customer,

Thank you for purchasing from Trivium Test Prep! We're honored to help you prepare for your HESI A² exam.

To show our appreciation, we're offering a **FREE *HESI A² Essential Test Tips* Video by Trivium Test Prep**.* Our video includes 35 test preparation strategies that will make you successful on the HESI A². All we ask is that you email us your feedback and describe your experience with our product. Amazing, awful, or just so-so: we want to hear what you have to say!

To receive your **FREE *HESI A² Essential Test Tips* Video**, please email us at 5star@ triviumtestprep.com. Include "Free 5 Star" in the subject line and the following information in your email:

1. The title of the product you purchased.
2. Your rating from 1 – 5 (with 5 being the best).
3. Your feedback about the product, including how our materials helped you meet your goals and ways in which we can improve our products.
4. Your full name and shipping address so we can send your **FREE *HESI A² Essential Test Tips* Video**.

If you have any questions or concerns please feel free to contact us directly at 5star@triviumtestprep.com.

Thank you!

- Trivium Test Prep Team

*To get access to the free video please email us at 5star@triviumtestprep.com, and please follow the instructions above.

HESI A^2 STUDY GUIDE 2019–2020

Test Prep and Practice Test Questions for the HESI Admission Assessment Exam

TABLE OF CONTENTS

INTRODUCTION

Congratulations on your decision to join the field of nursing—few other professions are so rewarding! By purchasing this book, you've already taken the first step toward succeeding in your career. The next step is to do well on the HESI Admission Assessment (HESI A^2) exam, which will require you to demonstrate knowledge of high-school level reading, writing, math, and science.

This book will walk you through the important concepts in each of these subjects and also provide you with insider information on test strategies and tactics. Even if it's been years since you graduated from high school or cracked open a textbook, don't worry—this book contains everything you'll need for the HESI A^2.

WHAT'S ON THE TEST?

The HESI A^2 is an eight-section, computer-based exam. Different schools will require different sections as part of their applications, so you'll want to make sure you know what sections you need to take on test day.

You can work through the sections on the HESI A^2 in any order, so you should plan in advance how you'd like to tackle the test. Some students like to start with the section they find the hardest, while others like to focus their efforts on sections they know they'll do well on. The time limits listed below are recommendations by the administrators of the HESI A^2 exam. You do not need to strictly adhere to these suggestions, but these limits may be helpful as you practice pacing yourself for other board certification exams.

1. **Mathematics: 55 questions, 50 minutes**

   The Mathematics section of the HESI A^2 focuses on skills required for health care professionals. You will see questions on basic addition, subtraction, multiplication, and division. You will also need to have knowledge of roman numerals, calculating dosages, measurements, fractions, and proportions.

2. **Reading: 55 questions, 60 minutes**

   The Reading section assesses your ability to read, analyze, and comprehend short passages related to health and medicine. You will need to be able to identify the main idea of a passage, make inferences about that passage, and interpret information in the passage from context clues.

3. **Vocabulary: 55 questions, 50 minutes**

   You will be tested on your knowledge of words, specifically those relating to the health field (although not all questions will be health related).

4. **Grammar: 55 questions, 50 minutes**

   The Grammar section will test your knowledge of basic grammar, parts of speech, common grammatical errors, and sentence structure.

5. **Biology: 30 questions, 25 minutes**

   The Biology section covers topics such as cellular respiration, photosynthesis, genetics, biological molecules, and cells. This, and the other science sections, can be tricky because there are only thirty questions that cover a wide range of material.

6. **Chemistry: 30 questions, 25 minutes**

   The Chemistry section covers topics such as the periodic table, chemical equations, atomic structure, chemical bonding, nuclear chemistry, and chemical reactions.

7. **Anatomy and Physiology: 30 questions, 25 minutes**

   The Anatomy and Physiology section covers a wide spectrum of body systems, including the muscular, skeletal, nervous, renal/urinary, reproductive, endocrine, circulatory, and respiratory systems.

8. **Physics: 30 questions, 25 minutes**

   Very few test takers will actually have the physics section on their exam, as this is excluded by many colleges. If you do encounter it, you will be tested on mechanics, energy, forces, waves, and light. Even if you do have this section on your test, do not focus your efforts here, as mathematics and the other sciences are typically much more important.

   Other Unscored Sections

   You may also encounter other unscored sections on the HESI A^2 called *learner profile* exams. These exams will not be used as part of your score. Instead, they are designed to help students better understand their strengths and weaknesses, learning styles and habits, and other personality traits.

Each scored section on the HESI A^2 includes five pilot questions that are not scored. These questions are used by the writers of the HESI A^2 to test new material and will not count toward your final score. However, you won't know which questions these are as you're taking the test, so treat every question like it counts.

How is the HESI A^2 scored?

You cannot "pass" or "fail" the HESI A^2. Your score is simply indicative of your current level of comprehension. However, each school has its own entrance requirements, so check the requirements of the institutions that you want to attend. Also, each institution has different requirements regarding the sections of the test you will take; make sure to check that you're taking the proper exam before you spend your time studying for a subject that you won't necessarily need.

HOW DOES THIS BOOK WORK?

The subsequent chapters in this book are divided into those subjects covered on the HESI A^2 exam. This book is not intended to teach brand-new concepts—there is no way to cram all of that material into one book! Instead, we will help you recall all the information that you've already learned. Even more importantly, we'll show you how to apply that knowledge on the test. Each chapter includes an extensive review, with plenty of examples to make sure you understand the concepts. Finally, you'll have a full practice test at the end so you know for sure you're ready.

Now that you have a firm understanding of the exam and what is included our book, don't forget that learning how to study, as well as how to successfully pass an exam, is just as important as the content. Trivium Test Prep would like to remind you as you begin your studies that we are offering a **FREE *From Stress to Success* DVD**. Our DVD includes 35 test preparation strategies that will help keep you calm and collected before and during your big exam. All we ask is that you email us your feedback and describe your experience with our product. Amazing, awful, or just so-so: we want to hear what you have to say!

To receive your **FREE *From Stress to Success* DVD**, please email us at 5star@triviumtestprep.com. Include

"Free 5 Star" in the subject line and the following information in your email:

1. The title of the product you purchased.
2. Your rating from 1 – 5 (with 5 being the best).
3. Your feedback about the product, including how our materials helped you meet your goals and ways in which we can improve our products.
4. Your full name and shipping address so we can send your **FREE *From Stress to Success* DVD**.

We hope you find the rest of this study guide helpful.

MATHEMATICS

THE MOST COMMON MISTAKES

People make little mistakes all the time, but during a test those tiny mistakes can make the difference between a good score and a poor one. Watch out for these common mistakes that people make on the math section of the HESI A²:

- answering with the wrong sign (positive/negative)
- mixing up the order of operations
- misplacing a decimal
- not reading the question thoroughly (and therefore providing an answer that was not asked for)
- circling the wrong letter or filling in wrong circle choice

If you're thinking, *those ideas are just common sense*, that's exactly the point. Most of the mistakes made on the HESI A² are simple ones. But no matter how silly the mistake, a wrong answer still means a lost point on the test.

STRATEGIES FOR THE MATHEMATICS SECTION

Go Back to the Basics

First and foremost, practice your basic skills: sign changes, order of operations, simplifying fractions, and equation manipulation. These are the skills used most on the HESI A², though they are applied in different contexts. Remember that when it comes down to it, all math problems rely on the four basic skills of addition, subtraction, multiplication, and division. All you need to figure out is the order in which they're used to solve a problem.

Don't Rely on Mental Math

Using mental math is great for eliminating answer choices, but ALWAYS WRITE DOWN YOUR WORK! This cannot be stressed enough. Use whatever paper is provided; by writing and/or drawing out the problem, you are more likely to catch any mistakes. The act of writing things down also forces you to organize your calculations, leading to an improvement in your HESI A² score.

The Three-Times Rule

You should read each question at least three times to ensure you're using the correct information and answering the right question:

> Step one: Read the question and write out the given information.

> Step two: Read the question, set up your equation(s), and solve.

> Step three: Read the question and check that your answer makes sense (is the amount too large or small; is the answer in the correct unit of measure, etc.).

Make an Educated Guess

Eliminate those answer choices which you are relatively sure are incorrect, and then guess from the remaining choices. Educated guessing is critical to increasing your score.

NUMBERS AND OPERATIONS

Roman Numerals

The roman numeral system uses letters to represent numerical values, as shown below.

Table 1.1. Roman numerals

ROMAN NUMERAL	VALUE
I	1
V	5
X	10
L	50
C	100
D	500
M	1000

These seven numerals are combined to form numbers. Numerals are always arranged from greatest to least in value starting with the largest possible number. For example, the number 157 would be written as: 100 + 50 + 5 + 1 + 1 = CLVII, and the number 3,621 is written as 1000 + 1000 + 1000 + 500 + 100 + 10 + 10 + 1 = MMMDCXXI.

To avoid adding four of the same numeral in a row, subtraction is used. If a numeral with a smaller value is placed before a numeral with a larger value, the smaller number is subtracted from the bigger number. For example, the number 9 is written as IX (10 − 1 = 9). Since I has a value of 1 and it is placed before X, which has a value of 10, the number is found by subtracting 1 from 10.

Examples

1. Express the number 538 in roman numerals.

   538 = 500 + 30 + 8

   538 = 500 + 10 + 10 + 10 + 5 + 1 + 1 + 1

   538 = **DXXXVIII**

2. What number is expressed by the roman numeral CDVII?

   C = 100, D = 500, V = 5, I = 1, I = 1

   Since C comes before D, 100 is subtracted from 500.

   500 − 100 + 5 + 1 +1 = **407**

Positive and Negative Number Rules

Adding, multiplying, and dividing numbers can yield positive or negative values depending on the signs of the original numbers. Knowing these rules can help determine if your answer is correct.

(+) + (−) = the sign of the larger number

(−) + (−) = negative number

(−) × (−) = positive number

(−) × (+) = negative number

(−) ÷ (−) = positive number

(−) ÷ (+) = negative number

Examples

1. Find the product of −10 and 47.

   (−) × (+) = (−)

   −10 × 47 = **−470**

2. What is the sum of −65 and −32?

   (−) + (−) = (−)

   −65 + −32 = **−97**

3. Is the product of −7 and 4 less than −7, between −7 and 4, or greater than 4?

   (−) × (+) = (−)

   −7 × 4 = −28, which is **less than −7**

4. What is the value of −16 divided by 2.5?

$(−) ÷ (+) = (−)$

$−16 ÷ 2.5 = \mathbf{−6.4}$

Can you come up with a mnemonic device to help yourself remember the order of operations?

Order of Operations

Operations in a mathematical expression are always performed in a specific order, which is described by the acronym PEMDAS:

1. Parentheses
2. Exponents
3. Multiplication
4. Division
5. Addition
6. Subtraction

Perform the operations within parentheses first, and then address any exponents. After those steps, perform all multiplication and division. These are carried out from left to right as they appear in the problem.

Finally, do all required addition and subtraction, also from left to right as each operation appears in the problem.

Examples

1. Solve: $[−(2)^2 − (4 + 7)]$

First, complete operations within parentheses:

$−(2)^2 − (11)$

Second, calculate the value of exponential numbers:

$−(4) − (11)$

Finally, do addition and subtraction:

$−4 − 11 = \mathbf{−15}$

2. Solve: $(5)^2 ÷ 5 + 4 × 2$

First, calculate the value of exponential numbers:

$(25) ÷ 5 + 4 × 2$

Second, calculate division and multiplication from left to right:

$5 + 8$

Finally, do addition and subtraction:

$5 + 8 = \mathbf{13}$

3. Solve the expression: $15 × (4 + 8) − 3^3$

First, complete operations within parentheses:

$15 × (12) − 3^3$

Second, calculate the value of exponential numbers:

$15 \times (12) - 27$

Third, calculate division and multiplication from left to right:

$180 - 27$

Finally, do addition and subtraction from left to right:

$180 - 27 = \textbf{153}$

4. Solve the expression: $\left(\frac{5}{2} \times 4\right) + 23 - 4^2$

First, complete operations within parentheses:

$(10) + 23 - 4^2$

Second, calculate the value of exponential numbers:

$(10) + 23 - 16$

Finally, do addition and subtraction from left to right:

$(10) + 23 - 16$

$33 - 16 = \textbf{17}$

Greatest Common Factor

The greatest common factor (GCF) of a set of numbers is the largest number that can evenly divide into all of the numbers in the set. To find the GCF of a set, find all of the factors of each number in the set. A factor is a whole number that can be multiplied by another whole number to result in the original number. For example, the number 10 has four factors: 1, 2, 5, and 10. (When listing the factors of a number, remember to include 1 and the number itself.) The largest number that is a factor for each number in the set is the GCF.

Examples

1. Find the greatest common factor of 24 and 18.

   Factors of 24: 1, 2, 3, 4, 6, 8, 12, 24

   Factors of 18: 1, 2, 3, 6, 9, 18

   The greatest common factor is 6.

2. Find the greatest common factor of 121 and 44.

   Since these numbers are larger, it's easier to start with the smaller number when listing factors.

   Factors of 44: 1, 2, 4, 11, 22, 44

   Now, it's not necessary to list all of the factors of 121. Instead, we can eliminate those factors of 44 which do not divide evenly into 121:

   121 is not evenly divisible by 2, 4, 22, or 44 because it is an odd number. This leaves only 1 and 11 as common factors, so the **GCF is 11**.

3. First aid kits are being assembled at a summer camp. A complete first aid kit requires bandages, sutures, and sterilizing swabs, and each of the kits must be identical to other kits. If the camp's total supplies include 52 bandages, 13 sutures, and 39 sterilizing swabs, how many complete first aid kits can be assembled without having any leftover materials?

This problem is asking for the greatest common factor of 52, 13, and 39. The first step is to find all of the factors of the smallest number, 13.

Factors of 13: 1, 13

13 is a prime number, meaning that its only factors are 1 and itself. Next, we check to see if 13 is also a factor of 39 and 52:

$13 \times 2 = 26$

$13 \times 3 = 39$

$13 \times 4 = 52$

We can see that 39 and 52 are both multiples of 13. This means that **13 first aid kits can be made without having any leftover materials.**

4. Elena is making sundaes for her friends. She has 20 scoops of chocolate ice cream and 16 scoops of strawberry. If she wants to make identical sundaes and use all of her ice cream, how many sundaes can she make?

Arranging things into identical groups with no leftovers is always a tip that the problem calls for finding the greatest common factor. To find the GCF of 16 and 20, the first step is to factor both numbers:

Factors of 16: 1, 2, 4, 8, 16

Factors of 20: 1, 2, 4, 5, 10, 20

From these lists, we see that 4 **is the GCF**. Elena can make 4 sundaes, each with 5 scoops of chocolate ice cream and 4 scoops of strawberry. Any other combination would result in leftover ice cream or sundaes that are not identical.

Comparison of Rational Numbers

Number comparison problems present numbers in different formats and ask which is larger or smaller, or whether the numbers are equivalent. The important step in solving these problems is to convert the numbers to the same format so that it is easier to see how they compare. If numbers are given in the same format, or after they have been converted, determine which number is smaller or if the numbers are equal. Remember that for negative numbers, higher numbers are actually smaller.

The strategies for comparing numbers can also be used to put numbers in order from least to greatest (or vice versa).

Examples

1. Is $4\frac{3}{4}$ greater than, equal to, or less than $\frac{18}{4}$?

These numbers are in different formats—one is a mixed fraction and the other is just a fraction. So, the first step is to convert the mixed fraction to a fraction:

$$4\frac{3}{4} = 4 \times \frac{4}{4} + \frac{3}{4} = \frac{19}{4}$$

Once the mixed number is converted, it is easier to see that **$\frac{19}{4}$ is greater than $\frac{18}{4}$.**

2. Which of the following numbers has the greatest value: 104.56, 104.5, or 104.6?

These numbers are already in the same format, so the decimal values just need to be compared. Remember that zeros can be added after the decimal without changing the value, so the three numbers can be rewritten as:

104.56

104.50

104.60

From this list, it is clearer to see that **104.60 is the greatest** because 0.60 is larger than 0.50 and 0.56.

3. Is 65% greater than, less than, or equal to $\frac{13}{20}$?

The first step is to convert the numbers into the same format. 65% is the same as $\frac{65}{100}$.

Next, the fractions need to be converted to have the same denominator. It is difficult to compare fractions with different denominators. Using a factor of $\frac{5}{5}$ on the second fraction will give common denominators:

$$\frac{13}{20} \times \frac{5}{5} = \frac{65}{100}.$$

Now, it is easy to see that **the numbers are equivalent**.

Units of Measurement

You are expected to memorize some units of measurement. These are given below. When doing unit conversion problems (i.e., when converting one unit to another), find the conversion factor, then apply that factor to the given measurement to find the new units.

You'll be given conversion factors if they're needed for a problem, but it's still good to familiarize yourself with common ones before the test.

CONTINUE

Table 1.2. Unit prefixes

PREFIX	SYMBOL	MULTIPLICATION FACTOR
tera	T	1,000,000,000,000
giga	G	1,000,000,000
mega	M	1,000,000
kilo	k	1,000
hecto	h	100
deca	da	10
base unit	--	--
deci	d	0.1
centi	c	0.01
milli	m	0.001
micro	μ	0.0000001
nano	n	0.0000000001
pico	p	0.0000000000001

Table 1.3. Units and conversion factors

DIMENSION	AMERICAN	SI
length	inch/foot/yard/mile	meter
mass	ounce/pound/ton	gram
volume	cup/pint/quart/gallon	liter
force	pound-force	newton
pressure	pound-force per square inch	pascal
work and energy	cal/British thermal unit	joule
temperature	Fahrenheit	kelvin
charge	faraday	coulomb

CONVERSION FACTORS

1 in. = 2.54 cm	1 lb. = 0.454 kg
1 yd. = 0.914 m	1 cal = 4.19 J
1 mi. = 1.61 km	$1°F = \frac{5}{9}(°F - 32°C)$
1 gal. = 3.785 L	$1 cm^3 = 1 mL$
1 oz. = 28.35 g	1 hr = 3600 s

Examples

1. A fence measures 15 ft. long. How many yards long is the fence?

   1 yd. = 3 ft.

   $\frac{15}{3} =$ **5 yd.**

2. A pitcher can hold 24 cups. How many gallons can it hold?

   1 gal. = 16 cups

   $\frac{24}{16} =$ **1.5 gallons**

3. A spool of wire holds 144 in. of wire. If Mario has 3 spools, how many feet of wire does he have?

12 in. = 1 ft.

$\frac{144}{12} = 12$ ft.

12 ft. × 3 spools = **36 ft. of wire**

4. A ball rolling across a table travels 6 inches per second. How many feet will it travel in 1 minute?

This problem can be worked in two steps: finding how many inches are covered in 1 minute, and then converting that value to feet. It can also be worked the opposite way, by finding how many feet it travels in 1 second and then converting that to feet traveled per minute. The first method is shown below.

1 min. = 60 sec.

(6 in.)/(sec.) × 60 s = 360 in.

1 ft. = 12 in.

(360 in.)/(12 in.) = **30 ft.**

5. How many millimeters are in 0.5 m?

1 meter = 1000 mm

0.5 meters = **500 mm**

6. A lead ball weighs 38 g. How many kilograms does it weigh?

1 kg = 1000 g

$\frac{38}{1000}$ g = **0.038 kg**

7. How many cubic centimeters are in 10 L?

1 L = 1000 ml

10 L = 1000 ml × 10

10 L = **10,000 ml or cm³**

8. Jennifer's pencil was initially 10 centimeters long. After she sharpened it, it was 9.6 centimeters long. How many millimeters did she lose from her pencil by sharpening it?

1 cm = 10 mm

10 cm − 9.6 cm = 0.4 cm lost

0.4 cm = 10 × .4 mm = **4 mm were lost**

Decimals and Fractions

ADDING AND SUBTRACTING DECIMALS

When adding and subtracting decimals, line up the numbers so that the decimals are aligned. You want to subtract the ones place from the ones place, the tenths place from the tenths place, etc.

Examples

1. Find the sum of 17.07 and 2.52.

$$\begin{array}{r} 17.07 \\ +\ \ 2.52 \\ \hline = \mathbf{19.59} \end{array}$$

2. Jeannette has 7.4 gallons of gas in her tank. After driving, she has 6.8 gallons. How many gallons of gas did she use?

$$\begin{array}{r} 7.4 \\ -\ 6.8 \\ \hline = \mathbf{0.6\ gal.} \end{array}$$

Multiplying and Dividing Decimals

When multiplying decimals, start by multiplying the numbers normally. You can then determine the placement of the decimal point in the result by adding the number of digits after the decimal in each of the numbers you multiplied together.

When dividing decimals, you should move the decimal point in the divisor (the number you're dividing by) until it is a whole. You can then move the decimal in the dividend (the number you're dividing into) the same number of places in the same direction. Finally, divide the new numbers normally to get the correct answer.

Examples

1. What is the product of 0.25 and 1.4?

   $25 \times 14 = 350$

   There are 2 digits after the decimal in 0.25 and one digit after the decimal in 1.4. Therefore the product should have 3 digits after the decimal: **0.350** is the correct answer.

2. Find $0.8 \div 0.2$.

   Change 0.2 to 2 by moving the decimal one space to the right.

   Next, move the decimal one space to the right on the dividend. 0.8 becomes 8.

   Now, divide 8 by 2. $8 \div 2 = \mathbf{4}$

3. Find the quotient when 40 is divided by 0.25.

   First, change the divisor to a whole number: 0.25 becomes 25.

   Next, change the dividend to match the divisor by moving the decimal two spaces to the right, so 40 becomes 4000.

   Now divide: $4000 \div 25 = \mathbf{160}$

WORKING WITH FRACTIONS

FRACTIONS are made up of two parts: the **NUMERATOR**, which appears above the bar, and the **DENOMINATOR**, which is below it. If a fraction is in its **SIMPLEST FORM**, the numerator and the denominator share no common factors. A fraction with a numerator larger than its denominator is an **IMPROPER FRACTION**; when the denominator is larger, it's a **PROPER FRACTION**.

Improper fractions can be converted into proper fractions by dividing the numerator by the denominator. The resulting whole number is placed to the left of the fraction, and the remainder becomes the new numerator; the denominator does not change. The new number is called a **MIXED NUMBER** because it contains a whole number and a fraction. Mixed numbers can be turned into improper fractions through the reverse process: multiply the whole number by the denominator and add the numerator to get the new numerator.

Examples

1. Simplify the fraction $\frac{121}{77}$.

121 and 77 share a common factor of 11. So, if we divide each by 11 we can simplify the fraction:

$$\frac{121}{77} = \frac{11}{11} \times \frac{11}{7} = \frac{11}{7}$$

2. Convert $\frac{37}{5}$ into a proper fraction.

Start by dividing the numerator by the denominator:

$37 \div 5 = 7$ with a remainder of 2

Now build a mixed number with the whole number and the new numerator:

$$\frac{37}{5} = 7\frac{2}{5}$$

MULTIPLYING AND DIVIDING FRACTIONS

To multiply fractions, convert any mixed numbers into improper fractions and multiply the numerators together and the denominators together. Reduce to lowest terms if needed.

To divide fractions, first convert any mixed fractions into single fractions. Then, invert the second fraction so that the denominator and numerator are switched. Finally, multiply the numerators together and the denominators together.

Inverting a fraction changes multiplication to division:
$$\frac{a}{b} \div \frac{c}{d} = \frac{a}{b} \times \frac{d}{c} = \frac{ad}{bc}$$

Examples

1. What is the product of $\frac{1}{12}$ and $\frac{6}{8}$?

Simply multiply the numerators together and the denominators together, then reduce:

$$\frac{1}{12} \times \frac{6}{8} = \frac{6}{96} = \frac{1}{16}$$

Sometimes it's easier to reduce fractions before multiplying if you can:

$$\frac{1}{12} \times \frac{6}{8} = \frac{1}{12} \times \frac{3}{4} = \frac{3}{48} = \frac{1}{16}$$

2. Find $\frac{7}{8} \div \frac{1}{4}$.

For a fraction division problem, invert the second fraction and then multiply and reduce:

$$\frac{7}{8} \div \frac{1}{4} = \frac{7}{8} \times \frac{4}{1} = \frac{28}{8} = \frac{7}{2}$$

The quotient is the result you get when you divide two numbers.

3. What is the quotient of $\frac{2}{5} \div 1\frac{1}{5}$?

This is a fraction division problem, so the first step is to convert the mixed number to an improper fraction:

$$1\frac{1}{5} = \frac{5 \times 1}{5} + \frac{1}{5} = \frac{6}{5}$$

Now, divide the fractions. Remember to invert the second fraction, and then multiply normally:

$$\frac{2}{5} \div \frac{6}{5} = \frac{2}{5} \times \frac{5}{6} = \frac{10}{30} = \frac{1}{3}$$

4. A recipe calls for $\frac{1}{4}$ cup of sugar. If 8.5 batches of the recipe are needed, how many cups of sugar will be used?

This is a fraction multiplication problem: $\frac{1}{4} \times 8\frac{1}{2}$.

First, we need to convert the mixed number into a proper fraction:

$$8\frac{1}{2} = \frac{8 \times 2}{2} + \frac{1}{2} = \frac{17}{2}$$

Now, multiply the fractions across the numerators and denominators, and then reduce:

$$\frac{1}{4} \times 8\frac{1}{2} = \frac{1}{4} \times \frac{17}{2} = \frac{17}{8} \text{ cups of sugar}$$

ADDING AND SUBTRACTING FRACTIONS

Adding and subtracting fractions requires a COMMON DENOMINATOR. To find the common denominator, you can multiply each fraction by the number 1. With fractions, any number over itself (e.g., $\frac{5}{5}$, $\frac{12}{12}$, etc.) is equivalent to 1, so multiplying by such a fraction can change the denominator without changing the value of the fraction. Once the denominators are the same, the numerators can be added or subtracted.

To add mixed numbers, you can first add the whole numbers and then the fractions. To subtract mixed numbers, convert each number to an improper fraction, then subtract the numerators.

Examples

1. Simplify the expression $\frac{2}{3} - \frac{1}{5}$.

   First, multiply each fraction by a factor of 1 to get a common denominator. How do you know which factor of 1 to use? Look at the other fraction and use the number found in that denominator:

   $$\frac{2}{3} - \frac{1}{5} = \frac{2}{3}\left(\frac{5}{5}\right) - \frac{1}{5}\left(\frac{3}{3}\right) = \frac{10}{15} - \frac{3}{15}$$

   Once the fractions have a common denominator, simply subtract the numerators:

   $$\frac{10}{15} - \frac{3}{15} = \frac{\textbf{7}}{\textbf{15}}$$

🔒

The phrase *simplify the expression* just means you need to perform all the operations in the expression.

2. Find $2\frac{1}{3} - \frac{3}{2}$.

   This is a fraction subtraction problem with a mixed number, so the first step is to convert the mixed number to an improper fraction:

   $$2\frac{1}{3} = \frac{2 \times 3}{3} + \frac{1}{3} = \frac{7}{3}$$

   Next, convert each fraction so they share a common denominator:

   $$\frac{7}{3} \times \frac{2}{2} = \frac{14}{6}$$
   $$\frac{3}{2} \times \frac{3}{3} = \frac{9}{6}$$

   Now, subtract the fractions by subtracting the numerators:

   $$\frac{14}{6} - \frac{9}{6} = \frac{\textbf{5}}{\textbf{6}}$$

3. Find the sum of $\frac{9}{16}$, $\frac{1}{2}$, and $\frac{7}{4}$.

   For this fraction addition problem, we need to find a common denominator. Notice that 2 and 4 are both factors of 16, so 16 can be the common denominator:

   $$\frac{1}{2} \times \frac{8}{8} = \frac{8}{16}$$
   $$\frac{7}{4} \times \frac{4}{4} = \frac{28}{16}$$
   $$\frac{9}{16} + \frac{8}{16} + \frac{28}{16} = \frac{\textbf{45}}{\textbf{16}}$$

4. Sabrina has $\frac{2}{3}$ of a can of red paint. Her friend Amos has $\frac{1}{6}$ of a can. How much red paint do they have combined?

   To add fractions, make sure that they have a common denominator. Since 3 is a factor of 6, 6 can be the common denominator:

   $$\frac{2}{3} \times \frac{2}{2} = \frac{4}{6}$$

   Now, add the numerators:

   $$\frac{4}{6} + \frac{1}{6} = \frac{\textbf{5}}{\textbf{6}} \textbf{ of a can}$$

→
CONTINUE

CONVERTING FRACTIONS TO DECIMALS

Calculators are not allowed on the HESI A², which can make handling fractions and decimals intimidating for many test takers. However, there are several techniques you can use to help you convert between the two forms.

The first thing to do is simply memorize common decimals and their fractional equivalents; a list of these is given in Table 3.4. With these values, it's possible to convert more complicated fractions as well. For example, $\frac{2}{5}$ is just $\frac{1}{5}$ multiplied by 2, so $\frac{2}{5} = 0.2 \times 2 = 0.4$.

Table 1.4. Common decimals and fractions

FRACTION	DECIMAL
$\frac{1}{2}$	0.5
$\frac{1}{3}$	$0.\overline{33}$
$\frac{1}{4}$	0.25
$\frac{1}{5}$	0.2
$\frac{1}{6}$	$0.1\overline{66}$
$\frac{1}{7}$	$0.\overline{142857}$
$\frac{1}{8}$	0.125
$\frac{1}{9}$	$0.\overline{11}$
$\frac{1}{10}$	0.1

Knowledge of common decimal equivalents to fractions can also help you estimate. This skill can be particularly helpful on multiple-choice tests like the HESI A², where excluding incorrect answers can be just as helpful as knowing how to find the right one. For example, to find $\frac{5}{8}$ in decimal form for an answer, you can eliminate any answers less than 0.5 because $\frac{4}{8} = 0.5$. You may also know that $\frac{6}{8}$ is the same as $\frac{3}{4}$ or 0.75, so anything above 0.75 can be eliminated as well.

Another helpful trick can be used if the denominator is easily divisible by 100: in the fraction $\frac{9}{20}$, you know 20 goes into 100 five times, so you can multiply the top and bottom by 5 to get $\frac{45}{100}$ or 0.45.

If none of these techniques work, you'll need to find the decimal by dividing the denominator by the numerator using long division.

Examples

1. Write $\frac{8}{18}$ as a decimal.

   The first step here is to simplify the fraction:
   $\frac{8}{18} = \frac{4}{9}$

Now it's clear that the fraction is a multiple of $\frac{1}{9}$, so you can easily find the decimal using a value you already know:

$$\frac{4}{9} = \frac{1}{9} \times 4 = 0.\overline{11} \times 4 = \mathbf{0.\overline{44}}$$

2. Write the fraction $\frac{3}{16}$ as a decimal.

None of the tricks above will work for this fraction, so you need to do long division:

```
        0.1875
  16 | 3.0000
     - 1 6
       1 40
     - 1 28
         120
     -   112
          80
     -    80
           0
```

The decimal will go in front of the answer, so now you know that $\frac{3}{16} = \mathbf{0.1875}$.

CONVERTING DECIMALS TO FRACTIONS

Converting a decimal into a fraction is more straightforward than the reverse process is. To convert a decimal, simply use the numbers that come after the decimal as the numerator in the fraction. The denominator will be a power of 10 that matches the place value for the original decimal. For example, the numerator for 0.46 would be 100 because the last number is in the tenths place; likewise, the denominator for 0.657 would be 1000 because the last number is in the thousandths place. Once this fraction has been set up, all that's left is to simplify it.

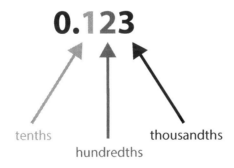

Figure 1.1. Simplified decimal

Example

Convert 0.45 into a fraction.

The last number in the decimal is in the hundredths place, so we can easily set up a fraction:

$$0.45 = \frac{45}{100}$$

The next step is to simply reduce the fraction down to the lowest common denominator. Here, both 45 and 100 are divisible by 5: 45 divided by 5 is 9, and 100 divided by 5 is 20. Therefore, you're left with:

$$\frac{45}{100} = \mathbf{\frac{9}{20}}$$

Ratios

A **RATIO** tells you how many of one thing exists in relation to the number of another thing. Unlike fractions, ratios do not give a part relative to a whole; instead, they compare two values. For example, if you have 3 apples and 4 oranges, the ratio of apples to oranges is 3 to 4. Ratios can be written using words (3 to 4), fractions $\left(\frac{3}{4}\right)$, or colons (3:4).

In order to work with ratios, it's helpful to rewrite them as a fraction expressing a part to a whole. For example, in the example above you have 7 total pieces of fruit, so the fraction of your fruit that are apples is $\frac{3}{7}$, and oranges make up $\frac{4}{7}$ of your fruit collection.

One last important thing to consider when working with ratios is the units of the values being compared. On the HESI A², you may be asked to rewrite a ratio using the same units on both sides. For example, you might have to rewrite the ratio 3 minutes to 7 seconds as 180 seconds to 7 seconds.

Examples

1. There are 90 voters in a room, and each is either a Democrat or a Republican. The ratio of Democrats to Republicans is 5:4. How many Republicans are there?

   We know that there are 5 Democrats for every 4 Republicans in the room, which means for every 9 people, 4 are Republicans.

   $5 + 4 = 9$

   Fraction of Democrats: $\frac{5}{9}$

   Fraction of Republicans: $\frac{4}{9}$

   If $\frac{4}{9}$ of the 90 voters are Republicans, then:

   $\frac{4}{9} \times 90 = \mathbf{40\ voters\ are\ Republicans}$

2. The ratio of students to teachers in a school is 15:1. If there are 38 teachers, how many students attend the school?

   To solve this ratio problem, we can simply multiply both sides of the ratio by the desired value to find the number of students that correspond to having 38 teachers:

   $\frac{15\ students}{1\ teacher} \times 38\ teachers = \mathbf{570\ students}$

Proportions

A **PROPORTION** is an equation which states that 2 ratios are equal. Proportions are usually written as 2 fractions joined by an equal sign $\left(\frac{a}{b} = \frac{c}{d}\right)$, but they can also be written using colons ($a : b :: c : d$). Note that in a proportion, the units must be the same in both numerators and in both denominators.

Often you will be given 3 of the values in a proportion and asked to find the 4th. In these types of problems, you can solve for the missing variable by cross-multiplying—multiply the numerator of each fraction by the denominator of the other to get an equation with no fractions as shown below. You can then solve the equation using basic algebra. (For more on solving basic equations, see *Algebraic Expressions and Equations*.)

$$\frac{a}{b} = \frac{c}{d} \ \rightarrow \ ad = bc$$

You'll see ratios written using fractions and colons on the test.

Examples

1. A train traveling 120 miles takes 3 hours to get to its destination. How long will it take for the train to travel 180 miles?

   Start by setting up the proportion:

   $$\frac{120 \text{ miles}}{3 \text{ hours}} = \frac{180 \text{ miles}}{x \text{ hours}}$$

   Note that it doesn't matter which value is placed in the numerator or denominator, as long as it is the same on both sides. Now, solve for the missing quantity through cross–multiplication:

   120 miles × x hours = 3 hours × 180 miles

   Now solve the equation:

   $$x \text{ hours} = \frac{(3 \text{ hours}) \times (180 \text{ miles})}{120 \text{ miles}}$$

   x = 4.5 hours

2. One acre of wheat requires 500 gallons of water. How many acres can be watered with 2600 gallons?

   Set up the equation:

   $$\frac{1 \text{ acre}}{500 \text{ gal.}} = \frac{x \text{ acres}}{2600 \text{ gal.}}$$

   Then solve for x:

   $$x \text{ acres} = \frac{1 \text{ acre} \times 2600 \text{ gal.}}{500 \text{ gal.}}$$

   $x = \frac{26}{5}$ or **5.2 acres**

3. If $35 : 5 :: 49 : x$, find x.

   This problem presents two equivalent ratios that can be set up in a fraction equation:

   $$\frac{35}{5} = \frac{49}{x}$$

You can then cross-multiply to solve for x:

$$35x = 49 \times 5$$

$$x = 7$$

Percentages

A **PERCENT** is the ratio of a part to the whole. Questions may give the part and the whole and ask for the percent, or give the percent and the whole and ask for the part, or give the part and the percent and ask for the value of the whole. The equation for percentages can be rearranged to solve for any of these:

$$percent = \frac{part}{whole}$$

$$part = whole \times percent$$

$$whole = \frac{part}{percent}$$

In the equations above, the percent should always be expressed as a decimal. In order to convert a decimal into a percentage value, simply multiply it by 100. So, if you've read 5 pages (the part) of a 10-page article (the whole), you've read $\frac{5}{10}$ = 0.5 or 50%. (The percent sign (%) is used once the decimal has been multiplied by 100.)

Note that when solving these problems, the units for the part and the whole should be the same. If you're reading a book, saying you've read 5 pages out of 15 chapters doesn't make any sense.

The word *of* usually indicates what the whole is in a problem. For example, the problem might say *Ella ate two slices of the pizza*, which means the pizza is the whole.

Examples

1. 45 is 15% of what number?

   Set up the appropriate equation and solve. Don't forget to change 15% to a decimal value:

   $$whole = \frac{part}{percent} = \frac{45}{0.15} = \mathbf{300}$$

2. Jim spent 30% of his paycheck at the fair. He spent $15 for a hat, $30 for a shirt, and $20 playing games. How much was his check? (Round to nearest dollar.)

   Set up the appropriate equation and solve:

   $$whole = \frac{part}{percent} = \frac{15 + 30 + 20}{.30} = \mathbf{\$217.00}$$

3. What percent of 65 is 39?

   Set up the equation and solve:

   $$percent = \frac{part}{whole} = \frac{39}{65} = \mathbf{0.6 \text{ or } 60\%}$$

4. Greta and Max sell cable subscriptions. In a given month, Greta sells 45 subscriptions and Max sells 51. If 240 total subscriptions were sold in that month, what percent were not sold by Greta or Max?

You can use the information in the question to figure out what percentage of subscriptions were sold by Max and Greta:

$$percent = \frac{part}{whole} = \frac{(51 + 45)}{240} = \frac{96}{240} = 0.4 \text{ or } 40\%$$

However, the question asks how many subscriptions weren't sold by Max or Greta. If they sold 40%, then the other salespeople sold 100% − 40% = **60%**.

5. Grant needs to score 75% on an exam. If the exam has 45 questions, at least how many does he need to answer correctly?

Set up the equation and solve. Remember to convert 75% to a decimal value:

$part = whole \times percent = 45 \times 0.75 = 33.75$, so he needs to answer at least **34 questions correctly**.

Percent Change

PERCENT CHANGE problems will ask you to calculate how much a given quantity changed. The problems are solved in a similar way to regular percent problems, except that instead of using the *part* you'll use the *amount of change*. Note that the sign of the *amount of change* is important: if the original amount has increased the change will be positive, and if it has decreased the change will be negative. Again, in the equations below the percent is a decimal value; you need to multiply by 100 to get the actual percentage.

$$percent\ change = \frac{amount\ of\ change}{original\ amount}$$

$$amount\ of\ change = original\ amount \times percent\ change$$

$$original\ amount = \frac{amount\ of\ change}{percent\ change}$$

Examples

1. A computer software retailer marks up its games by 40% above the wholesale price when it sells them to customers. Find the price of a game for a customer if the game costs the retailer $25.

Set up the appropriate equation and solve:

amount of change = original amount x percent change = $25 \times 0.4 = 10$

If the amount of change is 10, that means the store adds a markup of $10, so the game costs:

$25 + $10 = **$35**

2. A golf shop pays its wholesaler $40 for a certain club, and then sells it to a golfer for $75. What is the markup rate?

First, calculate the amount of change:

$75 − 40 = 35$

Words that indicate a percent change problem:
- discount
- markup
- sale
- increase
- decrease

The same steps shown here can be used to find percent change for problems that don't involve money as well.

Now you can set up the equation and solve. (Note that *markup rate* is another way of saying *percent change*):

$$percent\ change = \frac{amount\ of\ change}{original\ amount} = \frac{35}{40} = 0.875 = \textbf{87.5\%}$$

3. A store charges a 40% markup on the shoes it sells. How much did the store pay for a pair of shoes purchased by a customer for $63?

   You're solving for the original price, but it's going to be tricky because you don't know the amount of change; you only know the new price. To solve, you need to create an expression for the amount of change:

   If *original amount* = x

   Then *amount of change* = $63 - x$

   Now you can plug these values into your equation:

   $$original\ amount = \frac{amount\ of\ change}{percent\ change}$$

   $$x = \frac{63 - x}{0.4}$$

   The last step is to solve for x:

   $$0.4x = 63 - x$$

   $$1.4x = 63$$

   $$x = 45$$

   The store paid **$45 for the shoes**.

4. An item originally priced at $55 is marked 25% off. What is the sale price?

   You've been asked to find the sale price, which means you need to solve for the amount of change first:

   amount of change = *original amount* × *percent change* → $55 \times 0.25 = 13.75$

   Using this amount, you can find the new price. Because it's on sale, we know the item will cost less than the original price:

   $$55 - 13.75 = 41.25$$

   The sale price is $41.25.

5. James wants to put in an 18 foot by 51 foot garden in his backyard. If he does, it will reduce the size of this yard by 24%. What will be the area of the remaining yard?

   This problem is tricky because you need to figure out what each number in the problem stands for. 24% is obviously the percent change, but what about the measurements in feet? If you multiply these values you get the area of the garden (for more on area see *Area and Perimeter*):

   $$18\ ft. \times 51\ ft. = 918\ ft.^2$$

   This 918 ft.² is the amount of change—it's how much smaller the lawn is. Now we can set up an equation:

   $$original\ amount = \frac{amount\ of\ change}{percent\ change} = \frac{918}{.24} = 3825$$

If the original lawn was 3825 ft.² and the garden is 918 ft.², then the remaining area is

$3825 - 918 = 2907$

The remaining lawn covers **2907 ft.²**

Probabilities

A **PROBABILITY** is found by dividing the number of desired outcomes by the number of total possible outcomes. As with percentages, a probability is the ratio of a part to a whole, with the whole being the total number of things that could happen, and the part being the number of those things that would be considered a success. Probabilities can be written using percentages (40%), decimals (0.4), fractions $\left(\frac{2}{5}\right)$, or in words (probability is 2 in 5).

$$probability = \frac{desired\ outcomes}{total\ possible\ outcomes}$$

Examples

1. A bag holds 3 blue marbles, 5 green marbles, and 7 red marbles. If you pick one marble from the bag, what is the probability it will be blue?

   Because there are 15 marbles in the bag (3 + 5 + 7), the total number of possible outcomes is 15. Of those outcomes, 3 would be blue marbles, which is the desired outcome. With that information you can set up an equation:

   $$probability = \frac{desired\ outcomes}{total\ possible\ outcomes} = \frac{3}{15} = \frac{1}{5}$$

   The probability is **1 in 5 or 0.2 that a blue marble is picked.**

2. A bag contains 75 balls. If the probability that a ball selected from the bag will be red is 0.6, how many red balls are in the bag?

   Because you're solving for desired outcomes (the number of red balls), first you need to rearrange the equation:

   $$probability = \frac{desired\ outcomes}{total\ possible\ outcomes} \rightarrow$$
   $$desired\ outcomes = probability \times total\ possible\ outcomes$$

   In this problem, the desired outcome is choosing a red ball, and the total possible outcomes are represented by the 75 total balls.

   $desired\ outcomes = 0.6 \times 75 = 45$

   There are **45 red balls in the bag.**

3. A theater has 230 seats: 75 seats are in the orchestra area, 100 seats are in the mezzanine, and 55 seats are in the balcony. If a ticket is selected at random, what is the probability that it will be for either a mezzanine or balcony seat?

In this problem, the desired outcome is a seat in either the mezzanine or balcony area, and the total possible outcomes are represented by the 230 total seats, so the equation should be written as:

$$probability = \frac{desired\,outcomes}{total\,possible\,outcomes} = \frac{100 + 55}{230} = \textbf{0.67}$$

4. The probability of selecting a student whose name begins with the letter *s* from a school attendance log is 7%. If there are 42 students whose names begin with *s* enrolled at the school, how many students attend the school?

Because you're solving for total possible outcomes (total number of students), first you need to rearrange the equation:

$$total\,possible\,outcomes = \frac{desired\,outcomes}{probability}$$

In this problem, you are given a probability (7% or 0.07) and the number of desired outcomes (42). These can be plugged into the equation to solve:

$$total\,possible\,outcomes = \frac{42}{0.07} = \textbf{600 students}$$

ALGEBRA

Algebraic Expressions and Equations

Algebraic expressions and equations include a VARIABLE, which is a letter standing in for a number. These expressions and equations are made up of TERMS, which are groups of numbers and variables (e.g., $2xy$). An EXPRESSION is simply a set of terms (e.g., $3x + 2xy$), while an EQUATION includes an equal sign (e.g., $3x + 2xy = 17$). When simplifying expressions or solving algebraic equations, you'll need to use many different mathematical properties and operations, including addition, subtraction, multiplication, division, exponents, roots, distribution, and the order of operations.

EVALUATING ALGEBRAIC EXPRESSIONS

To evaluate an algebraic expression, simply plug the given value(s) in for the appropriate variable(s) in the expression.

Example

Evaluate $2x + 6y - 3z$ if , $x = 2$, $y = 4$, and $z = -3$.

Plug in each number for the correct variable and simplify:

$2x + 6y - 3z = 2(2) + 6(4) - 3(-3) = 4 + 24 + 9 = \textbf{37}$

ADDING AND SUBTRACTING TERMS

Only LIKE TERMS, which have the exact same variable(s), can be added or subtracted. CONSTANTS are numbers without variables attached, and those can be added and subtracted together as well. When simplifying an expression, like terms should be added or subtracted so that no individual group of variables occurs in more than one term. For example, the expression $5x + 6xy$ is in its simplest form, while $5x + 6xy - 11xy$ is not because the term xy appears more than once.

Example

Simplify the expression $5xy + 7y + 2yz + 11xy - 5yz$.

Start by grouping together like terms:

$(5xy + 11xy) + (2yz - 5yz) + 7y$

Now you can add together each set of like terms:

$16xy + 7y - 3yz$

MULTIPLYING AND DIVIDING TERMS

To multiply a single term by another, simply multiply the coefficients and then multiply the variables. Remember that when multiplying variables with exponents, those exponents are added together. For example, $(x^5y)(x^3y^4) = x^8y^5$.

When multiplying a term by a set of terms inside parentheses, you need to **DISTRIBUTE** to each term inside the parentheses as shown below:

$$a(b + c) = ab + ac$$

Figure 1.2. Distribution

When variables occur in both the numerator and denominator of a fraction, they cancel each other out. So, a fraction with variables in its simplest form will not have the same variable on the top and bottom.

Examples

1. Simplify the expression $(3x^4y^2z)(2y^4z^5)$.

   Multiply the coefficients and variables together:

   $3 \times 2 = 6$

   $y^2 \times y^4 = y^6$

   $z \times z^5 = z^6$

   Now put all the terms back together:

   $6x^4y^6z^6$

2. Simplify the expression: $(2y^2)(y^3 + 2xy^2z + 4z)$

   Multiply each term inside the parentheses by the term $2y^2$:

   $(2y^2)(y^3 + 2xy^2z + 4z)$

   $(2y^2 \times y^3) + (2y^2 \times 2xy^2z) \times (2y^2 \times 4z)$

   $2y^5 + 4xy^4z + 8y^2z$

3. Simplify the expression: $(5x + 2)(3x + 3)$

   Use the acronym FOIL—First, Outer, Inner, Last—to multiply the terms:

First: $5x \times 3x = 15x^2$

Outer: $5x \times 3 = 15x$

Inner: $2 \times 3x = 6x$

Last: $2 \times 3 = 6$

Now combine like terms:

$15x^2 + 21x + 6$

4. Simplify the expression: $\frac{2x^4y^3z}{8x^2z^2}$

Simplify by looking at each variable and crossing out those that appear in the numerator and denominator:

$\frac{2}{8} = \frac{1}{4}$

$\frac{x^4}{x^2} = \frac{x^2}{1}$

$\frac{z}{z^2} = \frac{1}{z}$

$\frac{2x^4y^3z}{8x^2z^2} = \frac{x^2y^3}{4z}$

When multiplying terms, add the exponents. When dividing, subtract the exponents.

Solving Equations

To solve an equation, you need to manipulate the terms on each side to isolate the variable, meaning if you want to find x, you have to get the x alone on one side of the equal sign. To do this, you'll need to use many of the tools discussed above: you might need to distribute, divide, add, or subtract like terms, or find common denominators.

Think of each side of the equation as the two sides of a see-saw. As long as the two people on each end weigh the same amount the see-saw will be balanced: if you have a 120 lb. person on each end, the see-saw is balanced. Giving each of them a 10 lb. rock to hold changes the weight on each end, but the see-saw itself stays balanced. Equations work the same way: you can add, subtract, multiply, or divide whatever you want as long as you do the same thing to both sides.

Most equations you'll see on the HESI A[2] can be solved using the same basic steps:

1. Distribute to get rid of parentheses.
2. Use the least common denominator to get rid of fractions.
3. Add/subtract like terms on either side.
4. Add/subtract so that constants appear on only one side of the equation.
5. Multiply/divide to isolate the variable.

Examples

1. Solve for x: $25x + 12 = 62$

   This equation has no parentheses, fractions, or like terms on the same side, so you can start by subtracting 12 from both sides of the equation:

   $25x + 12 = 62$

   $(25x + 12) - 12 = 62 - 12$

   $25x = 50$

   Now, divide by 25 to isolate the variable:

   $\frac{25x}{25} = \frac{50}{25}$

   $\mathbf{x = 2}$

2. Solve the following equation for x: $2x - 4(2x + 3) = 24$

   Start by distributing to get rid of the parentheses (don't forget to distribute the negative):

   $2x - 4(2x + 3) = 24 \rightarrow$

   $2x - 8x - 12 = 24$

   There are no fractions, so now you can join like terms:

   $2x - 8x - 12 = 24 \rightarrow$

   $-6x - 12 = 24$

   Now add 12 to both sides and divide by -6.

   $-6x - 12 = 24$

   $(-6x - 12) + 12 = 24 + 12 \rightarrow$

   $-6x = 36 \rightarrow$

   $\frac{-6x}{-6} = \frac{36}{-6}$

   $\mathbf{x = -6}$

3. Solve the following equation for x: $\frac{x}{3} + \frac{1}{2} = \frac{x}{6} - \frac{5}{12}$

   Start by multiplying by the least common denominator to get rid of the fractions:

   $\frac{x}{3} + \frac{1}{2} = \frac{x}{6} - \frac{5}{12} \rightarrow$

   $12\left(\frac{x}{3} + \frac{1}{2}\right) = 12\left(\frac{x}{6} - \frac{5}{12}\right) \rightarrow$

   $4x + 6 = 2x - 5$

   Now you can isolate x:

   $(4x + 6) - 6 = (2x - 5) - 6 \rightarrow$

   $4x = 2x - 11 \rightarrow$

   $(4x) - 2x = (2x - 11) - 2x \rightarrow$

   $2x = -11$

   $\mathbf{x = -\frac{11}{2}}$

4. Find the value of x: $2(x + y) - 7x = 14x + 3$

   This equation looks more difficult because it has 2 variables, but you can use the same steps to solve for x.

First, distribute to get rid of the parentheses and combine like terms:

$2(x + y) - 7x = 14x + 3 \rightarrow$

$2x + 2y - 7x = 14x + 3 \rightarrow$

$-5x + 2y = 14x + 3$

Now you can move the x terms to one side and everything else to the other, and then divide to isolate x:

$-5x + 2y = 14x + 3 \rightarrow$

$-19x = -2y + 3 \rightarrow$

$x = \dfrac{2y - 3}{19}$

Inequalities

INEQUALITIES look like equations, except that instead of having an equal sign, they have one of the following symbols:

> Greater than: The expression left of the symbol is larger than the expression on the right.

< Less than: The expression left of the symbol is smaller than the expression on the right.

≥ Greater than or equal to: The expression left of the symbol is larger than or equal to the expression on the right.

≤ Less than or equal to: The expression left of the symbol is less than or equal to the expression on the right.

Inequalities are solved like linear and algebraic equations. The only difference is that the symbol must be reversed when both sides of the equation are multiplied by a negative number.

See *Solving Equations* for step-by-step instructions on solving basic equations.

Example

Solve for x: $-7x + 2 < 6 - 5x$

Collect like terms on each side as you would for a regular equation:

$-7x + 2 < 6 - 5x \rightarrow$

$-2x < 4$

The direction of the sign switches when you divide by a negative number:

$-2x < 4 \rightarrow$

$x > -2$

Absolute Value

The ABSOLUTE VALUE of a number (represented by the symbol $|x|$) is its distance from zero, not its value. For example, $|3| = 3$, and $|-3| = 3$ because both 3 and –3 are three units from zero. The absolute value of a number is always positive.

Equations with absolute values will have two answers, so you need to set up two equations. The first is simply the equation with the absolute value symbol removed. For the second equation, isolate the absolute value on one side of the equation and multiply the other side of the equation by -1.

Examples

1. Solve for x: $|2x - 3| = x + 1$

Set up the first equation by removing the absolute value symbol, then solve for x:

$|2x - 3| = x + 1$

$2x - 3 = x + 1$

$x = 4$

For the second equation, remove the absolute value and multiply by -1:

$|2x - 3| = x + 1 \rightarrow$

$2x - 3 = -(x + 1) \rightarrow$

$2x - 3 = -x - 1 \rightarrow$

$3x = 2$

$x = \frac{2}{3}$

Both answers are correct, so the complete answer is **$x = 4$ or $\frac{2}{3}$**.

2. Solve for y: $2|y + 4| = 10$

Set up the first equation:

$2(y + 4) = 10 \rightarrow$

$y + 4 = 5 \rightarrow$

$y = 1$

Set up the second equation. Remember to isolate the absolute value before multiplying by -1:

$2|y + 4| = 10 \rightarrow$

$|y + 4| = 5 \rightarrow$

$y + 4 = -5$

$y = -9$

$y = 1$ or -9

Solving Word Problems

Any of the math concepts discussed here can be turned into a word problem, and you'll likely see word problems in various forms throughout the test. (In fact, you may have noticed that several examples in the ratio and proportion sections were word problems.)

The most important step in solving any word problem is to read the entire problem before beginning to solve it: one of the most commonly made mistakes on word problems is providing an answer to a question that wasn't asked. Also, remember that not all of the information given in a problem is always needed to solve it.

When working multiple-choice word problems like those on the HESI A², it's important to check your answer. Many of the incorrect choices will be answers that test takers arrive at by making common mistakes. So even if an answer you calculated is given as an answer choice, that doesn't necessarily mean you've worked the problem correctly—you have to check your own work to make sure.

GENERAL STEPS FOR WORD PROBLEM SOLVING

Step 1: Read the entire problem and determine what the question is asking for.

Step 2: List all of the given data and define the variables.

Step 3: Determine the formula(s) needed or set up equations from the information in the problem.

Step 4: Solve.

Step 5: Check your answer. (Is the amount too large or small? Are the answers in the correct unit of measure?)

KEY WORDS

Word problems generally contain key words that can help you determine what math processes may be required in order to solve them.

- Addition: added, combined, increased by, in all, total, perimeter, sum, and more than
- Subtraction: how much more, less than, fewer than, exceeds, difference, and decreased
- Multiplication: of, times, area, and product
- Division: distribute, share, average, per, out of, percent, and quotient
- Equals: is, was, are, amounts to, and were

BASIC WORD PROBLEMS

A word problem in algebra is just an equation or a set of equations described using words. Your task when solving these problems is to turn the "story" of the problem into mathematical equations.

Examples

1. A store owner bought a case of 48 backpacks for $476.00. He sold 17 of the backpacks in his store for $18 each, and the rest were sold to a school for $15 each. What was the salesman's profit?

   Start by listing all the data and defining the variable:

   total number of backpacks = 48

   cost of backpacks = $476.00

backpacks sold in store at price of $18 = 17

backpacks sold to school at a price of $15 = 48 − 17 = 31

total profit = x

Now set up an equation:

total profit = income − cost = $(306 + 465) − 476 = 295$

The store owner made a profit of **$295**.

2. Thirty students in Mr. Joyce's room are working on projects over 2 days. The first day, he gave them $\frac{3}{5}$ hour to work. On the second day, he gave them half as much time as the first day. How much time did each student have to work on the project?

   Start by listing all the data and defining your variables. Note that the number of students, while given in the problem, is not needed to find the answer:

   time on 1st day = $\frac{3}{5}$ hr. = 36 min.

   time on 2nd day = $\frac{1}{2}(36)$ = 18 min.

   total time = x

   Now set up the equation and solve:

   total time = time on 1st day + time on 2nd day

   $x = 36 + 18 = 54$

   The students had **54 minutes** to work on the projects.

⚠

Converting units can often help you avoid operations with fractions when dealing with time.

DISTANCE WORD PROBLEMS

Distance word problems involve something traveling at a constant or average speed. Whenever you read a problem that involves *how fast*, *how far*, or *for how long*, you should think of the distance equation, $d = rt$, where d stands for distance, r for rate (speed), and t for time.

These problems can be solved by setting up a grid with d, r, and t along the top and each moving object on the left. When setting up the grid, make sure the units are consistent. For example, if the distance is in meters and the time is in seconds, the rate should be meters per second.

Examples

1. Will drove from his home to the airport at an average speed of 30 mph. He then boarded a helicopter and flew to the hospital with an average speed of 60 mph. The entire distance was 150 miles, and the trip took 3 hours. Find the distance from the airport to the hospital.

   The first step is to set up a table and fill in a value for each variable:

   Table 1.5. Drive Time

	d	r	t
driving	d	30	t
flying	$150 - d$	60	$3 - t$

You can now set up equations for driving and flying. The first row gives the equation $d = 30t$, and the second row gives the equation $150 - d = 60(3 - t)$.

Next, you can solve this system of equations. Start by substituting for d in the second equation:

$d = 30t$

$150 - d = 60(3 - t) \rightarrow 150 - 30t = 60(3 - t)$

Now solve for t:

$150 - 30t = 180 - 60t$

$-30 = -30t$

$1 = t$

Although you've solved for t, you're not done yet. Notice that the problem asks for distance. So, you need to solve for d: what the problem asked for. It does not ask for time, but the time is needed to solve the problem.

Driving: $30t = 30$ miles

Flying: $150 - d = 120$ miles

The distance from the airport to the hospital is **120 miles**.

2. Two cyclists start at the same time from opposite ends of a course that is 45 miles long. One cyclist is riding at 14 mph and the second cyclist is riding at 16 mph. How long after they begin will they meet?

First, set up the table. The variable for time will be the same for each, because they will have been on the road for the same amount of time when they meet:

Table 1.6. Cyclist Times

	d	r	t
Cyclist #1	d	14	t
Cyclist #2	$45 - d$	16	t

Next set up two equations:

Cyclist #1: $d = 14t$

Cyclist #2: $45 - d = 16t$

Now substitute and solve:

$d = 14t$

$45 - d = 16t \rightarrow 45 - 14t = 16t$

$45 = 30t$

$t = 1.5$

They will meet **1.5 hr.** after they begin.

WORK PROBLEMS

WORK PROBLEMS involve situations where several people or machines are doing work at different rates. Your task is usually to figure out how long it will take these people or machines to complete a task while working together. The trick to doing work problems is to figure out how much of the project each person or machine completes in the same unit of time. For example, you might calculate how much of a wall a person can paint in 1 hour, or how many boxes an assembly line can pack in 1 minute.

Once you know that, you can set up an equation to solve for the total time. This equation usually has a form similar to the equation for distance, but here *work = rate × time*.

Examples

1. Bridget can clean an entire house in 12 hours while her brother Tom takes 8 hours. How long would it take for Bridget and Tom to clean 2 houses together?

   Start by figuring out how much of a house each sibling can clean on his or her own. Bridget can clean the house in 12 hours, so she can clean $\frac{1}{12}$ of the house in an hour. Using the same logic, Tom can clean $\frac{1}{8}$ of a house in an hour.

   By adding these values together, you get the fraction of the house they can clean together in an hour:

   $$\frac{1}{12} + \frac{1}{8} = \frac{5}{24}$$

   They can do $\frac{5}{24}$ of the job per hour.

   Now set up variables and an equation to solve:

   t = time spent cleaning (in hours)

   h = number of houses cleaned = 2

   work = rate × time

   $$h = \frac{5}{24}t \rightarrow$$

   $$2 = \frac{5}{24}t \rightarrow$$

   $$t = \frac{48}{5} = 9\frac{3}{5} \text{ hours}$$

See *Adding and Subtracting Fractions* for step-by-step instruction on operations with fractions.

2. Farmer Dan needs to water his cornfield. One hose can water a field 1.25 times faster than a second hose. When both hoses are opened, they water the field in 5 hours. How long would it take to water the field if only the second hose is used?

   In this problem you don't know the exact time, but you can still find the hourly rate as a variable:

   The first hose completes the job in f hours, so it waters $\frac{1}{f}$ field per hour. The slower hose waters the field in $1.25f$, so it waters the field in $\frac{1}{1.25f}$ hours. Together, they take 5 hours to water the field, so they water $\frac{1}{5}$ of the field per hour.

   Now you can set up the equations and solve:

   $$\frac{1}{f} + \frac{1}{1.25f} = \frac{1}{5} \rightarrow$$

   $$1.25f\left(\frac{1}{f} + \frac{1}{1.25f}\right) = 1.25f\left(\frac{1}{5}\right) \rightarrow$$

   $$1.25 + 1 = 0.25f$$

$$2.25 = 0.25f$$

$$f = 9$$

The fast hose takes 9 hours to water the cornfield. The slower hose takes $1.25(9) =$ **11.25 hours**.

3. Alex takes 2 hours to shine 500 silver spoons, and Julian takes 3 hours to shine 450 silver spoons. How long will they take, working together, to shine 1000 silver spoons?

Calculate how many spoons each man can shine per hour:

Alex: $\dfrac{500 \text{ spoons}}{2 \text{ hours}} = \dfrac{250 \text{ spoons}}{\text{hour}}$

Julian: $\dfrac{450 \text{ spoons}}{3 \text{ hours}} = \dfrac{150 \text{ spoons}}{\text{hour}}$

Together: $\dfrac{(250 + 150) \text{ spoons}}{\text{hour}} = \dfrac{400 \text{ spoons}}{\text{hour}}$

Now set up an equation to find the time it takes to shine 1000 spoons:

total time $= \dfrac{1 \text{ hour}}{400 \text{ spoons}} \times 1000 \text{ spoons} = \dfrac{1000}{400}$ hours $=$ **2.5 hours**

STATISTICS AND GEOMETRY

Graphs and Charts

These questions require you to interpret information from graphs and charts; they will be pretty straightforward as long as you pay careful attention to detail. There are several different graph and chart types that may appear on the HESI A².

BAR GRAPHS

BAR GRAPHS present the numbers of an item that exist in different categories. The categories are shown on the x-axis, and the number of items is shown on the y-axis. Bar graphs are usually used to easily compare amounts.

🔒 On the test you'll need to both read graphs and determine what kinds of graphs are appropriate for different situations.

Examples

1. The graph below shows rainfall in inches per month. Which month had the least amount of rainfall? Which had the most?

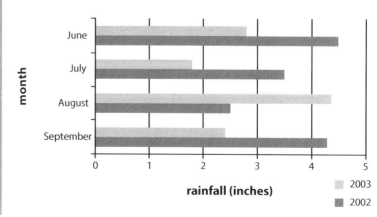

The shortest bar represents the month with the least rain, and the longest bar represents the month with the most rain: **July 2003 had the least**, and **June 2002 had the most**.

2. Using the graph below, how many more ice cream cones were sold in July than in September?

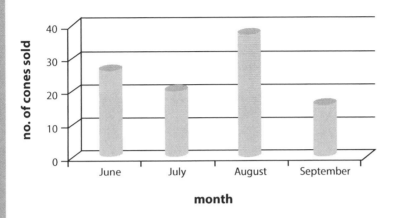

Tracing from the top of each bar to the scale on the left shows that sales in July were 20 and September sales were 15. So, **5 more cones were sold in July**.

Pie Charts

Pie charts present parts of a whole, and are often used with percentages. Together, all the slices of the pie add up to the total number of items, or 100%.

Examples

1. The pie chart below shows the distribution of birthdays in a class of students. How many students have birthdays in the spring or summer?

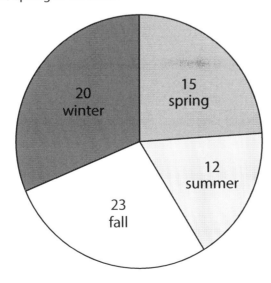

Fifteen students have birthdays in spring and 12 in winter, so there are **27 students** with birthdays in spring or summer.

2. Using the same Birthday Pie Chart in the example before, what percentage of students have birthdays in winter?

Use the equation for percent:

$$percent = \frac{part}{whole} = \frac{winter\ birthdays}{total\ birthdays} =$$

$$\frac{20}{20 + 15 + 23 + 12} = \frac{20}{70} = \frac{2}{7} = .286\ \text{or}\ \mathbf{28.6\%}$$

LINE GRAPHS

LINE GRAPHS show trends over time. The number of each item represented by the graph will be on the y-axis, and time will be on the x-axis.

Examples

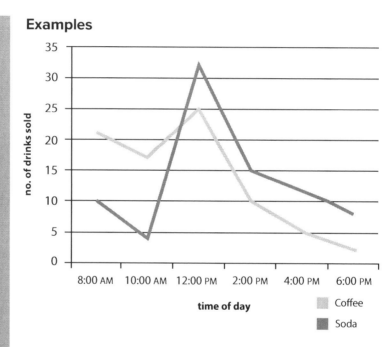

1. The line graph above shows beverage sales at an airport snack shop throughout the day. Which beverage sold more at 4:00 p.m.?

At 4:00 p.m., approximately 12 sodas and 5 coffees were sold, so more **soda** was sold.

2. At what time of day were the most beverages sold?

This question is asking for the time of day with the most sales of coffee and soda combined. It is not necessary to add up sales at each time of day to find the answer. Just from looking at the graph, you can see that sales for both beverages were highest at noon, so the answer must be **12:00 p.m.**

MEAN, MEDIAN, AND MODE

MEAN is a math term for average. To find the mean, total all the terms and divide by the number of terms. The MEDIAN is the middle number of a given set. To find the median, put the terms in numerical order; the middle number will be the median. In the case of a set of even numbers, the middle two numbers are averaged. MODE is the number which occurs most frequently within a given set.

It is possible to have more than one mode.

Examples

1. Find the mean of 24, 27, and 18.

   Add the terms, then divide by the number of terms:

   $mean = \frac{24 + 27 + 18}{3} = \textbf{23}$

2. The mean of three numbers is 45. If two of the numbers are 38 and 43, what is the third number?

   Set up the equation for mean with x representing the third number, then solve:

   $mean = \frac{38 + 43 + x}{3} = 45$

   $38 + 43 + x = 135$

   $x = \textbf{54}$

3. What is the median of 24, 27, and 18?

   Place the terms in order, then pick the middle term:

   18, 24, 27

   The median is **24**.

4. What is the median of 24, 27, 18, and 19?

   Place the terms in order. Because there are an even number of terms, the median will be the average of the middle 2 terms:

   18, 19, 24, 27

   $median = \frac{19 + 24}{2} = \textbf{21.5}$

5. What is the mode of 2, 5, 4, 4, 3, 2, 8, 9, 2, 7, 2, and 2?

   The mode is 2 because it appears the most within the set.

Area and Perimeter

AREA and PERIMETER problems will require you to use the equations shown in the table below to find either the area inside a shape or the distance around it (the perimeter). These equations will not be given on the test, so you need to have them memorized on test day.

Table 1.7. Equations

SHAPE	AREA	PERIMETER
circle	$A = \pi r^2$	$C = 2\pi r = \pi d$
triangle	$A = \dfrac{b \times h}{2}$	$P = s^1 + s^2 + s^3$
square	$A = s^2$	$P = 4s$
rectangle	$A = l \times w$	$P = 2l + 2w$

🔒
These equations aren't given to you on test day—you need to have them memorized.

Examples

1. A farmer has purchased 100 m of fencing to put around his rectangular garden. If one side of the garden is 20 m long and the other is 28 m, how much fencing will the farmer have left over?

   The perimeter of a rectangle is equal to twice its length plus twice its width:

   $P = 2(20) + 2(28) = 96$ m

   The farmer has 100 m of fencing, so he'll have 100 − 96 = **4 m** left.

2. Taylor is going to paint a square wall that is 3.5 m tall. What is the total area that Taylor will be painting?

   Each side of the square wall is 3.5 m:

   $A = 3.5^2 =$ **12.25 m²**

Pythagorean Theorem

Shapes with 3 sides are known as TRIANGLES. In addition to knowing the formulas for their area and perimeter, you should also know the Pythagorean theorem, which describes the relationship between the three sides (*a*, *b*, and *c*) of a right triangle:

$$a^2 + b^2 = c^2$$

Example

Erica is going to run a race in which she'll run 3 miles due north and 4 miles due east. She'll then run back to the starting line. How far will she run during this race?

One leg of her route (the triangle) is missing, but you can find its length using the Pythagorean theorem:

$a^2 + b^2 = c^2$

$3^2 + 4^2 = c^2$

$25 = c^2$

$c = 5$

Adding all 3 sides gives the length of the whole race:

$3 + 4 + 5 =$ **12 miles**

2

READING

The HESI A[2] Reading section will require you to read both non-fiction and fiction passages and then answer questions about them. These questions will fall into three main categories:

ABOUT THE AUTHOR: The question will ask about the author's attitude, thoughts, and opinions. When encountering a question asking specifically about the author, pay attention to context clues in the article. The answer may not be explicitly stated, but instead conveyed in the overall message.

PASSAGE FACTS: You must distinguish between facts and opinions presented in the passage. You may also be asked to identify specific information supplied by the author of the passage.

ADDITIONAL INFORMATION: These questions will have you look at what kind of information could be added to or was missing from the passage. They may also ask in what direction the passage was going. Questions may ask what statement could be added to strengthen the author's statement, or weaken it; they may also provide a fill-in-the-blank option to include a statement that is missing from, but fits with, the rest of the passage.

STRATEGIES

Despite the different types of questions you will face, there are some strategies for reading comprehension which apply across the board:

- Read the answer choices first, then read the passage. This will save you time, as you will know what to look out for as you read.

- Use the process of elimination. Some answer choices are obviously incorrect and are relatively easy to detect. After reading the passage, eliminate those blatantly incorrect answer choices; this increases your chance of finding the correct answer much more quickly.

- Avoid negative statements. Generally, test-makers will not make negative statements about anyone or anything. Statements will be either neutral or positive, so if it seems like an answer choice has a negative connotation, it is very likely that the answer is false.

THE MAIN IDEA

The main idea of a text is the purpose behind why a writer would choose to write a book, article, story, etc. Being able to find and understand the main idea is a critical skill necessary to comprehend and appreciate what you're reading.

Consider a political election. A candidate is running for office and plans to deliver a speech asserting her position on tax reform. The topic of the speech—tax reform—is clear to voters, and probably of interest to many. However, imagine that the candidate believes that taxes should be lowered. She is likely to assert this argument in her speech, supporting it with examples proving why lowering taxes would benefit the public and how it could be accomplished. While the topic of the speech would be tax reform, the benefit of lowering taxes would be the main idea. Other candidates may have different perspectives on the topic; they may believe that higher taxes are necessary, or that current taxes are adequate. It is likely that their speeches, while on the same topic of tax reform, would have different main ideas: different arguments likewise supported by different examples. Determining what a speaker, writer, or text is asserting about a specific issue will reveal the MAIN IDEA.

One more quick note: the HESI A² may also ask about a passage's THEME, which is similar to, but distinct from its topic. While a TOPIC is usually a specific *person, place, thing,* or *issue,* the theme is an *idea* or *concept* that the author refers back to frequently. Examples of common themes include ideas like the importance of family, the dangers of technology, and the beauty of nature.

There will be many questions on the HESI A² that require you to differentiate between the topic, theme, and main idea of a passage. Let's look at an example passage to see how you would answer these questions:

Topic: The subject of the passage.
Theme: An idea or concept the author refers to repeatedly.
Main idea: The argument the writer is making about the topic.

Babe Didrikson Zaharias, one of the most decorated female athletes of the twentieth century, is an inspiration for everyone. Born in 1911 in Beaumont, Texas, Zaharias lived in a time when women were considered second-class to men, but she never let that stop her from becoming a champion. Babe was one of seven children in a poor immigrant family and was competitive from an early age. As a child she excelled at most things she tried, especially sports, which continued into high school and beyond. After high school, Babe played amateur basketball for two years, and soon after began training in track and field. Despite the fact that women were only allowed to enter in three events, Babe represented the United States in the 1932 Los Angeles Olympics, and won two gold medals and one silver for track and field events.

In the early 1930s, Babe began playing golf, which earned her a legacy. The first tournament she entered was a men's only tournament; however she did not make the cut to play. Playing golf as an amateur was the only option for a woman at this time, since there was no professional women's league. Babe played as an amateur for a little over a decade, until she turned pro in 1947 for the Ladies Professional Golf Association (LPGA) of which she was a founding member. During her career as a golfer, Babe won eighty-two tournaments, amateur and professional, including the U.S. Women's Open, All-American Open, and British Women's Open Golf Tournament. In 1953, Babe was diagnosed with cancer, but fourteen weeks later, she played in a tournament. That year she won her third U.S. Women's Open. However by 1955, she didn't have the physicality to compete anymore, and she died of the disease in 1956.

The topic of this paragraph is obviously Babe Zaharias—the whole passage describes events from her life. Determining the main idea, however, requires a little more analysis. The passage describes Babe Zaharias' life, but the main idea of the paragraph is what it says about her life. To figure out the main idea, consider what the writer is saying about Babe Zaharias. The writer is saying that she's someone to admire—that's the main idea and what unites all the information in the paragraph. Lastly, what might the theme of the passage be? The writer refers to several broad concepts, including never giving up and overcoming the odds, both of which could be themes for the passage.

Two major indicators of the main idea of a paragraph or passage follow:

- It is a general idea; it applies to the more specific ideas in the passage. Every other sentence in a paragraph should be able to relate in some way to the main idea.

- It asserts a specific viewpoint that the author supports with facts, opinions, or other details. In other words, the main idea takes a stand.

Example

From so far away it's easy to imagine the surface of our solar system's planets as enigmas—how could we ever know what those far-flung planets really look like? It turns out, however, that scientists have a number of tools at their disposal that allow them to paint detailed pictures of many planets' surfaces. The topography of Venus, for example, has been explored by several space probes, including the Russian Venera landers and NASA's Magellan orbiter. These craft used imaging and radar to map the surface of the planet, identifying a whole host of features including volcanoes, craters, and a complex system of channels. Mars has similarly been mapped by space probes, including the famous Mars Rovers, which are automated vehicles that actually landed on the surface of Mars. These rovers have been used by NASA and other space agencies to study the geology, climate, and possible biology of the planet.

In addition to these long-range probes, NASA has also used its series of orbiting telescopes to study distant planets. These four massively powerful telescopes include the famous Hubble Space Telescope as well as the Compton Gamma Ray Observatory, Chandra X-Ray Observatory, and the Spitzer Space Telescope. Scientists can use these telescopes to examine planets using not only visible light but also infrared and near-infrared light, ultraviolet light, x-rays, and gamma rays.

Powerful telescopes aren't just found in space: NASA makes use of Earth-bound telescopes as well. Scientists at the National Radio Astronomy Observatory in Charlottesville, VA, have spent decades using radio imaging to build an incredibly detailed portrait of Venus' surface. In fact, Earth-bound telescopes offer a distinct advantage over orbiting telescopes because they allow scientists to capture data from a fixed point, which in turn allows them to effectively compare data collected over a long period of time.

Which of the following sentences best describes the main idea of the passage?

A) It's impossible to know what the surfaces of other planets are really like.

B) Telescopes are an important tool for scientists studying planets in our solar system.

C) Venus' surface has many of the same features as the Earth's, including volcanoes, craters, and channels.

D) Scientists use a variety of advanced technologies to study the surface of the planets in our solar system.

Answer A) can be eliminated because it directly contradicts the rest of the passage. Answers B) and C) can also be eliminated because they offer only specific details from the passage—while both choices contain details from the passage, neither is general enough to encompass the passage as a whole. **Only answer D) provides an assertion that is both backed up by the passage's content and general enough to cover the entire passage.**

Topic and Summary Sentences

The main idea of a paragraph usually appears within the topic sentence. The TOPIC SENTENCE introduces the main idea to readers; it indicates not only the topic of a passage, but also the writer's perspective on the topic.

Notice, for example, how the first sentence in the example paragraph about Babe Zaharias states the main idea: *Babe Didrikson Zaharias, one of the most decorated female athletes of the twentieth century, is an inspiration for everyone.*

Even though paragraphs generally begin with topic sentences due to their introductory nature, on occasion writers build up to the topic sentence by using supporting details in order to generate interest or build an argument. Be alert for paragraphs when writers do not include a clear topic sentence at all; even without a clear topic sentence, a paragraph will still have a main idea. You may also see a SUMMARY SENTENCE at the end of a passage. As its name suggests, this sentence sums up the passage, often by restating the main idea and the author's key evidence supporting it.

Example

In the following paragraph, what are the topic and summary sentences?

The Constitution of the United States establishes a series of limits to rein in centralized power. Separation of powers distributes federal authority among three competing branches: the executive, the legislative, and the judicial. Checks and balances allow the branches to check the usurpation of power by any one branch. States' rights are protected under the Constitution from too much encroachment by the federal government. Enumeration of powers names the specific and few powers the federal government has. These four restrictions have helped sustain the American republic for over two centuries.

The topic sentence is the first sentence in the paragraph. It introduces the topic of discussion, in this case the constitutional limits aimed at restricting centralized power. **The summary sentence is the last sentence in the paragraph.** It sums up the information that was just presented: here, that constitutional limits have helped sustain the United States of America for over two hundred years.

Implied Main Idea

A paragraph without a clear topic sentence still has a main idea; rather than clearly stated, it is implied. Determining the IMPLIED MAIN IDEA requires some detective work: you will need to look at the author's word choice and tone in addition to the content of the passage to find his or her main idea. Let's look at a few example paragraphs.

Examples

One of my summer reading books was *Mockingjay*. I was captivated by the adventures of the main character and the complicated plot of the book. However, I felt like the ending didn't reflect the excitement of the story. Given what a powerful personality the main character has, I felt like the ending didn't do her justice.

1. Even without a clear topic sentence, this paragraph has a main idea. What is the writer's perspective on the book—what is the writer saying about it?

   A) *Mockingjay* is a terrific novel.

   B) *Mockingjay* is disappointing.

   C) *Mockingjay* is full of suspense.

   D) *Mockingjay* is a lousy novel.

   The correct answer is B): the novel is disappointing. How can you tell that this is the main idea? First, you can eliminate choice C) because it's too specific to be a main idea. It only deals with one specific aspect of the novel (its suspense).

   Sentences A), B), and D), on the other hand, all express a larger idea about the quality of the novel. However, only one of these statements can actually serve as a "net" for the whole paragraph. Notice that while the first few sentences praise the novel, the last two criticize it. Clearly, this is a mixed review.

   Therefore, the best answer is B). Sentence A) is too positive and doesn't account for the *letdown* of an ending. Sentence D), on the other hand, is too negative and doesn't account for the reader's sense of suspense and interest in the main character. But sentence B) allows for both positive and negative aspects—when a good thing turns bad, we often feel disappointed.

Fortunately, none of Alyssa's coworkers have ever seen inside the large filing drawer in her desk. Disguised by the meticulous neatness of the rest of her workspace, there was no sign of the chaos beneath. To even open it, she had to struggle for several minutes with the enormous pile of junk jamming the drawer, until it would suddenly give way, and papers, folders, and candy wrappers spilled out of the top and onto the floor. It was an organizational nightmare, with torn notes and spreadsheets haphazardly thrown on top of each other, and melted candy smeared across pages. She was worried the odor would soon permeate to her coworkers' desks, revealing her secret.

2. Which sentence best describes the main idea of the paragraph above?

A) Alyssa wishes she could move to a new desk.

B) Alyssa wishes she had her own office.

C) Alyssa is glad none of her coworkers know about her messy drawer.

D) Alyssa is sad because she doesn't have any coworkers.

Clearly, Alyssa has a messy drawer, and C) is the right answer. The paragraph begins by indicating her gratitude that her coworkers do not know about her drawer (*Fortunately, none of Alyssa's coworkers have ever seen inside the large filing drawer in her desk.*) Plus, notice how the drawer is described: *it was an organizational nightmare*, and it apparently doesn't even function properly: *to even open the drawer, she had to struggle for several minutes.* The writer reveals that it has an odor, with melted candy inside. Alyssa is clearly ashamed of her drawer and fearful of being judged by her coworkers about it.

SUPPORTING DETAILS

SUPPORTING DETAILS provide more support for the author's main idea. For instance, in the Babe Zaharias example, the writer makes the general assertion that *Babe Didrikson Zaharias, one of the most decorated female athletes of the twentieth century, is an inspiration for everyone.* The rest of the paragraph provides supporting details with facts showing why she is an inspiration: the names of the illnesses she overcame, and the specific years she competed in the Olympics.

Be alert for SIGNAL WORDS, which can be helpful in identifying supporting details. These signal words tell you that a supporting fact or idea will follow, and so can be helpful in identifying supporting details. Signal words can also help you rule out sentences that are not the main idea or topic sentence: if a sentence begins with one of these phrases, it will likely be too specific to be a main idea.

SIGNAL WORDS
- for example
- specifically
- in addition
- furthermore
- for instance
- others
- in particular
- some

Examples

From so far away it's easy to imagine the surface of our solar system's planets as enigmas—how could we ever know what those far-flung planets really look like? It turns out, however, that scientists have a number of tools at their disposal that allow them to paint detailed pictures of many planets' surfaces. The topography of Venus, for example, has been explored by several space probes, including the Russian Venera landers and NASA's Magellan orbiter. These craft used imaging and radar to map the surface of the planet, identifying a whole host of features including volcanoes, craters, and a complex system of channels. Mars has similarly been mapped by space probes, including the famous Mars Rovers, which are automated vehicles that actually landed on the surface of Mars. These rovers have been used by NASA and other space agencies to study the geology, climate, and possible biology of the planet.

In addition to these long-range probes, NASA has also used its series of orbiting telescopes to study distant planets. These four massively powerful telescopes include the famous Hubble Space Telescope as well as the Compton Gamma Ray Observatory, Chandra X-Ray Observatory, and the Spitzer Space Telescope. Scientists can use these telescopes to examine planets using not only visible light but also infrared and near-infrared light, ultraviolet light, x-rays, and gamma rays.

Powerful telescopes aren't just found in space: NASA makes use of Earth-bound telescopes as well. Scientists at the National Radio Astronomy Observatory in Charlottesville, VA, have spent decades using radio imaging to build an incredibly detailed portrait of Venus' surface. In fact, Earth-bound telescopes offer a distinct advantage over orbiting telescopes because they allow scientists to capture data from a fixed point, which in turn allows them to effectively compare data collected over a long period of time.

1. Which sentence from the text best develops the idea that scientists make use of many different technologies to study the surfaces of other planets?

   A) These rovers have been used by NASA and other space agencies to study the geology, climate, and possible biology of the planet.

   B) From so far away it's easy to imagine the surface of our solar system's planets as enigmas—how could we ever know what those far-flung planets really look like?

   C) In addition to these long-range probes, NASA has also used its series of orbiting telescopes to study distant planets.

   D) These craft used imaging and radar to map the surface of the planet, identifying a whole host of features including volcanoes, craters, and a complex system of channels.

You're looking for details from the passage that supports the main idea—scientists make use of many different technologies to study the surfaces of other planets. Answer A) includes a specific detail about rovers, but does not offer any details that support the idea of multiple technologies being used. Similarly, answer D) provides another specific detail about space probes. Answer B) doesn't provide any supporting details; it simply introduces the topic of the passage. **Only answer C) provides a detail that directly supports the author's assertion that scientists use multiple technologies to study the planets.**

2. If true, which detail could be added to the passage above to support the author's argument that scientists use many different technologies to study the surface of planets?

A) Because the Earth's atmosphere blocks x-rays, gamma rays, and infrared radiation, NASA needed to put telescopes in orbit above the atmosphere.

B) In 2015, NASA released a map of Venus which was created by compiling images from orbiting telescopes and long-range space probes.

C) NASA is currently using the Curiosity and Opportunity rovers to look for signs of ancient life on Mars.

D) NASA has spent over $2.5 billion to build, launch, and repair the Hubble Space Telescope.

You can eliminate answers C) and D) because they don't address the topic of studying the surface of planets. Answer A) can also be eliminated because it only addresses a single technology. **Only choice B) would add support to the author's claim about the importance of using multiple technologies.**

3. The author likely included the detail *Earth-bound telescopes offer a distinct advantage over orbiting telescopes because they allow scientists to capture data from a fixed point* in order to:

A) explain why it has taken scientists so long to map the surface of Venus

B) suggest that Earth-bound telescopes are the most important equipment used by NASA scientists

C) prove that orbiting telescopes will soon be replaced by Earth-bound telescopes

D) demonstrate why NASA scientists rely on many different types of scientific equipment

Only answer D) speaks directly to the author's main argument. The author doesn't mention how long it has taken to map the surface of Venus (answer A), nor does he say that one technology is more important than the others (answer B). And while this detail does highlight the advantages of using Earth-bound telescopes, the author's argument is that many technologies are being used at the same time, so there's no reason to think that orbiting telescopes will be replaced (answer C).

FACTS VS. OPINIONS

On HESI A² reading passages you might be asked to identify a statement in a passage as either a fact or an opinion, so you'll need to know the difference between the two. A **FACT** is a statement or thought that can be proven to be true. The statement *Wednesday comes after Tuesday* is a fact—you can point to a calendar to prove it. In contrast, an **OPINION** is an assumption that is not based in fact and cannot be proven to be true. The assertion that *television is more*

Which of the following words would be associated with opinions?

- for example
- studies have shown
- I believe
- in fact
- the best/worst
- it's possible that

entertaining than feature films is an opinion—people will disagree on this, and there's no reference you can use to prove or disprove it.

Example

Exercise is critical for healthy development in children. Today, there is an epidemic of unhealthy children in the United States who will face health problems in adulthood due to poor diet and lack of exercise as children. This is a problem for all Americans, especially with the rising cost of health care.

It is vital that school systems and parents encourage their children to engage in a minimum of thirty minutes of cardiovascular exercise each day, mildly increasing their heart rate for a sustained period. This is proven to decrease the likelihood of developmental diabetes, obesity, and a multitude of other health problems. Also, children need a proper diet rich in fruits and vegetables so that they can grow and develop physically, as well as learn healthy eating habits early on.

Which of the following is a fact in the passage, not an opinion?

A) Fruits and vegetables are the best way to help children be healthy.

B) Children today are lazier than they were in previous generations.

C) The risk of diabetes in children is reduced by physical activity.

D) Children should engage in thirty minutes of exercise a day.

Answer C) is a simple fact stated by the author; it's introduced by the word *proven* to indicate that you don't need to just take the author's word for it. Choice B) can be discarded immediately because it is not discussed anywhere in the passage, and also because it is negative. Answers A) and D) are both opinions—the author is promoting exercise, fruits, and vegetables as a way to make children healthy. (Notice that these incorrect answers contain words that hint at being an opinion such as *best*, *should*, or other comparisons.)

MAKING INFERENCES

In addition to understanding the main idea and factual content of a passage, you'll also be asked to take your analysis one step further and anticipate what other information could logically be added to the passage. In a non-fiction passage, for example, you might be asked which statement the author of the passage would agree with. In an excerpt from a fictional work, you might be asked to anticipate what the character would do next.

To answer these questions, you need to have a solid understanding of the topic, theme, and main idea of the passage; armed with this information, you can figure out which of the answer choices best fits within those criteria (or alternatively, which ones do not). For example, if the author of the passage is advocating for safer working conditions in textile factories, any supporting details that would be added to the passage should support that idea. You might add sentences that contain information about the number of accidents that occur in textile factories or that outline a new plan for fire safety.

Example

Exercise is critical for healthy development in children. Today, there is an epidemic of unhealthy children in the United States who will face health problems in adulthood due to poor diet and lack of exercise as children. This is a problem for all Americans, especially with the rising cost of health care.

It is vital that school systems and parents encourage their children to engage in a minimum of thirty minutes of cardiovascular exercise each day, mildly increasing their heart rate for sustained period. This is proven to decrease the likelihood of developmental diabetes, obesity, and a multitude of other health problems. Also, children need a proper diet rich in fruits and vegetables so that they can grow and develop physically, as well as learn healthy eating habits early on.

What other information might the author have provided to strengthen the argument?

A) an example of how fruits and vegetables can improve a child's development

B) how much health insurance costs today vs. ten years ago

C) a detailed explanation of how diabetes affects the endocrine and digestive systems

D) how many calories the average person burns during thirty minutes of exercise

All of the choices would provide additional information, **but only one pertains specifically to the improvement of health in children: choice A).**

TYPES OF PASSAGES

Whenever an author writes a text, she always has a purpose, whether that's to entertain, inform, explain, or persuade. A short story, for example, is meant to entertain, while an online news article would be designed to inform the public about a current event.

Each of these different types of writing has a specific name. On the HESI A², you will be asked to identify which of these categories a passage fits into:

- **NARRATIVE WRITING** tells a story (novel, short story, play).
- **EXPOSITORY WRITING** informs people (newspaper and magazine articles).

- **TECHNICAL WRITING** explains something (product manual, directions).
- **PERSUASIVE WRITING** tries to convince the reader of something (opinion column on a blog).

You may also be asked about primary and secondary sources. These terms describe not the writing itself but the author's relationship to what's being written about. A **PRIMARY SOURCE** is an unaltered piece of writing that was composed during the time when the events being described took place; these texts are often written by the people involved. A **SECONDARY SOURCE** might address the same topic but provides extra commentary or analysis. These texts can be written by people not directly involved in the events. For example, a book written by a political candidate to inform people about his or her stand on an issue is a primary source; an online article written by a journalist analyzing how that position will affect the election is a secondary source.

Example

Elizabeth closed her eyes and braced herself on the armrests that divided her from her fellow passengers. Take-off was always the worst part for her. The revving of the engines, the way her stomach dropped as the plane lurched upward: it made her feel sick. Then, she had to watch the world fade away beneath her, getting smaller and smaller until it was just her and the clouds hurtling through the sky. Sometimes (but only sometimes) it just had to be endured. She focused on the thought of her sister's smiling face and her new baby nephew as the plane slowly pulled onto the runway.

The passage above is reflective of which type of writing?

A) narrative

B) expository

C) technical

D) persuasive

The passage is telling a story—we meet Elizabeth and learn about her fear of flying—**so it's a narrative text.** There is no factual information presented or explained, nor is the author trying to persuade the reader.

TEXT STRUCTURE

Authors can structure passages in a number of different ways. These distinct organizational patterns, referred to as **TEXT STRUCTURE**, use the logical relationships between ideas to improve the readability and coherence of a text. The most common ways passages are organized include:

- **PROBLEM-SOLUTION**: the author presents a problem and then discusses a solution.

- **COMPARISON-CONTRAST**: the author presents two situations and then discusses the similarities and differences.
- **CAUSE-EFFECT**: the author presents an action and then discusses the resulting effects.
- **DESCRIPTIVE**: an idea, object, person, or other item is described in detail.

Example

The issue of public transportation has begun to haunt the fast-growing cities of the southern United States. Unlike their northern counterparts, cities like Atlanta, Dallas, and Houston have long promoted growth out and not up—these are cities full of sprawling suburbs and single-family homes, not densely concentrated skyscrapers and apartments. What to do then, when all those suburbanites need to get into the central business districts for work? For a long time it seemed highways were the answer: twenty-lane wide expanses of concrete that would allow commuters to move from home to work and back again. But these modern miracles have become time-sucking, pollution-spewing nightmares. They may not like it, but it's time for these cities to turn toward public transport like trains and buses if they want their cities to remain livable.

The organization of this passage can best be described as:

A) a comparison of two similar ideas

B) a description of a place

C) a discussion of several effects all related to the same cause

D) a discussion of a problem followed by the suggestion of a solution

You can exclude answer choice C) because the author provides no root cause or a list of effects. From there this question gets tricky, because the passage contains structures similar to those described above. For example, it compares two things (cities in the North and South) and describes a place (a sprawling city). However, if you look at the overall organization of the passage, you can see that it starts by presenting a problem (transportation) and then presents a solution (trains and buses), **making answer D) the only choice that encompasses the entire passage.**

VOCABULARY

On the Reading section you may also be asked to provide definitions or intended meanings for words within passages. You may have never encountered some of these words before the test, but there are tricks you can use to figure out what they mean.

Context Clues

The most fundamental vocabulary skill is using the context in which a word is used to determine its meaning. Your ability to observe sentences closely is extremely useful when it comes to understanding new vocabulary words.

There are two types of context that can help you understand the meaning of unfamiliar words: situational context and sentence context. Regardless of which context is present, these types of questions are not really testing your knowledge of vocabulary; rather, they test your ability to comprehend the meaning of a word through its usage.

SITUATIONAL CONTEXT is context that is presented by the setting or circumstances in which a word or phrase occurs. SENTENCE CONTEXT occurs within the specific sentence that contains the vocabulary word. To figure out words using sentence context clues, you should first determine the most important words in the sentence.

There are four types of clues that can help you understand the context, and therefore the meaning of a word:

- RESTATEMENT clues occur when the definition of the word is clearly stated in the sentence.
- POSITIVE/NEGATIVE CLUES can tell you whether a word has a positive or negative meaning.
- CONTRAST CLUES include the opposite meaning of a word. Words like *but, on the other hand,* and *however* are tip-offs that a sentence contains a contrast clue.
- SPECIFIC DETAIL CLUES provide a precise detail that can help you understand the meaning of the word.

It is important to remember that more than one of these clues can be present in the same sentence. The more there are, the easier it will be to determine the meaning of the word. For example, the following sentence uses both restatement and positive/negative clues: *Janet suddenly found herself destitute, so poor she could barely afford to eat.* The second part of the sentence clearly indicates that *destitute* is a negative word. It also restates the meaning: very poor.

Examples

Select the answer that most closely matches the definition of the underlined word or phrase as it is used in the sentence.

1. I had a hard time reading her <u>illegible</u> handwriting.
   A) neat
   B) unsafe
   C) sloppy
   D) educated

Already, you know that this sentence is discussing something that is hard to read. Look at the word that *illegible* is describing: handwriting. Based on context clues, you can tell that *illegible* means that her handwriting is hard to read.

Next, look at the answer choices. Choice A), *neat,* is obviously a wrong answer because neat handwriting would not be difficult to read. Choices B) and D), *unsafe* and *educated,* don't make sense. **Therefore, choice C), *sloppy*, is the best answer.**

2. The dog was <u>dauntless</u> in the face of danger, braving the fire to save the girl trapped inside the building.

   A) difficult

   B) fearless

   C) imaginative

   D) startled

   Demonstrating bravery in the face of danger would be B) *fearless*. In this case, the restatement clue (braving the fire) tells you exactly what the word means.

3. Beth did not spend any time preparing for the test, but Tyrone kept a <u>rigorous</u> study schedule.

   A) strict

   B) loose

   C) boring

   D) strange

   In this case, the contrast word *but* tells us that Tyrone studied in a different way than Beth, which means it's a contrast clue. If Beth did not study hard, then Tyrone did. **The best answer, therefore, is choice A).**

Analyzing Words

As you no doubt know, determining the meaning of a word can be more complicated than just looking in a dictionary. A word might have more than one DENOTATION, or definition; which one the author intends can only be judged by looking at the surrounding text. For example, the word *quack* can refer to the sound a duck makes, or to a person who publicly pretends to have a qualification which he or she does not actually possess.

A word may also have different CONNOTATIONS, which are the implied meanings and emotion a word evokes in the reader. For example, a cubicle is simply a walled desk in an office, but for many the word implies a constrictive, uninspiring workplace. Connotations can vary greatly between cultures and even between individuals.

Lastly, authors might make use of FIGURATIVE LANGUAGE, which is the use of a word to imply something other than the word's literal definition. This is often done by comparing two things. If you say *I felt like a butterfly when I got a new haircut*, the listener knows you don't resemble an insect but instead felt beautiful and transformed.

Examples

Select the answer that most closely matches the definition of the underlined word or phrase as it is used in the sentence.

1. The uneven <u>pupils</u> suggested that brain damage was possible.

    A) part of the eye

    B) student in a classroom

    C) walking pace

    D) breathing sounds

    Only answer choice A (part of the eye) matches both the definition of the word and context of the sentence. Choice B is an alternative definition for pupil, but does not make sense in the sentence. Both C and D could be correct in the context of the sentence, but neither is a definition of pupil.

2. Aiden examined the antique lamp and worried that he had been <u>taken for a ride</u>. He had paid a lot for the vintage lamp, but it looked like it was worthless.

    A) transported

    B) forgotten

    C) deceived

    D) hindered

    It's clear from the context of the sentence that Aiden was not literally taken for a ride. Instead, this phrase is an example of figurative language. **From context clues it can be figured out that Aiden paid too much for the lamp, so he was deceived (answer choice C).**

Word Structure

Although you are not expected to know every word in the English language for your test, you will need the ability to use deductive reasoning to find the choice that is the best match for the word in question, which is why we are going to explain how to break a word into its parts to determine its meaning. Many words can be broken down into three main parts:

PREFIX — ROOT — SUFFIX

Roots are the building blocks of all words. Every word is either a root itself or has a root. Just as a plant cannot grow without roots, neither can vocabulary, because a word must have a root to give it meaning. The root is what is left when you strip away all the prefixes and suffixes from a word. For example, in the word *unclear*, if you take away the prefix *un-*, you have the root *clear*.

Check out the chapter *Human Body Science* for a list of medical roots and prefixes that are commonly tested on the HESI A².

Roots are not always recognizable words, because they generally come from Latin or Greek words, such as *nat*, a Latin root meaning born. The word *native*, which means a person born in a referenced place, comes from this root; so does the word *prenatal*, meaning *before birth*. It's important to keep in mind, however, that roots do not always match the exact definitions of words, and they can have several different spellings.

PREFIXES are syllables added to the beginning of a word and **SUFFIXES** are syllables added to the end of the word. Both carry assigned meanings and can be attached to a word to completely change the word's meaning or to enhance the word's original meaning.

Let's use the word *prefix* itself as an example: *fix* means to place something securely and *pre-* means before. Therefore, *prefix* means to place something before or in front of. Now let's look at a suffix: in the word *feminism*, *femin* is a root which means female. The suffix *-ism* means act, practice, or process. Thus, *feminism* is the process of establishing equal rights for women.

Although you cannot determine the meaning of a word by a prefix or suffix alone, you can use this knowledge to eliminate answer choices; understanding whether the word is positive or negative can give you the partial meaning of the word.

✔

Can you figure out the definitions of the following words using their parts?

- ambidextrous
- anthropology
- diagram
- egocentric
- hemisphere
- homicide
- metamorphosis
- nonsense
- portable
- rewind
- submarine
- triangle
- unicycle

Table 2.1. Common roots and affixes

ROOT	DEFINITION	EXAMPLE
ast(er)	star	asteroid, astronomy
audi	hear	audience, audible
auto	self	automatic, autograph
bene	good	beneficent, benign
bio	life	biology, biorhythm
cap	take	capture
ced	yield	secede
chrono	time	chronometer, chronic
corp	body	corporeal
crac or crat	rule	autocrat
demo	people	democracy
dict	say	dictionary, dictation
duc	lead or make	ductile, produce
gen	give birth	generation, genetics
geo	earth	geography, geometry
grad	step	graduate
graph	write	graphical, autograph
ject	throw	eject
jur or jus	law	justice, jurisdiction
log or logue	thought	logic, logarithm
luc	light	lucidity
man	hand	manual
mand	order	remand
mis	send	transmission
mono	one	monotone
omni	all	omnivore
path	feel	pathology
phil	love	philanthropy
phon	sound	phonograph
port	carry	export
qui	rest	quiet
scrib or script	write	scribe, transcript
sense or sent	feel	sentiment
tele	far away	telephone
terr	earth	terrace
uni	single	unicode
vac	empty	vacant
vid	see	video
vis	see	vision

Table 2.2. Common prefixes

PREFIX	DEFINITION	EXAMPLE
a- (also an-)	not, without; to, towards; of, completely	atheist, anemic, aside, aback, anew, abashed
ante-	before, preceding	antecedent, ante-room
anti-	opposing, against	antibiotic, anticlimax
com- (also co-, col-, con-, cor-)	with, jointly, completely	combat, codriver, collude, confide
dis- (also di-)	negation, removal	disadvantage, disbar
en- (also em-)	put into or on; bring into the condition of; intensify	engulf, entomb
hypo-	under	hypoglycemic, hypothermia
in- (also il-, im-, ir-)	not, without; in, into, towards, inside	infertile, impossible, influence, include
intra-	inside, within	intravenous, intrapersonal
out-	surpassing, exceeding; external, away from	outperform, outdoor
over-	excessively, completely; upper, outer, over, above	overconfident, overcast
pre-	before	precondition, pre-adolescent, prelude
re-	again	reapply, remake
semi-	half, partly	semicircle, semi-conscious
syn- (also sym-)	in union, acting together	synthesis, symbiotic
trans-	across, beyond	transatlantic
trans-	into a different state	translate
under-	beneath, below	underarm, undersecretary
under-	not enough	underdeveloped

Examples

Select the answer that most closely matches the definition of the underlined word or phrase as it is used in the sentence.

1. The <u>bellicose</u> dog will be sent to training school next week.

   A) misbehaved

   B) friendly

   C) scared

   D) aggressive

Both misbehaved and aggressive look like possible answers given the context of the sentence. **However, the prefix *belli*, which means warlike, can be used to confirm that aggressive (choice D) is the right answer.**

2. The new menu <u>rejuvenated</u> the restaurant and made it one of the most popular spots in town.

   A) established

   B) invigorated

   C) improved

   D) motivated

All of the answer choices could make sense in the context of the sentence, so it's necessary to use word structure to find the definition. The root *juven* means young and the prefix *re* means again, so *rejuvenate* means to be made young again. **The answer choice with the most similar meaning is *invigorated*, which means to give something energy.**

3

VOCABULARY

The HESI A² vocabulary section will test your knowledge of general vocabulary as well as terms commonly used in the medical profession. The test will consist of the following types of questions:

- Select the correct definition of the term.
- Match the stated definition to the correct term.
- Infer the definition of the term from its use in a sentence.
- Select the term that will make the sentence grammatically correct.
- Select the correct synonym of the term.
- Identify the incorrectly spelled term.
- Select the correct order of the terms to be used in the sentence structure.

WORD LIST

abate: become less in amount or intensity

abbreviate: to shorten or abridge

abdicate: to give up or leave

abrupt: changing or terminating suddenly

abstain: refrain; choose to avoid or not participate

access: means of approach or admission

accountable: liable or responsible

adhere: hold closely to an idea or course; be devoted

adverse: harmful to one's interests; unfortunate

adversity: a state of burden or hardship

affect: change or influence

anecdote: a short story or account of an event

annual: occurring or returning once a year

apply: bring into physical contact; lay on; bring into operation

assiduous: very careful and hardworking

audible: loud enough to be heard

benevolent: showing sympathy, understanding, and generosity

bias: an unfair preference or dislike

bilateral: having two sides

boisterous: rough, rowdy, unruly

brazen: bold or unrestrained by normal standards

brusque: attitude of shortness or rudeness; gruff

capacious: large in size or capacity

cardiac: pertaining to the heart

cast: a molded protective device used to support broken bones

cavity: any hollow place or space

cease: stop doing an action, discontinue

circuitous: lengthy due to being indirect or roundabout

collaborate: work together on a common project

collateral: adjoining or accompanying

compassion: awareness and sympathy for the suffering of others

compensatory: making up for; offsetting; paying for

complication: something intricate, involved, or aggravating

comply: acquiesce to another's wish, command, etc.

compromise: an accommodation in which both sides make concessions

concave: with an outline or surface curved inward

concise: brief and compact

condescending: an attitude of superiority or being snobby toward others

conditional: dependent on something else being done

consistency: state of being congruous; conforming to regular patterns, habits, principles, etc.

constrict: cause to shrink, cramp, crush

contingent: depending on something not certain; conditional

contour: the outline of a figure or shape

contract: legal or business agreement; acquire a habit or disease

contraindication: discouragement of the use of a treatment

copious: abundant and plentiful

defecate: have a bowel movement

deficit: shortage; excess of liabilities over assets

deleterious: harmful or deadly to living things

depress: weaken; sadden

depth: deepness; distance measured downward, inward, or backward

deter: to prevent or discourage

deteriorating: growing worse; reducing in worth; impairing

device: a gadget; a mechanical apparatus

diagnosis: analysis of a present condition

diameter: a line dividing a circle into halves; its length

digression: a deviation or detour from the central topic or focus

dilate: expand; make larger; distend

diligent: persistent and hardworking

dilute: weaken by a mixture of water or other liquid; reduce in strength

discrete: separate; discontinuous

disdain: lack of respect or intense dislike

distended: dilated, expanded, or swollen

dysfunction: impaired functioning

elevate: raise; lift up

empathy: understanding of another's feelings

endogenous: something produced within the body

enervating: causing debilitation or weakness

enhance: to improve; to increase clarity

ephemeral: lasting only for a short period of time

exacerbate: make more bitter, angry, or violent; irritate or aggravate

exasperate: worsen, make angry, or frustrate

excess: the state of being more or too much; a surplus or remainder

exemplary: worthy of imitation; setting the example

exogenous: something produced outside the body

expand: increase in extent, bulk, or amount; spread or stretch out; unfold

exposure: the state of being exposed or open to external environments

extenuating: diminish the seriousness of something

external: located outside of something and/ or apart from something

fatal: causing death or ruin

fatigue: weariness from physical or mental exertion

flaccid: soft; flabby

flushed: suffused with color; washed out with a copious flow of water

fortitude: strength and endurance during a difficult situation

fortuitous: occurring by happy chance

gaping: to be open; to have a break in continuity

garble: confusing, not understandable

gastrointestinal: pertaining to the stomach and intestines

gender: the classification of masculine or feminine

hematologic: dealing with the blood

hydration: the act of meeting body fluid demands

hygiene: the science that deals with the preservation of health

hyperbole: exaggerating; making something more than it is

hypothesis: a theory that has not yet been tested or investigated

imminent: very likely to happen

impaired: made worse, damaged, or weakened

impending: the point of occurring; imminent

impetuous: undue haste without thought of consequences

incidence: frequency or range of occurrence; extent of effects

incompatible: unable to be or work together

inconsequential: something without importance or significance

inevitable: impossible to avoid or prevent from happening

infection: tainted with germs or disease

inflamed: condition in which the body is inflicted with heat, swelling, and redness

ingest: take into the body for digestion

initiate: set going; begin; originate

innocuous: harmless

insidious: operating stealthily with evil effect; deceitful; treacherous

intact: remaining uninjured, unimpaired, whole, or complete

integrity: doing what is right, honest, or decent

internal: situated within something; enclosed; inside

intuitive: to know by instinct alone

invasive: being intrusive or encroaching upon

labile: apt to lapse or err; unstable

laceration: a rough tear; an affliction

languid: tired and slow

latent: hidden; dormant; undeveloped

lethargic: not wanting to move; sluggish

longevity: having a long life

manifestation: a demonstration or display

musculoskeletal: pertaining to muscles and the skeleton

neurologic: dealing with the nervous system

neurovascular: pertaining to the nervous system and blood vessels

novice: a beginner; inexperienced

nutrient: something affording nutrition

occluded: shut in or out; closed; absorbed

ominous: foretelling disaster; threatening

ongoing: continuous; constant

oral: spoken, not written; pertaining to the mouth

overt: plain to the view; open

paradox: appearing conflicting or contradictory

parameter: a variable quantity whose values depend on the special case

paroxysmal: having to do with a spasm or violent outburst

patent: open for all to read; plain; obvious

pathogenic: causing disease

pathology: the science of the nature and origin of disease

posterior: located in the back or rear

potent: wielding power; strong; effective

potential: possible; possibility

pragmatic: concerned with practical matters and results

precaution: an act done in advance to ensure safety or benefit; prudent foresight

precipitous: overhasty; rash; uncontrolled

precocious: showing advanced development or maturity at an early age

predispose: give a tendency or inclination to; dispose in advance

preexisting: already in place; already occurring

primary: first; earliest; most important

priority: right of precedence; order of importance

procrastinate: to postpone doing something

prognosis: a forecast

prudent: careful and sensible; using good judgment

rationale: rational basis for something; justification

recur: appear again; return

renal: pertaining to the kidneys

resilient: quick to recover

respiration: breathing

restrict: attach limitations to; restrain

retain: hold or keep in possession, use, or practice

sagacity: sound knowledge, judgment, and foresight

scrutinize: examine closely and carefully

site: location

status: relative standing; position; condition

strict: precise; exacting; severe

sublingual: beneath the tongue

subtle: understated, not obvious

superficial: shallow in character and attitude; only concerned with things on the surface

superfluous: more than is needed, desired, or necessary

supplement: an addition to something substantially completed; to add to

suppress: restrain; abolish; repress

symmetric: similar proportion in the size or shape of something

symptom: a sign or indication of a problem or disease

syndrome: a set of symptoms that characterize a certain disease or condition

tactful: showing concern to not offend others

tenacious: determined without change or doubt from the plan

terse: to the point; concise

therapeutic: pertaining to the curing of disease; having remedial effect

transdermal: passing through the skin

transient: lasting for only a short time or duration

transmission: the act or result of sending something along or onward to a recipient or destination

trauma: a bodily injury or mental shock

triage: the act of sorting or categorizing conditions and diseases in preparation for treatment

trite: dull; common

untoward: unfavorable; troublesome

urinate: discharge urine

vascular: pertaining to bodily ducts that convey fluid

venerable: worthy of respect because of wisdom or age

venerate: to regard with much respect

verbal: expressed in words; oral, not written

virus: an agent of infection

vital: pertaining to life; alive; essential to existence or well-being

void: empty; evacuate

volume: a space filled by a fluid

wary: to be cautious or suspicious

Examples

Select the correct definition of the underlined term.

1. The medication had an <u>adverse</u> effect.
   A) harmful
   B) beneficial
   C) limiting
   D) none of the above

2. The documentation was <u>concise</u>.
   A) long
   B) short
   C) irrelevant
   D) none of the above

3. When assessing the patient, the nurse found several areas that had undergone <u>trauma</u>.
   A) injury
   B) shock
   C) both A and B
   D) neither A nor B

4. Before surgery, the patient had to <u>void</u> his bladder.

A) empty

B) fill

C) check

D) remove

Match the definition in the sentence to the correct term.

5. The number of surgeries was <u>more than necessary</u>.

A) contraindicated

B) excessive

C) invasive

D) reasonable

6. The patient was too <u>weakened and damaged</u> to drive.

A) assiduous

B) prudent

C) impaired

D) labile

Select the correct synonym of the underlined term.

7. The <u>neurologic</u> assessment was completed before the diagnosis.

A) nervous system

B) skeletal system

C) gastrointestinal system

D) urinary system

8. The <u>main</u> nurse had just finished caring for the patient.

A) primary

B) secondary

C) priority

D) none of the above

Select the term that correctly completes the sentence.

9. Nurses should avoid _____ a patient as often as possible.
   A) attending to
   B) accommodating
   C) restricting
   D) assisting

10. The patient showed many _____ of Down's syndrome.
    A) symptoms
    B) rejections
    C) contraindications
    D) none of the above

Answers: 1. A) 2. B) 3. C) 4. A) 5. B) 6. C) 7. A) 8. A) 9. C) 10. A)

4

GRAMMAR

The first step in getting ready for the grammar section of the test is to review parts of speech and the rules that accompany them. The good news is that you have been using these rules since you first began to speak; even if you don't know a lot of the technical terms, many of these rules may be familiar to you. Some of the topics you might see include:

- matching pronouns with their antecedents
- matching verbs with their subjects
- ensuring that verbs are in the correct tense
- spelling irregular, hyphenated, and commonly misspelled words
- using correct capitalization
- distinguishing between types of sentences
- correcting sentence structure
- changing passive to active voice

PARTS OF SPEECH

Nouns and Pronouns

NOUNS are people, places, or things. They are typically the subject of a sentence. For example, in the sentence *The hospital was very clean*, the noun is *hospital*; it is a place. PRONOUNS replace nouns and make sentences sound less repetitive. Take the sentence *Sam stayed home from school because Sam was not feeling well*. The word *Sam* appears twice in the same sentence. Instead, you can use a pronoun and say *Sam stayed at home because he did not feel well.* Sounds much better, right?

Because pronouns take the place of nouns, they need to agree both in number and gender with the noun they replace. So, a

SINGULAR PRONOUNS
- I, me, mine, my
- you, your, yours
- he, him, his
- she, her, hers
- it, its

PLURAL PRONOUNS
- we, us, our, ours
- they, them, their, theirs

plural noun needs a plural pronoun, and a feminine noun needs a feminine pronoun. In the previous sentence, for example, the plural pronoun *they* replaced the plural noun *pronouns*. There will usually be several questions on the English and Language Usage section that cover pronoun agreement, so it's good to get comfortable spotting pronouns.

Examples

Wrong: If a student forgets their homework, it is considered incomplete.

Correct: If a student forgets his or her homework, it is considered incomplete.

Student is a singular noun, but *their* is a plural pronoun. So, this first sentence is grammatically incorrect. To correct it, replace *their* with the singular pronoun *his* or *her*.

Wrong: Everybody will receive their paychecks promptly.

Correct: Everybody will receive his or her paycheck promptly.

Everybody is a singular noun, but *their* is a plural pronoun. So, this sentence is grammatically incorrect. To correct it, replace *their* with the singular pronoun *his* or *her*.

Wrong: When a nurse begins work at a hospital, you should wash your hands.

Correct: When a nurse begins work at a hospital, he or she should wash his or her hands.

This sentence begins in third-person perspective and finishes in second-person perspective. So, this sentence is grammatically incorrect. To correct it, ensure the sentence finishes in third-person perspective.

Wrong: After the teacher spoke to the student, she realized her mistake.

Correct: After Mr. White spoke to his student, she realized her mistake (*she* and *her* referring to student).

Correct: After speaking to the student, the teacher realized her own mistake (*her* referring to teacher).

This sentence refers to a teacher and a student. But whom does *she* refer to, the teacher or the student? To improve clarity, use specific names or state more specifically who spotted the mistake.

Verbs

Remember the old commercial, *Verb: It's what you do*? That sums up verbs in a nutshell. A *verb* is the action of a sentence; verbs *do* things. Verbs must be conjugated to match the context of the sentence; this can sometimes be tricky because English has many irregular verbs. For example, *runs* is an action verb in the present tense that becomes *ran* in the past tense; the linking verb *is* (which describes a state of being) becomes *was* in the past tense.

Table 4.1. Conjugations of the verb *to be*

	PAST	PRESENT	FUTURE
SINGULAR	was	is	will be
PLURAL	were	are	will be

As mentioned, verbs must use the correct tense, and that tense must make sense in the context of the sentence. For example, the sentence *I was baking cookies and eat some dough* sounds strange, right? That's because the two verbs *was baking* and *eat* are in different tenses. *Was baking* occurred in the past; *eat*, on the other hand, occurs in the present. Instead, it should be *ate some dough*.

Like pronouns, verbs must agree in number with the noun they refer back to. In the example above, the verb *was* refers back to the singular *I*. If the subject of the sentence was plural, it would need to be modified to read *They were baking cookies and ate some dough*. Note that the verb *ate* does not change form; this is common for verbs in the past tense.

Examples

Wrong: The cat chase the ball while the dogs runs in the yard.

Correct: The cat chases the ball while the dogs run in the yard.

Cat is singular, so it takes a singular verb (which confusingly ends with an s); *dogs* is plural, so it needs a plural verb.

Wrong: The cars that had been recalled by the manufacturer was returned within a few months.

Correct: The cars that had been recalled by the manufacturer were returned within a few months.

Sometimes, the subject and verb are separated by clauses or phrases. Here, the subject *cars* is separated from the verb phrase *were returned*, making it more difficult to conjugate the verb.

Correct: The deer hid in the trees.

Correct: The deer are not all the same size.

The subject of these sentences is a collective noun, which describes a group of people or items. This noun can be singular if it's referring to the group as a whole, or plural if it refers to each item in the group as a separate entity.

Correct: The doctor and nurse work in the hospital.

Correct: Neither the nurse nor her boss was scheduled to take a vacation.

Correct: Either the patient or her parents need to sign the release forms.

Think of the subject and the verb as sharing a single *s*. If the noun ends with an *s*, the verb shouldn't, and vice versa.

If the subject is separated from the verb, cross out the phrases between them to make conjugation easier.

Adjectives and Adverbs

ADJECTIVES are words that describe a noun. Take the sentence *The boy hit the ball.* If you want to know more about the noun *boy*, then you could use an adjective to describe him: *The little boy hit the ball.* An adjective simply provides more information about a noun or subject in a sentence.

For some reason, many people have a difficult time with adverbs, but don't worry! They are really quite simple. ADVERBS and adjectives are similar because they provide more information about a part of a sentence; however, adverbs do not describe nouns—that's an adjective's job. Instead, adverbs describe verbs, adjectives, and even other adverbs. For example, in the sentence *The doctor had recently hired a new employee,* the adverb *recently* tells us more about how the action *hired* took place.

Adjectives, adverbs, and MODIFYING PHRASES (groups of words that together modify another word) should always be placed as close as possible to the word they modify. Separating words from their modifiers can create incorrect or confusing sentences.

Examples

Wrong: Running through the hall, the bell rang and the student knew she was late.

Correct: Running through the hall, the student heard the bell ring and knew she was late.

The phrase *running through the hall* should be placed next to *student*, the noun it modifies.

Wrong: Of my two friends, Clara is the most smartest.

Correct: Of my two friends, Clara is more smart.

The first sentence above has two mistakes. First, the word *most* should only be used when comparing three or more things. Second, the adjective should only be modified with *more/most* or the suffix *-er/-est*, not both.

Other Parts of Speech

PREPOSITIONS express the location of a noun or pronoun in relation to other words and phrases in a sentence. For example, in the sentence *The nurse parked her car in a parking garage*, the preposition *in* describes the position of the car in relation to the garage. Together, the preposition and the noun that follow it are called a PREPOSITIONAL PHRASE. In the example above, the prepositional phrase is *in a parking garage*.

CONJUNCTIONS connect words, phrases, and clauses. The conjunctions summarized in the acronym FANBOYS—For, And, Nor, But, Or, Yet, So—are called COORDINATING CONJUNCTIONS and are used to join INDEPENDENT CLAUSES (clauses that can stand alone as a complete sentence). For example, in the sentence *The nurse prepared the patient for surgery, and the doctor performed the surgery*, the conjunction *and* joins together the two independent clauses. Other conjunctions, like *although*, *because*, and *if*, join together an independent and DEPENDENT CLAUSE (which cannot stand on its own). In the sentence *She had to ride the subway because her car was broken*, the conjunction *because* joins together the two clauses.

INTERJECTIONS, like *wow* and *hey*, express emotion and are most commonly used in conversation and casual writing.

⚠️ An independent (or main) clause can stand alone as its own sentence. A dependent (or subordinate) clause must be attached to an independent clause to make a complete sentence.

Examples

Choose the word that best completes the sentence.

1. Her love _____ blueberry muffins kept her coming back to the bakery every week.

   A) to

   B) with

   C) of

   D) about

   The correct preposition is *of* (choice C).

2. Christine left her house early on Monday morning, _____ she was still late for work.

   A) but

   B) and

   C) for

   D) or

   In this sentence, the conjunction is joining together two contrasting ideas, so the correct answer is *but* (choice A).

SENTENCE STRUCTURE

Punctuation

The basic rules for using the major punctuation marks are given in the table below.

Table 4.2. How to use punctuation

PUNCTUATION	USED FOR...	EXAMPLE
period	ending sentences	Periods go at the end of complete sentences.
question mark	ending questions	What's the best way to end a sentence?
exclamation point	ending sentences that show extreme emotion	I'll never understand how to use commas!
comma	joining two independent clauses (always with a coordinating conjunction)	Commas can be used to join clauses, but they must always be followed by a coordinating conjunction.
	setting apart introductory and nonessential words and phrases	Commas, when used properly, set apart extra information in a sentence.
	separating items in a list	My favorite punctuation marks include the colon, semicolon, and period.
semicolon	joining together two independent clauses (never with a conjunction)	I love exclamation points; they make sentences seem so exciting!
colon	introducing a list, explanation, or definition	When I see a colon I know what to expect: more information.
apostrophe	form contractions	It's amazing how many people can't use apostrophes correctly.
	show possession	Parentheses are my sister's favorite punctuation; she finds commas' rules confusing.
quotation marks	indicate a direct quote	I said to her, "Tell me more about parentheses."

Capitalization

- The first word of a sentence is always capitalized.
- The first letter of a proper noun is always capitalized. (We're going to Chicago on Wednesday.)

- Titles are capitalized if they precede the name they modify. (President Obama met with Joe Biden, his vice president.)
- Months are capitalized, but not the names of the seasons. (Snow fell in March even though winter was over.)

Sentence Classification

TYPES OF CLAUSES

A sentence can be classified as simple, compound, complex, or compound-complex based on the type and number of clauses it has.

Table 4.3. Types of clauses

SENTENCE TYPE	NUMBER OF INDEPENDENT CLAUSES	NUMBER OF SUBORDINATE CLAUSES
simple	1	0
compound	2+	0
complex	1	1+
compound-complex	2+	1+

A **SIMPLE SENTENCE** consists of only one independent clause. Because there are no dependent clauses in a simple sentence, it can simply be a two-word sentence, with one word being the subject and the other word being the verb (e.g., *I ran.*). However, a simple sentence can also contain prepositions, adjectives, and adverbs. Even though these additions can extend the length of a simple sentence, it is still considered a simple sentence as long as it doesn't contain any dependent clauses.

COMPOUND SENTENCES have two or more independent clauses and no dependent clauses. Usually a comma and a coordinating conjunction (*and, or, but, nor, for, so,* and *yet*) join the independent clauses, though semicolons can be used as well. For example, the sentence *My computer broke, so I took it to be repaired* is compound.

COMPLEX SENTENCES have one independent clause and at least one dependent clause. In the complex sentence *If you lie down with dogs, you'll wake up with fleas*, the first clause is dependent (because of the subordinating conjunction *if*), and the second is independent.

COMPOUND-COMPLEX SENTENCES have two or more independent clauses and at least one subordinate clause. For example, the sentence *Even though David was a vegetarian, he went with his friends to steakhouses, but he focused on the conversation instead of the food*, is compound-complex.

On the test you'll have to both identify and construct different kinds of sentences.

Can you write a simple, compound, complex, and compound-complex sentence using the same independent clause?

Examples

Classify: San Francisco in the springtime is one of my favorite places to visit.

Although the sentence is lengthy, it is simple because it contains only one subject and verb (*San Francisco... is*) modified by additional phrases.

Classify: I love listening to the radio in the car because I can sing along as loud as I want.

The sentence has one independent clause (*I love... car*) and one dependent (*because I . . . want*), so it's complex.

Classify: I wanted to get a dog, but I have a fish because my roommate is allergic to pet dander.

This sentence has three clauses: two independent (*I wanted... dog* and *I have a fish*) and one dependent (*because my... dander*), so it's compound-complex.

Classify: The game was canceled, but we will still practice on Saturday.

This sentence is made up of two independent clauses joined by a conjunction (*but*), so it's compound.

Clause Placement

In addition to these classifications, sentences can also be defined by the location of the main clause. In a PERIODIC SENTENCE, the main idea of the sentence is held until the end. In a CUMULATIVE SENTENCE, the independent clause comes first, and any modifying words or clauses follow it. Note that this type of classification—periodic or cumulative—is not used in place of the simple, compound, complex, or compound-complex classifications. A sentence can be both cumulative and complex, for example.

Examples

Classify: To believe your own thought, to believe that what is true for you in your private heart is true for all men, that is genius.

In this sentence the main independent clause—*that is genius*—is held until the very end, so it's periodic. It's also simple because it has one independent clause.

Classify: We need the tonic of wildness—to wade sometimes in marshes where the bittern and meadow-hen lurk, and hear the booming of the snipe; to smell the whispering sedge where only some wilder and more solitary fowl builds her nest, and the mink crawls with its belly close to the ground.

Here, the main clause—*we need the tonic of wildness*—is at the beginning, so the sentence is cumulative. It's also simple because it has one main clause.

Active and Passive Voice

Sentences can be written in active voice or passive voice. ACTIVE VOICE means that the subjects of the sentences are performing the action of the sentence. In a sentence in PASSIVE VOICE, the subjects are being acted on. So, the sentence *Justin wrecked my car* is in the active voice because the subject (*Justin*) is doing the action (*wrecked*). The sentence can be rewritten in passive voice by using a *to be* verb: *My car was wrecked by Justin.* Now the subject of the sentence (*car*) is being acted on. Notice that it's possible to write the sentence so that the person performing the action is not identified: *My car was wrecked.*

Generally, good writing will make more use of the active than passive voice. However, passive voice can sometimes be the better choice. For example, if it's not known who or what performed the action of the sentence, it's necessary to use passive voice.

Examples

1. Rewrite the following sentence in active voice: *I was hit with a stick by my brother.*

   To rewrite a sentence in active voice, first take the person or object performing the action (usually given in a prepositional phrase) and make it the subject. Then, the subject of the original sentence becomes the object and the **to be** verb disappears: **My brother hit me with a stick**.

2. Rewrite the following sentence in passive voice: *My roommate made coffee this morning.*

   To rewrite a sentence in passive voice, the object (**coffee**) becomes the subject, and the subject gets moved to a prepositional phrase at the end of the sentence. Lastly, the **to be** verb is added: **The coffee was made this morning by my roommate.**

Point of View

A sentence's POINT OF VIEW is the perspective from which it is written. Point of view is described as either first, second, or third person.

Table 4.4. Point of view

PERSON	PRONOUNS USED	WHO'S ACTING?	EXAMPLE
first	I, we	the writer	I take my time when shopping for shoes.
second	you	the reader	You prefer to shop online.
third	he, she, it, they	the subject	She buys shoes from her cousin's store.

Using first person is best for writing in which the writer's personal experiences, feelings, and opinions are an important element. Second person is best for writing in which the author directly addresses the reader. Third person is most common in formal and academic writing; it creates distance between the writer and the reader. A sentence's point of view has to remain consistent throughout the sentence.

Look for pronouns to help you identify which point of view a sentence is using.

Example

Wrong: If someone wants to be a professional athlete, you have to practice often.

Correct: If you want to be a professional athlete, you have to practice often.

Correct: If someone wants to be a professional athlete, he or she has to practice often.

In the first sentence, the person shifts from third (*someone*) to second (*you*). It needs to be rewritten to be consistent.

HOMOPHONES AND SPELLING

The HESI A² will include questions that ask you to identify the correct **HOMOPHONE**, which is a set of words that are pronounced similarly but have different meanings. Bawl and ball, for example, are homophones. You will also be tested on spelling, so it's good to familiarize yourself with commonly misspelled words.

COMMON HOMOPHONES
- bare/bear
- brake/break
- die/dye
- effect/affect
- flour/flower
- heal/heel
- insure/ensure
- morning/mourning
- peace/piece
- poor/pour
- principal/principle
- sole/soul
- stair/stare
- suite/sweet
- their/there/they're
- wear/where

Examples

Choose the sentence that contains the correct spelling of the underlined word.

1. Her excellent <u>manors</u> and friendly personality <u>made</u> it easy for her to win new clients.
2. Her excellent <u>manners</u> and friendly personality <u>made</u> it easy for her to win new clients.
3. Her excellent <u>manors</u> and friendly personality <u>maid</u> it easy for her to win new clients.
4. Her excellent <u>manners</u> and friendly personality <u>maid</u> it easy for her to win new clients.

People's behavior towards others are *manners*, while a *manor* is a country house. A *maid* is a person who cleans and *made* is the past tense of make. **So, the correct answer is 2.**

1. The nurse has three <u>patents</u> to see before lunch.
2. The nurse has three <u>patience</u> to see before lunch.
3. The nurse has three <u>patients</u> to see before lunch.
4. The nurse has three <u>pateince</u> to see before lunch.

The correct spelling of *patients* is found in answer choice 3.

BIOLOGY

BIOLOGICAL MOLECULES

ORGANIC compounds are those that contain carbon. These compounds, such as glucose, triacylglycerol, and guanine, are used in day-to-day metabolic processes. Many of these molecules are POLYMERS formed from repeated smaller units called MONOMERS. INORGANIC compounds are those that do not contain carbon. These make up a very small fraction of mass in living organisms, and are usually minerals such as potassium, sodium, and iron.

There are several classes of organic compounds commonly found in living organisms. These biological molecules include carbohydrates, proteins, lipids, and nucleic acids, which combined make up more than 95 percent of non-water material in living organisms.

Carbohydrates

CARBOHYDRATES, also called sugars, are molecules made of carbon, hydrogen, and oxygen. Sugars are primarily used in organisms as a source of energy: they can be catabolized (broken down) to create energy molecules such as adenosine triphosphate (ATP) or nicotinamide adenine dinucleotide (NAD+), providing a source of electrons to drive cellular processes.

The basic formula for a carbohydrate is CH_2O, and the majority of carbohydrates are multiples of this empirical formula. For example, GLUCOSE is $C_6H_{12}O_6$. Carbohydrates can also bond together to form polymeric compounds. Some polymers of glucose include starch, which is used to store excess sugar, and cellulose, which is a support fiber responsible in part for the strength of plants.

HYDROCARBONS AND CARBOHYDRATES

alkanes:
C_nH_{2n+2}

alkenes:
C_nH_{2n}

alkynes:
C_nH_{2n-2}

monosaccharides:
$(CH_2O)_n$

Lipids

Lipids are compounds primarily composed of carbon and hydrogen with only a small percentage of oxygen. Lipids contain a **head**, usually formed of glycerol or phosphate, and a **tail**, which is a hydrocarbon chain. The composition of the head, whether it is a carboxylic acid functional group, a phosphate group, or some other functional group, is usually polar, meaning it is hydrophilic. The tail is composed of carbon and hydrogen, and is usually nonpolar, meaning it is hydrophobic.

The combined polarity of the lipid head and the non-polarity of the lipid tail is a unique feature of lipids critical to the formation of the phospholipid bilayer in the cell membrane. The fatty acid tails are all pointed inward, and the heads are pointed outward. This provides a semi-permeable membrane that allows a cell to separate its contents from the environment.

Figure 5.1. Free fatty acid lipid

The **saturation** of a lipid describes the number of double bonds in the tail of the lipid. The more double bonds a lipid tail has, the more unsaturated the molecule is, and the more bends there are in its structure. As a result, unsaturated fats (like oils) tend to be liquid at room temperature, whereas saturated fats (like lard or butter) are solid at room temperature.

Proteins

Proteins are large molecules composed of a chain of **amino acids**. The sequence of amino acids in the chain determines the protein's structure and function. Each amino acid is composed of three parts:

- Amino group ($-NH_2$): The amino group is found on all amino acids.
- Carboxyl group ($-COOH$): The carboxyl group is found on all amino acids.
- R group: The R group is a unique functional group that is different for each amino acid. For example, in the histidine amino acid seen in Figure 5.2, the R group is a cyclic imidazole group.

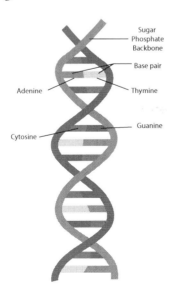

Figure 5.2. The amino acid histidine

The R group determines the amino acid's physiological function.

There are twenty-two amino acids used to produce proteins. It is not necessary to know each amino acid, but it is important to know that sequences of these amino acids form proteins, and that each amino acid has a unique R-functional group.

Nucleic Acids

NUCLEIC ACIDS, which include DNA and RNA, store all information necessary to produce proteins. These molecules are built using smaller molecules called NUCLEOTIDES, which are composed of a 5-carbon sugar, a phosphate group, and a nitrogenous base.

DNA is made from four nucleotides: adenine, guanine, cytosine, and thymine. Together, adenine and guanine are classified as PURINES while thymine and cytosine are classified as PYRIMIDINES. These nucleotides bond together in pairs; the pairs are then bonded together in a chain to create a double helix shape with the sugar as the outside and the nitrogenous base on the inside. In DNA, adenine and thymine always bond together as do guanine and cytosine. In RNA, thymine is replaced by a nucleotide called uracil, which bonds with adenine. RNA also differs from DNA in that it often exists as a single strand.

The major differences between DNA and RNA include:

- Uracil replaces thymine in RNA.

- RNA can exist as a single strand while DNA is double stranded.

- RNA contains ribose while DNA contains deoxyribose.

Figure 5.3. DNA

Examples

1. Match the polymer with the correct monomer.
    A) DNA; nucleic acid
    B) RNA; amino acid
    C) starch; lipid
    D) histidine; glucose

2. Which of the following is not found in DNA?
    A) adenine
    B) uracil
    C) thymine
    D) cytosine

3. Which of the following is not a compound created from sugar?
    A) glycogen
    B) starch
    C) cellulose
    D) guanine

4. An amino acid contains an R group, an amino group, and a:
    A) hydroxyl group
    B) carboxyl group
    C) phenyl group
    D) phosphate group

    Answers: 1. A) 2. B) 3. D) 4. B)

THE HISTORY OF LIFE

Scientists believe life on Earth started around 3.8 billion years ago. The exact time when the first living cells appeared is unknown, but observations in geology have indicated the type of environment when living cells first appeared. It is hypothesized that life began due to a sequence of events that created biological molecules and cell-like structures:

1. synthesis of amino acid molecules and sugars, possibly from interaction of lightning and high temperatures near volcanic vents

2. joining and interaction of these molecules in something resembling modern-day proteins

3. assembly of these molecules within a membrane, which started to resemble a cell

The researchers STANLEY MILLER and HAROLD UREY had a hypothesis that the above three steps could have happened in a primordial environment in which there was no oxygen. Note that higher concentrations of oxygen did not appear until the evolution of plants, so life must have started without a significant oxygen presence.

Miller-Urey Experiment

In the **MILLER-UREY EXPERIMENT**, the researchers placed a mixture of ingredients that included water, methane, ammonia, and hydrogen into an enclosed reactor bulb. The conditions were modified to simulate those that were thought to exist on Earth several billion years ago. A pair of electrodes was placed into the reactor vessel, and sparks that simulated lightning were fired through the mixture every few minutes.

Miller and Urey found that their reaction mixture turned pink in color within a day, and after two weeks, the reactor vessel contained a thick solution that included a number of important molecules. Among the compounds that formed were with some amino acids, including glycine, as well as sugars. After full characterization, the scientists found that the experiment created eleven of the twenty-two known amino acids.

Fossil Record

The **FOSSIL RECORD** is a history of species that existed throughout time that has been unearthed by archaeologists. The fossils, if well preserved, are able to show us the bone structures and the forms of animals, plants, and even cells that existed billions of years ago. The fossils can be used to understand how species evolved through time and, in some cases, even to see what they ate and the environments in which they lived.

The age of fossils is determined through a method called **RADIOMETRIC DATING**, which examines the amount of radioactive carbon remaining in the sample. The radioactive carbon isotope carbon-14 has a half-life of 5,730 years, which means that this isotope can be used to reliably date fossils that are up to about ten half-lives, or 50,000 years in age. For fossils older than that, an isotope with a longer half-life is used. In some fossils, the presence of small amounts of uranium-238, with a half-life of 4.5 billion years, can aid in dating.

Timeline of Earth

- 4.6 billion years ago: formation of Earth
- 3.7 billion years ago: prokaryotes first came into existence
- 2.6 billion years ago: oxygen is believed to be present in the atmosphere
- 2.1 billion years ago: eukaryotic organisms have evolved

- 1.5 billion years ago: multicellular organisms have evolved
- 800 million years ago: the first animals exist
- 500 million years ago: Paleozoic Era
- 260 million years ago: Mesozoic Era
- 65 million years ago: Cenozoic Era
- 10,000 years ago: early humans

The three eras, the Paleozoic, Mesozoic, and Cenozoic, were each characterized by an explosion of different species. Each era was responsible for the formation of a number of different species.

PALEOZOIC: The Paleozoic era was characterized by the colonization of land, with many types of plants appearing, and the diversification of fish and reptile species.

MESOZOIC: The Mesozoic era saw the first flowering plants appearing, as well as many land animals, including the dinosaurs. However, at the end of the Mesozoic era, the extinction of the dinosaurs occurred, likely due to a catastrophic event such as a huge meteorite striking the earth.

CENOZOIC: In the Cenozoic era, many of the animals and plants that we see today started to evolve, including mammals, many different angiosperm plants, and the direct ancestors of humans.

Examples

1. A student is attempting to replicate the Miller-Urey experiment. Which of the following reagents does he *not* need?

   A) ammonia

   B) carbon dioxide

   C) oxygen

   D) water vapor

2. In the Miller-Urey experiment, which attempted to replicate conditions that were existent in early Earth, which of the following compounds was *not* created?

   A) amino acids

   B) methane

   C) lipid precursors

   D) chlorophyll

   Answers: 1. C) 2. D)

THE BIOLOGICAL HIERARCHY
- atom
- molecule
- organelle
- cell
- tissue
- organ
- organ system
- organism
- population
- community
- ecosystem
- biome
- biosphere

THE BASICS OF THE CELL

The **CELL** is the most basic unit of life; all higher organisms are composed of cells. Most cells range from 20 μm to 100 μm in size, although some can be even larger. Cells were first discovered by the Englishman **Robert Hooke**, the inventor of the microscope, in the 1600s. However, cell theory truly began to develop when a Dutchman named **Antony van Leeuwenhoek** pioneered new developments in the field of microscopy, allowing scientists to view bacteria, protozoa, and other microorganisms.

Cell Subgroups

Cells are roughly divided into two large subgroups: prokaryotic cells and eukaryotic cells. The primary similarities and differences are listed in Table 5.1. below.

Table 5.1. Prokaryotic and eukaryotic cells

Traits unique to prokaryotic cells	Prokaryotic cells, such as bacteria, are the only types of cells which contain peptidoglycan, a sugar, and an amino acid layer that supports the cell membrane.	Prokaryotic cells do not have a nuclear membrane.	Many prokaryotic cells contain plasmids, which are circular rings of DNA that hold genetic information.
Traits shared by prokaryotic and eukaryotic cells	Both cells have cell membranes and often have cell walls.	Both types of cells contain DNA.	Both can have flagella and ribosomes.
Traits unique to eukaryotic cells	Eukaryotic cells have a nuclear membrane, and DNA is contained within the membrane.	Eukaryotic cells have a Golgi body, which is used for transport of proteins.	Some eukaryotic cells have lysosomes or peroxisomes, which are used in digestion.

Parts of the Cell

Although the cell is the smallest unit of life, there are many small bodies, called **organelles**, which exist in the cell. These organelles are required for the many process that takes place inside a cell.

- **Mitochondria:** The mitochondria are the organelles responsible for making ATP within the cell. A mitochondria has several layers of membranes used to assist the electron transport chain. This pathway uses energy provided by molecules such as glucose or fat (lipid) to generate ATP through the transfer of electrons.
- **Vacuole:** A vacuole is a small body used to transfer materials within and out of the cell. It has a membrane of its own and can carry things such as cell wastes, sugars, or proteins.
- **Nucleus:** The nucleus of a eukaryotic cell contains all of its genetic information in the form of DNA. In the nucleus, DNA replication and transcription occur. In the eukaryotic cell, after transcription, the mRNA is exported out of the nucleus into the cytosol for use.
- **Endoplasmic reticulum:** The ER, for short, is used for translation of mRNA into proteins, and

for the transport of proteins out of the cell. The rough endoplasmic reticulum has many ribosomes attached to it, which function as the cell's machinery in transforming RNA into protein. The smooth endoplasmic reticulum is associated with the production of fats and steroid hormones.

- **RIBOSOME**: The ribosome is a small two-protein unit that reads mRNA and, with the assistance of transport proteins, creates an amino acid.

Figure 5.4. Animal cell

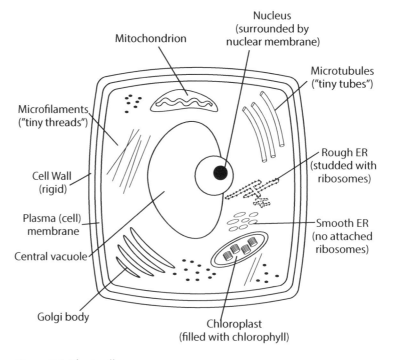

Figure 5.5. Plant cell

Cell Membrane

The CELL MEMBRANE is a unique layer that surrounds the cell and performs numerous functions. It is composed of compounds called PHOSPHOLIPIDS, which are amphipathic, and consist of an alkane tail and a phospho-group head. The alkane lipid tail is hydrophobic, meaning it will not allow water to pass through, and the phosphate group head is hydrophilic, which allows water to pass through. The arrangement of these molecules forms a bilayer, which has a hydrophobic middle layer. In this manner, the cell is able to control the import and export of various substances into the cell.

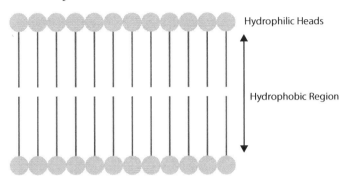

Figure 5.6. Cell membrane bilayer

In addition to the phospholipid bilayer, the cell membrane often includes proteins, which perform a variety of functions. Some proteins are used as receptors, which allow the cell to interact with its surroundings. Others are TRANSMEMBRANE PROTEINS, meaning that they cross the entire membrane. These types of proteins are usually channels which allow the transportation of molecules into and out of the cell.

Membrane proteins are also used in cell-to-cell interaction. This includes functions such as cell-cell joining or recognition, in which a cell membrane protein contacts a protein from another cell. A good example of this is the immune response in the human body. Due to the proteins found on the cell membrane of antigens, immune system cells can contact, recognize, and attempt to remove them.

Membrane Transport

A cell needs to be able to both import and export vital substances across the membrane while at the same time preventing harmful substances from entering the cell. Two major classes of transportation allow this process to occur: active transport and passive transport.

ACTIVE TRANSPORT uses ATP to accomplish one of two tasks: it can move a molecule against the concentration gradient (from low concentration to high), or it can be used to import or export a bulky molecule, such as a sugar or a protein, across the cell membrane. Active transport requires the use of proteins and energy in the form of ATP. The ATP produced by the cell binds to the proteins in the cell membrane and is hydrolyzed, producing the energy required to change the conformational structure of the protein. This change in the structure of the protein allows the protein to funnel molecules across the cell membrane.

PASSIVE TRANSPORT does not require energy and allows molecules such as water to passively diffuse across the cell membrane. Facilitated diffusion is a form of passive transport that does not require energy but does require the use of proteins located on the cell membrane. These transport proteins typically have a "channel" running through the core of a protein specific to a certain type of molecule. For example, a transport protein for sodium only allows sodium to flow through the channel.

Tonicity

The balance of water in the cell is one of the most important regulatory mechanisms for the cell. Water enters or exits the cell through a process called OSMOSIS. This movement of water does not usually require energy, and the movement is regulated by a factor called tonicity.

TONICITY is the concentration of solutes in the cell. Solutes can be salt ions, such as sodium or chlorine, or other molecules such as sugar, amino acids, or proteins. The difference in tonicity between the cell and its outside environment governs the transportation of water into and out of the cell. For example, if there is a higher tonicity inside the cell, then water will enter the cell. If there is a higher tonicity outside the cell, the water will leave the cell. This is due to a driving force called the CHEMIOSMOTIC POTENTIAL that attempts to make tonicity equal across a membrane.

There are three terms used to describe a cell's tonicity:

- An ISOTONIC cell has the same concentration of solutes inside and outside of the cell. There will be no transport of water in this case.

- A HYPERTONIC cell has a lower concentration of solutes inside than outside of the cell. The cell will lose water to the environment and shrivel. This is what happens if a cell is placed into a salty solution.

- A HYPOTONIC cell has a higher concentration of solutes inside than outside of the cell. The cell will absorb water from the environment and swell, becoming turgid.

Cell Interactions

With the vast number of cells in living organisms, (an estimated 100 trillion in the human body), how do they all interact and talk with one another? Cells are able to communicate with one other through cell signaling, which occurs via chemical signals excreted by the cell. It is also possible to have direct cell-to-cell communication through protein receptors located in the cell membrane. Important signaling molecules include CYCLIC AMP, which is best known for its function in the signaling cascade when epinephrine binds to a cell, and NEUROTRANSMITTERS such as glycine, aspartate, acetylcholine, dopamine, serotonin, and melatonin, among many others.

LOCAL or DIRECT SIGNALING is a signal that occurs between cells that are either right next to each other or within a few cells' distance. This communication can occur by two methods. First, GAP JUNCTIONS exist between the membranes of two cells that can allow signaling molecules to directly enter the cells. Second, the receptors on the membrane can bind with other cells that have membrane receptors to communicate.

The primary chemical used in long range signaling is called a HORMONE. In humans and animals, hormones are produced by organs and cells in the endocrine system such as the testes, hypothalamus, and pituitary glands. These hormones, once released, can travel throughout the organism through the circulatory system (blood). The hormones can then bind to other cells that have the appropriate receptor and cause a signal to start inside the cell.

One example of long range signaling in the human body is the production of insulin by the pancreas. Insulin spreads through the body via the blood, and when it binds to an insulin receptor on a cell, the cell begins to take in more glucose. This prcoess is called long range signaling because insulin is produced by cells in only one location (the pancreas) but is able to affect nearly all other cells in the body.

An example of long distance signaling in plants is the production of ethylene, a ripening chemical. It can be present in the air or diffuse through cell walls, and the production of ethylene by one plant can cause a chain reaction that causes nearby plants to also start ripening.

How do the hormones you studied in human body science act as long range signaling molecules?

Examples

1. The Golgi body is one of the largest organelles found in the cell, and is responsible for:

    A) protein synthesis

    B) intracellular and extracellular transport

    C) replication of DNA

    D) formation of ribosomes

2. In animal cell structure, the cell membrane is composed of a phospholipid bilayer that separates the cell from its surroundings. Which of the following is also present in the cell membrane?

   A) proteins

   B) ATP

   C) mitochondria

   D) vacuoles

3. A student places a cell with a 50 mM intracellular ion content into a solution containing 20 mM ion content. What will happen to the cell?

   A) The cell will shrink.

   B) The cell membrane will become porous.

   C) The cell will expand.

   D) The cell is isotonic, and nothing will occur.

4. Which of the following species cannot travel across a cell membrane without the use of energy?

   A) water

   B) potassium

   C) sodium

   D) glucose

5. Although plant cells and animal cells are roughly the same size, the volume of cytosol, or plasma, inside an animal cell is significantly larger than that seen in a plant cell. What is responsible for this difference?

   A) the presence of chlorophyll in plant cells

   B) the presence of an endoplasmic reticulum in plant cells

   C) the presence of a large storage vacuole in plant cells

   D) the presence of a cell wall in plant cells

6. The endoplasmic reticulum is broken up into the rough ER and the smooth ER. The rough ER is responsible for synthesis of proteins and some polysaccharides. What is the smooth ER responsible for?

   A) metabolism of carbohydrates and synthesis of lipids

   B) DNA replication and transcription

   C) modification of RNA after the transcription process

   D) degradation of residual amino acids and cell waste

7. Which of the following is not a type of cell connection or junction between cells?

A) tight junction

B) gap junction

C) desmosome

D) channel junction

Answers: 1. B) 2. A) 3. C) 4. D) 5. C) 6. D) 7. C)

ENZYMES

Enzymes are an important type of protein crucial for aiding various reactions in the cell. An ENZYME is a large protein that acts as a catalyst, which is a substance able to speed up a reaction by reducing the activation energy of a reaction or bringing reactants closer together.

All chemical reactions have something called an activation energy, which is the amount of energy required for a reaction to begin. For some reactions, this barrier is quite high, which is why enzymes are necessary. Enzymes can reduce the activation energy of a reaction through interaction with the bonds in the reactants. Many enzymes have something called an ACTIVE SITE, which is an area of the protein with certain functional groups that are able to bind with a reactant. This binding forms a stabilized intermediate that allows the reactant to more easily dissociate or react with another reagent.

Enzymes can also bring reactants closer together. Many reaction rates are limited by the concentration of reactants in the solution. For example, in a cell, the concentration of glucose is usually less than 0.5 mM. This means that the chance for a glucose molecule to contact another reactant is quite low. Enzymes can bind to a glucose molecule and then bind to the other reactant, forcing the reactants close enough together for the reaction to take place.

Some examples of important enzymes include:

- **DNA POLYMERASE**: the enzyme responsible for copying DNA. The enzyme binds to a single strand of DNA and assembles nucleotides to match the strand.

- **PYRUVATE KINASE**: the enzyme responsible for glycolysis, which is the initial breakdown of glucose in the human body (and other organisms).

- **ENDOGLUCANASE:** enzyme responsible for the breakdown of cellulose in fungi and bacteria. This enzyme breaks down the cellulose chain into smaller sugars.

CELLULAR METABOLISM

METABOLISM is the series of chemical reactions that produce the energy and molecules necessary for cellular activity. These processes can best be understood as a pathway. For example, a glucose molecule can be converted into an intermediate (pyruvate) which is then converted into a product (ATP). In a single cell, there are hundreds, if not thousands, of these metabolic pathways that all function to keep the cell alive.

Catabolism vs. Anabolism

A major function of metabolism is **CATABOLISM**, which is the breakdown of molecules. A catabolic pathway breaks down a larger molecule into smaller ones, often releasing energy. For example, the process of breaking down fat for energy is catabolic. **ANABOLISM** is the opposite of catabolism: in an anabolic pathway, energy and smaller molecules are used by the cell to build a more complicated molecule. A good example of an anabolic pathway is the synthesis of a protein.

ATP: The Most Important Energy Molecule

ATP is short for **ADENOSINE TRIPHOSPHATE**, which is the most common molecule used for energy. The ATP molecule is formed from ribose, a sugar, and three phosphate groups (a phosphate group is written as Pi). ATP is primarily used for energy, but is also used to form adenine.

ATP is able to store energy through the formation of high-energy bonds between the phosphate groups in the "tail" of the molecule. When the last phosphate bond in the group is broken through a hydrolysis reaction, a phosphate molecule is released. This exothermic reaction releases energy that can then be used to drive another cellular reaction. The product of the reaction is a phosphate molecule and a lower energy adenosine diphosphate (ADP) molecule. When two phosphate groups are removed from ATP in a unit called a pyrophosphate (PPi), the molecule adenosine monophosphate (AMP) is produced.

Under standard state conditions, the conversion of ATP to ADP releases 30.5 kilojoules per mole of energy. In a living cell, however, that value increases to 57 kilojoules per mole.

Figure 5.7. Adenosine triphosphate

Because ATP is highly reactive, it is not stored in the body in high quantities. Instead, ADP is recycled and converted to ATP by the addition of a phosphate group. This process of forming ATP is a catabolic pathway that largely occurs in the mitochondria. The energy for this process is stored in lipids, carbohydrates, and proteins.

Respiratory Pathways

ATP is produced through a catabolic process which can take place in one of two ways. The first method, in which oxygen is used, is called an AEROBIC RESPIRATORY PATHWAY. In a respiratory pathway, a food substance, such as glucose or amino acids, is broken down with the use of oxygen, and ATP is produced. The second method (addressed further below) is an anaerobic process called fermentation that does not use oxygen.

The basic overall process of aerobic cellular respiration is shown below:

Organic compound + Oxygen →
Carbon dioxide + Water + Energy

Because the reaction requires oxygen, animals that use aerobic respiration require oxygen to live. For example, humans breathe in oxygen using our lungs for respiration, and produce carbon dioxide and water as a byproduct. (Note that while the act of breathing is often called respiration, it is a different process than cellular respiration.)

The energy obtained from the breakdown of organic compounds comes from the bonds of the compound. This energy can vary widely, from about four kilocalories of energy per gram in carbohydrates to nine kilocalories per gram in lipids. The transfer of energy from the bonds breaking in these molecules occurs through an oxidation-reduction reaction, which involves the transfer of electrons from one species to another.

In respiration, there are two primary pathways that are important to know. The first is glycolysis, which breaks down glucose into two molecules of pyruvate and produces a small amount of ATP. The second is the citric acid cycle, which takes pyruvate and produces much more ATP, as well as the byproduct carbon dioxide.

Glycolysis

GLYCOLYSIS is the first step in the breakdown of sugars. The overall reaction of glycolysis is as follows:

Glucose + 2 [NAD]+ + 2 [ADP] + 2 [P]$_i$ →
2 Pyruvate + 2 [NADH] + 2H$^+$ + 2 [ATP] + 2H$_2$O

Overall, a glucose molecule is used to produce two pyruvate molecules (which are fed into the citric acid cycle), four energy

Cellular respiration is the conversion of energy into a form that can be used by cells. Physiological respiration is the exchange of oxygen and carbon dioxide between cells and the environment.

molecules (two NADH and two ATP molecules), and two molecules of water.

The conversion of glucose into these products takes place over a ten-step pathway, which involves two phases. The first phase uses energy in order to break apart the glucose molecule. The second phase then recovers energy in the form of ATP and NADH, and results in the production of the pyruvate molecules.

As a result of these steps, there is a production of four molecules of ATP and two molecules of NADH; there is a corresponding use of two molecules of ATP. This results in the net production of two ATP, two NADH, and two pyruvate molecules.

Citric Acid Cycle

The majority of the energy in the glucose molecule has not been released by glycolysis. Under aerobic conditions, the citric acid cycle and electron transport chain, which follow glycolysis, will produce more ATP. The citric acid cycle is also known as the Krebs cycle or the tricarboxylic acid (TCA) cycle.

In eukaryotic cells, the CITRIC ACID CYCLE takes place in the matrix of the mitochondria of the cell. The same reaction can occur in the cytosol/cytoplasm of prokaryotic cells. The citric acid cycle gets its name from the production and re-absorption of citric acid during the process. During the course of the TCA cycle, a molecule of pyruvate derived from glycolysis is transformed into three molecules of CO_2 and two molecules of ATP. The TCA cycle needs to run twice for each molecule of glucose, due to the two molecules of pyruvate obtained from a molecule of glucose. Thus, at the end of two turns of the cycle, four ATP have been produced.

- In each turn of the citric acid cycle, which includes the oxidation of pyruvate (Step 1), four NADH, one $FADH_2$, one GTP, and two CO_2 are produced. NADH and $FADH_2$ are used to feed the electron transport chain, during which the bulk of ATP is produced.
- Each glucose molecule requires two turns of the citric acid cycle, yielding eight NADH, two $FADH_2$, two GTP, and four CO_2. The GTP can be converted to ATP.
- After glycolysis and the citric acid cycle have been completed, there is a net of four ATP, ten NADH, and two $FADH_2$.

The Electron Transport Chain

The ELECTRON TRANSPORT CHAIN is located in the inner membrane of the mitochondria in the eukaryotic cell. In the chain, a series of electron carriers couple the movment of electrons with the transportation of hydrogen ions (H+) across a membrane to create an electrochemical gradient. The source of these electrons is usually NADH and FADH$_2$ generated from the citric acid cycle.

Figure 5.8. Cellular respiration

This electrochemical gradient is used by the molecule ATP synthase to create ATP from ADP: the flow of the hydrogen ions through the ATP synthase molecules provides the energy to generate ATP. Each NADH typically generates 2.5 ATP; each FADH$_2$ generates 1.5 ATP.

At the end of the Electron Transport Chain, 30 to 32 ATP have typically been produced. It is important to note, however, that this number can vary—up to 38 ATP are produced in plants— depending on what type of shuttles are used to transport the electrons from NADH across the membrane. (Plants don't spend an ATP to transport NADH into the mitochondria.)

Fermentation

Fermentation is an alternative process that can generate ATP in anaerobic conditions. Many organisms, such as yeast, can primarily use fermentation so they do not need oxygen to live. There are two primary forms of fermentation, alcohol and lactic acid fermentation.

ALCOHOL FERMENTATION is probably the most common type of fermentation. After glycolysis occurs, the pyruvate is converted into ethanol. 2-NADH is used in the process, but as acetaldehyde is converted into ethanol, 2-NADH is produced. Yeast are known to ferment sugars, producing ethanol and carbon dioxide, which is the source of the alcohol and carbonation in beer.

LACTIC ACID FERMENTATION differs only slightly from alcohol fermentation. Instead of acetaldehyde being produced, the pyruvate is directly fermented into lactic acid. This takes place in some fungi and bacteria, and can occur in the human body. When you use up your excess stores of ATP during strenuous exercise, and the citric acid cycle is unable to provide more ATP quickly, lactic acid fermentation occurs in your muscles to produce additional energy. This is what causes the "burning" feeling during exercise.

✔
What are some other conditions under which cells might need to use anaerobic respiration?

Examples

1. Which of the following processes produces the most ATP during cellular respiration?

   A) glycolysis

   B) citric acid cycle

   C) lactic acid fermentation

   D) the electron transport chain

2. Which of the following statements about the cycling of ATP is NOT true?

   A) $ATP \rightarrow ADP + P_i$

   B) $ATP \rightarrow ADP + PP_i$

   C) $ATP \rightarrow AMP + PP_i$

   D) $ADP \rightarrow AMP + P_i$

3. In the citric acid cycle, how many runs of the cycle are required to process one molecule of glucose?

   A) 1

   B) 2

   C) 3

   D) 4

4. During the process of aerobic respiration, the movement of which of these ions is responsible for the generation of a large amount of ATP?

   A) potassium

   B) hydrogen

   C) sodium

   D) chlorine

5. Which of the following compounds is not produced by the citric acid cycle?

A) NADH

B) GTP

C) ATP

D) FADH

Answers: 1. D) 2. B) 3. B) 4. B) 5. D)

THE CELL CYCLE

The cell cycle is the process cells go through as they live, grow, and divide to produce new cells. The cell cycle can be divided into four primary phases:

1. G1 phase: growth phase one
2. S phase: DNA replication
3. G2 phase: growth phase two
4. Mitotic phase: The cell undergoes mitosis and splits into two cells.

Together, the G1, S, and G2 phases are known as INTERPHASE. During these phases, which usually take up 80 to 90 percent of the total time in a cell cycle, the cell is growing and conducting normal cell functions.

Mitosis

The process of cell division is called MITOSIS. When a cell divides, it needs to make sure that each copy of the cell has a roughly equal amount of the necessary elements, including DNA, proteins, and organelles.

A cell has a lot of DNA: even the smallest human cell contains a copy of the entire human genome. In human cells, this copy of the genome is nearly two meters in length—quite long when you consider that the average cell is only 100 µm in diameter.

In the nucleus, DNA is organized around proteins called HISTONES; together, this protein and DNA complex is known as CHROMATIN. During interphase, chromatin is usually arranged loosely to allow access to DNA. During mitosis, however, DNA is tightly packaged into units called CHROMOSOMES. When DNA has replicated, the chromosome is composed of two CHROMATIDS joined together at the CENTROMERE.

The mitotic phase is separated into five substages:

- Prophase: In prophase, the DNA in the cell winds into chromatin and each pair of duplicated chromosomes becomes joined. The mitotic spindle, which pulls apart the chromosomes later, forms and drifts to each end of the cell.

THE CELL CYCLE
Go **S**ally **G**o, **M**ake **C**hildren!
- **g**rowth phase 1
- DNA **s**ynthesis
- **g**rowth phase 2
- **m**itosis
- **c**ytokinesis

- Prometaphase: In this phase, the nuclear membrane, which holds the DNA, dissolves, allowing the chromosomes to come free. The chromosomes now start to attach to microtubules linked to the centrioles.
- Metaphase: The centrioles, with microtubules attached to the chromosomes, are now on opposite sides of the cell. The chromosomes align in the middle of the cell, and the microtubules begin contracting.
- Anaphase: In anaphase, the chromosomes move to separate sides of the cell, and the cell structure begins to lengthen, pulling apart as it goes.
- Telophase: In this last part of the cell cycle, the cell membrane splits, and two new daughter cells are formed. The nucleolus, containing the DNA, reforms.

In this manner, cells are able to reproduce quite quickly. Many bacteria or yeast cells have a total cell cycle time of between twenty and thirty minutes, meaning they are able to double in number in that amount of time. This can lead to rapid proliferation of cells, assuming there is no food shortage. For example, a small colony of 200 *E.coli* cells can rapidly grow to more than 20 million cells in a matter of hours.

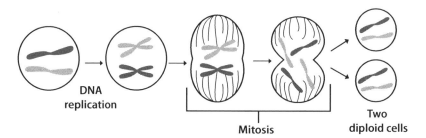

Figure 5.9. Mitosis

Meiosis

A somatic cell contains pairs of homologous chromosomes with one set of chromosomes coming from each parent. For example, humans have 23 pairs of chromosomes, for a total of 46 chromosomes. These cells are described as DIPLOID. Sex cells, on the other hand, have only one set of chromosomes (so, a human sex cell has 23 chromosomes), which is referred to as being HAPLOID. Meiosis is the process by which a diploid cell produces four haploid cells.

There are two consecutive stages of meiosis known as Meiosis I and Meiosis II. These two stages are further broken down into four stages each.

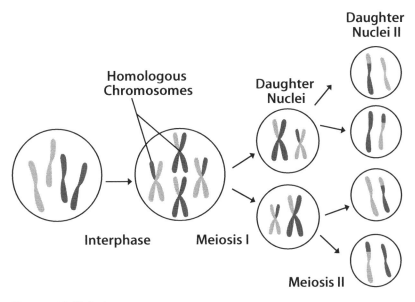

Figure 5.10. Meiosis

MEIOSIS I

1. Prophase I: In prophase, the chromosomes condense using histone proteins and become paired. The paired chromosomes will connect with each other via structures called the synaptonemal complexes. This is also known as synapsis. An important event called crossing-over occurs at this point. Genetic material is exchanged between sister chromatids, resulting in a random assembly of homologous chromosomes. After this is complete, microtubules attach to the chromosomes and centrioles and begin to align them in the middle of the cell.

2. Metaphase I: Similar to mitosis, the chromosomes align in the middle of the cell and begin to pull apart from one another.

3. Anaphase I: The sister chromatids separate and move toward opposite sides of the cell.

4. Telophase I: The cells separate, and each cell now has one copy each of a homologous chromosome.

MEIOSIS II

1. Prophase II: In prophase II, a spindle forms and aligns the chromosomes. No crossing-over occurs.

2. Metaphase II: In Metaphase II, the chromosomes again align at the metaphase plate. This time, however, when they are pulled apart, each daughter cell will not have the same copy of a sister chromatid. This is one of the causes of genetic variation among offspring.

3. Anaphase II: As in Anaphase I, the sister chromatids pull apart to opposite ends of the cell.

MITOSIS

I Passed **M**y **A**natomy **T**est

- Interphase
- Prophase
- Metaphase
- Anaphase
- Telophase

4. Telophase II: The cell splits apart, resulting in four unique daughter cells.

Table 5.2. Mitosis vs. meiosis

EVENT	MITOSIS	MEIOSIS
DNA replication	Occurs in interphase	Occurs in interphase
Number of Divisions	1	2
Synapsis	Does not occur	Occurs in prophase I
Number of Daughter Cells	2	4
Role in Animals	Cell growth and repair	Production of gametes for reproduction

Introduction of Genetic Variation in Meiosis

One of meiosis' most important roles is the introduction of genetic variation. The INDEPENDENT ASSORTMENT of chromosomes in this process gives each gamete a unique subset of genes from the parent. When the haploid gamete combines with another to form a zygote, the result is a genetically unique organism that has a different gene composition than either of the parents.

The process of meiosis also introduces genetic variation during CROSSING OVER, which occurs in prophase I when homologous chromosomes pair along their lengths. Each gene on each chromosome becomes aligned with its sister gene. Then, when crossing over occurs, the DNA sequence is broken and crisscrossed, creating a new chromatid with pieces of each of the original homologous chromosomes.

Finally, meiosis allows for RANDOM FERTILIZATION. Although the gametes produced by each gender are unique, the fact that millions of sperm are produced by the human male (and quite a bit more in other species), means that there are many different possible combinations. For this reason, even though we might cross an animal pair together hundreds of times, it is next to impossible to get two children that have the same genotype (except identical twins).

Apoptosis

APOPTOSIS is an elaborate cellular signaling mechanism that determines when a cell dies. In normal animals and cells, apoptosis is a well-regulated occurrence that prevents the overgrowth of cells. In the process of apoptosis, enzymes and other cellular agents break down materials in the cell until the membrane dissociates and nothing remains.

Apoptosis has been observed in nearly all living organisms, and is an essential part of growth and regrowth. For example, humans' skin cells undergo apoptosis every day with dead skin cells shedding off and new skin cells replacing them.

The mechanism of apoptosis is one of the most studied in biology due to its link to many cancers. Cancerous tumors can develop due to a failure of the apoptosis pathway, leading to the growth of cells that never die. (Note, however, that cancer can be caused by many things, not just a lack of apoptosis.)

Examples

1. A scientist takes DNA samples from a cell culture at two different times, each sample having the same cell count. In the first sample, he finds that there is 6.5 pg of DNA, whereas in the second sample he finds that there is 13 pg of DNA. Which stage of the cell cycle is the second sample in?

    A) interphase G1

    B) interphase S

    C) interphase G2

    D) none of the above

2. Which of the following processes will take place in both mitosis and meiosis?

    A) separation of homologous chromatids

    B) formation of new nuclei that each have half the number of chromosomes that exist in the parent nuclei

    C) tightening of chromatin into chromosomes

    D) separation of duplicated sister chromatids

3. Meiosis creates genetic variation in all of the following ways except:

    A) creating haploid sex cells that will be randomly fertilized

    B) allowing for the exchange of genetic material between chromosomes

    C) increasing the probability of mutations in the nucleotide sequence of DNA

    D) sorting each set of homologous chromosomes independently

    Answers: 1. C) 2. D) 3. C)

DNA REPLICATION

DNA REPLICATION is the process by which a copy of DNA is created in a cell.

The Basics of DNA

Deoxyribonucleic acid, or DNA, has a double helix structure consisting of two complementary strands of DNA. Each DNA strand has a deoxyribose sugar backbone and one of four nucleic acid bases: guanine, adenine, thymine, and cytosine (G, A, T, and C, respectively). These bases bind together to create DNA's two strands: A and T form a pair, and G and C form a pair.

The individual strands of DNA are directional, meaning it matters in which direction the DNA is read. The two ends of a DNA strand are called the 3' end and the 5' end, and these names are included when describing a section of DNA, as shown below:

5'-ATGAATTGCCT-3'

For two complementary strands of DNA, one end starts at 5' and the other starts at 3':

5'-ATGAATTGCCT-3'

3'-TACTTAACGGA-5'

This naming convention is needed to understand the direction of DNA replication, and where the enzymes bind during the process.

The Process of Replication

During DNA replication, three steps will occur. The first step is INITIATION, in which an initiator protein binds to regions of DNA known as origin sites. Once the initiation protein has been bound, the DNA polymerase complex will be able to attach. At this point, the DNA will unwind into two separate single strands.

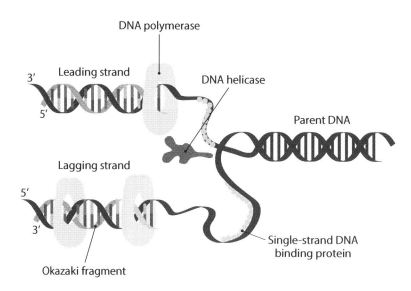

Figure 5.11. DNA replication

During the next step, ELONGATION, new strands of DNA are created. Single strand binding proteins (SSBs) will bind to each strand of the DNA. Then, DNA polymerase will attach and start replicating the strands by synthesizing a new, complementary strand. DNA polymerase reads the DNA in the 3' to 5' direction, meaning the new strand is synthesized in the 5' to 3' direction. This creates a problem, because the DNA can only be read in the 3' to 5' direction on one strand, known as the LEADING STRAND. The LAGGING STRAND, which runs from 5' to 3', has to be synthesized piece by piece in chunks called OKAZAKI FRAGMENTS. The breaks between these fragments are later filled in by DNA ligase.

The last step in the process of DNA replication is TERMINATION. After DNA polymerase completes the copying process, the replication forks meet and the process is terminated. There is one catch to this: because the DNA polymerase enzyme can never read or replicate the very end of a strand of DNA, every time a full chromosome is replicated, a small part of DNA is lost at the end. This piece of DNA is usually non-coding and is called a TELOMERE. The shortening of the telomeres is the reason why replication can only occur a limited number of times in somatic cells before DNA replication is no longer possible.

Table 5.3. Important enzymes in DNA replication

DNA HELICASE	Unwinds a section of DNA to create a segment with two single strands.
DNA POLYMERASE	DNA polymerase I is responsible for synthesizing Okasaki fragments. DNA polymerase III is responsible for the primary replication of the 5' to 3' strand.
DNA LIGASE	Ligase fixes small breaks in the DNA strand and is used to seal the finished DNA strands.
DNA TELOMERASE	In some cells, DNA telomerase lengthens the telomeres at the end of each strand of DNA, allowing it to be copied additional times.

Polymerase Chain Reaction (PCR)

PCR, which was developed in 1983, is a method used in biology to artificially replicate DNA. This can be useful when looking at the presence or size of a gene, or in order to get enough DNA to insert into a host organism. The PCR method uses primers, DNA polymerase, a template, and a machine called a thermocycler in order to replicate the DNA. The basic steps are as follows:

1. Denaturation: The DNA is heated to 90°C to denature it and cause it to form single strands.

2. Annealing: The reaction temperature is set to between 50 and 60°C, which allows the primers to anneal to the template.

3. Elongation: The reaction temperature is set between 70 and 80°C, which is an optimal temperature for a modified DNA polymerase called Taq polymerase. DNA replication occurs.

This set of steps is then repeated up to one hundred times in the thermocycler. As a result, one hundred copies of DNA can result in 1.1×10^{14} copies of DNA in forty cycles.

Examples

1. During DNA replication, the 3' strand and the 5' strand are simultaneously replicated. Which enzyme is responsible for replicated the 3' strand?

   A) DNA polymerase III

   B) DNA ligase

   C) DNA polymerase I

   D) DNA helicase

2. Small sections of DNA are lost during replication because

   A) the sections of DNA between Okazaki fragments cannot be recovered.

   B) DNA polymerase cannot replicate the end of the DNA strand.

   C) DNA cannot be read in the 5' to 3' direction.

   D) the initiator proteins bind to only one strand of DNA.

   Answers: 1. C) 2. B)

TRANSCRIPTION AND TRANSLATION

The processing of information stored in DNA to produce a protein takes place in two stages: transcription and translation. In transcription, an mRNA copy of the DNA is created. In translation, the mRNA strand is read by a ribosome to create an amino acid chain, which is folded into a protein.

Transcription

DNA TRANSCRIPTION is the process of making messenger RNA (mRNA) from a DNA strand. The steps for DNA transcription are similar to that of DNA replication, although different enzymes are used. The DNA strand provides a template for RNA polymerase: the DNA is first unwound, and then RNA polymerase makes a complementary transcript of the DNA sequence.

After the primary transcript has been made, the mRNA is sent to SPLICEOSOMES, which remove the non-coding regions of the RNA called INTRONS. The final RNA product is then available for translation into the actual protein.

Codons

The "message" contained in DNA and RNA is encoded in the nucleotides. Each amino acid is represented by a set of three base pairs in the nucleotide sequence called a CODON. There are 64 possible codons ($4 \times 4 \times 4$), which means many of the twenty-two amino acids are coded for with more than one codon. There is also a stop codon, which instructs the ribosome to stop processing the mRNA.

You will not need to memorize the codons, but you will need to identify corresponding codons and amino acids from a chart like the one shown here.

Table 5.4. Codons and amino acids									
1st base	2nd base								3rd base
	U		C		A		G		
U	UUU	(Phe/F) Phenylaline	UCU	(Ser/S) Serine	UAU	(Tyr/Y) Tyrosine	UGU	(Cys/C) Cysteine	U
	UUC		UCC		UAC		UGC		C
	UUA	(Leu/L) Leucine	UCA		UAA	Stop (Ochre)	UGA	Stop (Opal)	A
	UUG		UCG		UAG	Stop (Amber)	UGG	(Trp/W) Tryptophan	G
C	CUU		CCU	(Pro/P) Proline	CAU	(His/H) Histidine	CGU	(Arg/R) Arginine	U
	CUC		CCC		CAC		CGC		C
	CUA		CCA		CAA	(Gin/Q) Glutamine	CGA		A
	CUG		CCG		CAG		CGG		G
A	AUU	(Ile/I) Isoleucine	ACU	(Thr/T) Threon	AAU	(Asn/N) Asparagine	AGU	(Ser/Serine)	U
	AUC		ACC		AAC		AGC		C
	AUA		ACA		AAA	(Lys/K) Lysine	AGA	(Arg/R) Arginine	A
	AUG	(Met/M) Methionine	ACG		AAG		AGG		G
G	GUU	(Val/V) Valine	GCU	(Ala/A) Alanine	GAU	(Asp/D) Aspartic acid	GGU	(Gly/G) Glycine	U
	GUC		GCC		GAC		GGC		C
	GUA		GCA		GAA	(Glu/E) Glutamic acid	GGA		A
	GUG		GCG		GAG		GGG		G

Translation

The **TRANSLATION** process converts the mRNA transcript into a useable protein. This process occurs in a ribosome, which lines up the mRNA so it can bind to the appropriate tRNA (transfer RNA). Each tRNA includes an amino acid and an anti-codon, which matches to the complementary codon on the mRNA. When the tRNA is in place, the enzyme aminoacyl-tRNA synthetase uses a molecule of ATP to form a bond between the existing amino acid strand and the new amino acid brought in by the tRNA.

The translation process stops when a stop codon is reached in the sequence. These codons activate a protein called a release factor, which binds to the ribosome. The ribosome, which is made of two proteins, will split apart after the release factor binds. This releases the newly formed amino acid chain.

Protein Folding

After the amino acid chain has been produced, the process is still not complete: the amino acid chain needs to be folded into a protein. The polypeptide chain, now able to interact with itself due to hydrogen and disulfide bonds, will start to form a three-dimensional structure. A protein structure has four primary levels of structures:

1. The primary structure is the sequence of amino acids.
2. The secondary structure results from hydrogen bonds within the protein. These bonds create regular patterns called alpha helixes and beta sheets.
3. The tertiary structure is the overall three-dimensional structure and shape of the protein.
4. The quaternary structure results when multiple proteins interact. Not all proteins have a quarternary structure.

Mutations

The DNA or RNA sequence can sometimes undergo a MUTATION, which is a change in the base pair sequence of the DNA or RNA strand. A mutation can be benign or silent, meaning it has no effect, or it can cause a change in the protein structure.

An example of how a single POINT MUTATION can change the entire tertiary structure of a protein is sickle cell anemia. In sickle cell anemia, there is a single change in the base pair sequence from a T to an A. This results in an mRNA transcript codon change from GAA to GUA, which changes the amino acid from glutamate to valine. As a result, the protein is unable to fold properly, and the hemoglobin structure is longer than usual. When present in a red blood cell, this mutation causes the red blood cells to become elongated and sickle-like. As a result, oxygen is not carried as effectively in individuals who have sickle cell anemia.

On the other hand, many mutations will not result in any change in the protein sequence at all. For example, if the sequence CCG mutated to CCA, there would be no change, because the codon produced by both sequences corresponds to the amino acid glycine.

Gene Regulation

An important part of understanding metabolism is learning how genes are activated and deactivated. Studying gene expression and regulation is easier in bacteria due to their simple genomes and the simplicity of extracting their plasmids. Although human gene regulation is becoming more thoroughly understood, the vast complexity of the human metabolism and number of genes makes it difficult to get a full picture of all the interactions.

To understand gene regulation, it's necessary to understand the structure of the genetic code. Proteins are not produced from a single gene; instead, a set of genes, called an OPERON, is required. The operon includes a PROMOTER, which initiates transcription; an OPERATOR, to which an enzyme can bind to regulate transcription; and the protein coding sequence.

Either negative or positive regulation is used to control the operon. In negative regulation, a gene will be expressed unless a

How might mutations in DNA and RNA affect fitness and, consequently, natural selection?

repressor becomes attached. In positive regulation, genes are only expressed when an activator attaches to initiate expression.

In addition to interactions with the operon, the expression of DNA can be controlled by modifications to the chromatin. Because the location of the promoters in the chromatin sequence greatly affects access to the gene, expression can be regulated by managing how tightly bound the chromatin is in the nucleus. Modifications to histone proteins, small amino acid structures found only in eukaryotic cell nuclei, can also inhibit or allow access to DNA.

Lastly, gene expression can be controlled when DNA is methylated at the cytosine group. The methylation of DNA will prevent a DNA polymerase or RNA polymerase enzyme from attaching to the DNA, in effect preventing transcription.

Examples

1. A researcher has discovered a mutation in a sequence of mRNA, which changes a codon from AUG to AAG. What effect will this have on the sequence?

   A) There will be no effect.

   B) The codon sequence will start being translated at a different location than before.

   C) The codon sequence will stop being translated at a different location than before.

   D) The protein will no longer fold at all due to the mismatched codon.

2. Which of the following DNA sequences coding for an amino acid sequence does *not* include a stop codon?

   A) TTG-GTC-TAA-AAT

   B) TTT-GGC-AGA-CTC

   C) GTA-AUG-TAG-AGC

   D) TTC-CAT-CAC-TGA

3. Which of the following removes introns from mRNA?

   A) an operon

   B) an anti-codon

   C) a ribosome

   D) a spliceosome

4. Histone proteins can be found in which of these locations?

   A) eukaryotic cell nucleus

   B) prokaryotic cell nucleus

   C) mitochondria

   D) all of the above

5. Which of the following is not a method by which DNA expression can be controlled?

A) operon

B) methylation

C) promotion

D) sulfonation

Answers: 1. B) 2. B) 3. D) 4. A) 5. D)

GENETICS

GENETICS is the study of genes and how they are passed down to offspring. Before the discovery of genes, there were many theories about how traits are passed to offspring. One of the dominant theories in the 19th century was blending inheritence, which stated that the genetic material from the parents would mix to form that of the children in the same way that two colors might mix.

The idea was eventually displaced by the current theory, which is based on the concept of a **GENE**, which is a region of DNA that codes for a specific protein. Multiple versions of the same gene, called **ALLELES**, account for variation in a population.

During sexual reproduction, offspring receive a single copy of every gene from each parent. These two genes may be identical, making the individual **HOMOZYGOUS**, or they may be different, making the individual **HETEROZYGOUS** for that gene. In a heterozygous individual, the genes don't blend; instead they act separately, with one often being completely or partially suppressed.

Mendel's Laws

The idea that individual genes are passed down from parents to their children was conceived by **GREGOR MENDEL**. Mendel used various plants to test his ideas, but his best-known work is with pea plants.

Mendel became an Augustinian monk at the age of 21. He studied briefly at the University of Vienna, and after returning to the monastery, started work on breeding plants. During the course of his work, he discovered that the plants had heritable features, meaning features that were passed from parent to offspring. Because of the short generation time of peas, Mendel started working on identifying the traits that could be passed on in the pea plant. He tracked two characteristics: pea flower color and pea shape. From this, he found that the traits were independent of one another, meaning that the pea's flower color in no way affected the pea shape.

During the course of his work, Mendel came up with three laws to describe genetic inheritance: the laws of segregation, independent assortment, and dominance. The **LAW OF SEGREGATION** states that genes come in allele pairs (if the organism is diploid, which most

If an organism is described as true-breeding for a specific trait, it is homozygous for that trait and will pass it on to its offspring.

are), and that each parent can only pass a single allele down to its child. Thus, for a pair of alleles in a gene, one comes from the father and one comes from the mother in sexual reproduction. The law of segregation also states that the alleles must separate during the course of meiosis so that only one is given to each gamete.

The **LAW OF INDEPENDENT ASSORTMENT** states that genes responsible for different traits are passed on independently. Thus, there is not necessarily a correlation between two genes. For example, if a mother is tall and has brown hair, she might pass on her genes for tallness to her child, but perhaps not the ones for brown hair. This law can be seen in the use of the Punnett square, in which gene alleles are separated to determine inheritance.

Lastly, the **LAW OF DOMINANCE** states that some alleles are dominant and some are recessive. Dominant alleles will mask the behavior of recessive ones. For example, in a rose red might be dominant, and white recessive. Thus, if a homozygous red rose mates with a homozygous white rose, all of their offspring will be red. Although the white gene allele will be present, it will not be expressed.

Punnett Square

A **PUNNETT SQUARE** is a table-based diagram that can be used to predict the offspring outcome from the mating of a set of parents; it was developed by Reginald Punnett. In the square, the alleles from each parent (the P generation) are placed on the X and Y axes of the square, and the boxes are then filled in to represent the possible offspring gene combinations (F_1 for the first generation). Note that dominant genes are described with capital letters, and recessive genes with lower case letters.

Examples

1. Potatoes can be either round or oval. The dominant gene is oval. A heterozygous oval potato plant (Oo) is mated with a homozygous round potato plant (oo). What will be the distribution of this trait in the first generation of offspring?

	O	o
o	Oo	oo
o	Oo	oo

In the Punnett Square above, we have placed the parents on each side of the box. The heterozygous parent is seen on the X-axis as Oo, and the homozygous is on the Y-axis as oo. By separating the alleles (the law of segregation) and then recombining the possible combinations from the parents, we can predict what the genotype, and thus phenotype, of the offspring will be. **In this case, half of the offspring will be round (oo), and the other half will be oval (Oo).**

2. In the same plant described in problem #1, purple flowers are dominant, and pink flowers are recessive. If an OoPP parent is crossed with an ooPp parent, what would the resulting offspring look like?

	OP	OP	oP	oP
oP	OoPP	OoPP	ooPP	ooPP
oP	OoPP	OoPP	ooPP	ooPP
op	OoPp	OoPp	ooPp	ooPp
op	OoPp	OoPp	ooPp	ooPp

In this case, we separate out the alleles so that each one is matched with the other allele in all the possible combinations:

The four possible combinations for OoPP are OP, OP, oP, and oP. The four combinations for ooPp are oP, oP, op, and op. Filling in the squares gives all possible outcomes for the offpsring.

Half will be oval and purple, and half will be round and purple.

Phenotype vs. Genotype

A **PHENOTYPE** is an organism's observable characteristics, such as height, eye color, skin color, and hair color. **GENOTYPE** is an organism's genetic code. Although the genotype of two different people might be different, they could have the same phenotype, depending on which alleles are dominant or recessive. For example, the two types of roses Rr and RR are both red, meaning they have the same phenotype. However, they have a different genotype, with one rose type being heterozygous and the other being homozygous.

Individuals with the same genotype may also have different phenotypes. For example, the environment can have a large effect on phenotypic traits. Someone with light brown skin will tan in the sunlight, for instance, and a malnourished child may grow up to be shorter than expected.

Examples

1. In a type of plant newly discovered in South America, the seed color is controlled by the gene R. In these plants, those having the dominant allele R have bright red seeds, and those that have the homozygous recessive allele pair rr have pale pink seeds. In the first generation, a scientist crosses a true-breeding RR plant with a recessive rr plant. The F1 plant is then crossed with itself, resulting in the F2 generation. In the F2 generation, what percentage of the plants will have bright red seeds?

   A) 25%

   B) 50%

   C) 75%

   D) 100%

2. If a recessive trait is linked to the X-chromosome, it will most likely be seen in:

   A) males

   B) females

   C) both genders

   D) neither gender

3. A sex-linked trait primarily seen in males but sometimes seen in females is passed along on the:

   A) 22nd chromosome

   B) 18th chromosome

   C) X chromosome

   D) Y chromosome

4. Below are four statements regarding mutations. Which of these statements are true?

I.	Mutations are always harmful to the individual or species.
II.	Mutations can be beneficial.
III.	Mutations can occur randomly, without the aid of radiation or chemicals.
IV.	Mutations play an important role in evolution.

   A) I and II are true.

   B) Only II is true.

   C) II and III are true.

   D) II, III, and IV are true.

   Answers: 1. C) 2. A) 3. C) 4. D)

EVOLUTION

Evolution is best defined as descent from previous species with modification. That is, each generation changes slightly from the last until the difference is so great that a new species is formed. Evolution is why there is a diversity of life on Earth; it's the reason there are different species of animals and plants. This was what Charles Darwin meant by the title of his book *On the Origin of Species.*

Charles Darwin

CHARLES DARWIN was an Englishman with an intense interest in nature. Darwin enrolled at several universities, including Cambridge. He became interested in botany there, and had a chance to accompany the HMS *Beagle* on a voyage around the world. It was during this trip that he came across numerous species and started to form the theory of evolution.

Upon his return, Darwin published a book called *On the Origin of Species.* It is worth noting that Darwin did not coin the term evolution at this time, but rather called it "descent with modification." He stated that all organisms were inter-related, and could be traced to a distant ancestor. He was also one of the first to describe evolution as a tree, with different species branching off at different parts of the "tree."

Natural selection acts on an organism's phenotype, not its genotype. Only alleles that affect an organism's fitness will be selected for or against.

Based on his observations, Darwin proposed the theory of NATURAL SELECTION. Charles Darwin noticed that birds on the Galapagos Islands, while mostly similar, had unique beak shapes that allowed them to eat particular foods. Some beaks were small, some were wide and blunt, and some were needle like. Darwin hypothesized that these different beak shapes arose due to a selection process.

A selection process, whether natural or artificial, refers to the removal of inferior organisms that cannot survive in an environment. For example, farmers use artificial selection when they plant only seeds from plants that have produced a large yield in the past. This practice creates a field of plants that only produces large yields. Natural selection works in a similar fashion, except it is the conditions in nature that determine whether a particular individual will thrive and reproduce.

Darwin proposed the theory of natural selections based on specific observations. These were:

1. The members of a population of species have varied traits. For example, one species of monkey might have fur color varying from white to brown.
2. All species produce excess offspring. For example, if left uncontrolled, rabbit populations will more than double

in size every year. Secondly, not all offspring are able to survive.

3. The traits in an individual of a population that give it a higher chance of surviving also allow it to produce more offspring.

4. As a result, "more fit" individuals are more likely to pass on their traits; this will result in a change in the species over time.

This difference in reproduction is the basis of natural selection. Essentially, the traits of an individual determine whether it is "selected" by the environment. Individuals with superior traits are more likely to survive and reproduce, and thus pass on their genes. Individuals with inferior traits will not survive, and their genes will be lost. Over many generations, natural selection will lead to a species being driven toward a certain set of characteristics, which is how evolution occurs.

Speciation

SPECIATION is the process by which organisms evolve and become new species. A SPECIES is generally defined as a group of organisms in which two hybrids are able to produce fertile offspring. However, there is often debate and uncertainty about how species are defined and identified.

Speciation can occur under a number of different conditions. In ALLOPATRIC SPECIATION, a population becomes geographically separated, and the separated populations evolve to the point that they can no longer interbreed. In PERAPATRIC EVOLUTION, a new species is formed when a small portion of the population becomes isolated. PARAPATRIC SPECIATION occurs when populations are mostly separated but share a small area of overlap; selection pressures prevent interbreeding and eventually result in the development of new species.

Patterns of Evolution

Evolution can follow a number of different patterns depending on environmental factors. In DIVERGENT EVOLUTION, two species descended from the same ancestor develop different traits. In CONVERGENT EVOLUTION, two unrelated species develop similar traits, usually to meet the same basic need. For example, flight developed independently in a number of groups of organisms, including insects, birds, and bats. Finally, PARALLEL EVOLUTION occurs when two related species independently develop the same traits.

Case Study: Drug-Resistant Bacteria

Antibiotics and other chemicals are commonly used to treat infections. This has, over the course of the last twenty to thirty years, acted as a selection pressure on bacteria.

Staphylococcus aureus is a dangerous bacteria that resides on the skin of many people. It is ordinarily harmless, but if the individual has a weakened immune system, or the bacteria are allowed to enter the body in large amounts, *S. aureus* will eat away at the flesh of that person. This is the reason it is called the flesh-eating disease, or necrotizing fasciitis.

The best drug to treat *S. aureus* infections is methicillin, which was developed in 1959. However, just several years after the use of methicillin was introduced, methicillin-resistant *S. aureus* bacteria (called MRSA) began to appear. How did this happen?

The use of antibiotics will usually kill 99.9 percent of the bacteria, but some bacteria will manage to survive, through either genetic resistance or an insufficient dose. These bacteria have been artificially selected and will reproduce. Over time, as more and more people use the antibiotic, the small proportion of bacteria able to survive will thrive and multiply, eventually creating a population of methicillin-resistant bacteria.

Today, more than half of *S. aureus* infections are methicillin-resistant, causing doctors to have to look elsewhere for an effective method of treatment. This is a present-day study of evolution in progress.

Examples

1. In order for genetic drift to occur, in which a gene allele drops out of the population, which of the following must be true of the population?

    A) The population is large.

    B) The population is small.

    C) The population has many food sources.

    D) The population is able to survive in many niches.

2. Charles Darwin based his theory of natural selection on a number of logical observations and premises. Which of the following is *not* one of them?

    A) Organisms have many more offspring that the environment could be expected to support.

    B) Many species are able to mutate or alter their genes in order to adapt to the environment.

    C) Organisms are unique, and their offspring inherit traits from their parents.

    D) In a given environment, populations of species typically remain about the same throughout time.

3. Which of the following is an example of convergent evolution?

A) The evolution of tails in both whales and sharks

B) The evolution of pine cones in both southern pine and spruce trees

C) The evolution of pincers in both ants and termites

D) The evolution of feathers in both the sparrow and finch

Answers: 1. B) 2. B) 3. A)

PHYLOGENY AND SPECIES CLASSIFICATION

PHYLOGENY is the understanding of how species evolved through time. The study of phylogeny creates charts called phylogeny trees, which show the inter-relatedness of different species. For example, humans are quite closely related to many mammals, with our DNA being 90 percent similar to that of cats.

The Phylogenetic Tree

A PHYLOGENETIC TREE, shown in the diagram below, shows how groups of organisms are related to each other. The branches represent the relative point in time when each group of species, or family, diversified. For example, we can say according to the tree below that animals and fungi are more closely related than animals and flagellates, due to their relative distances on the tree.

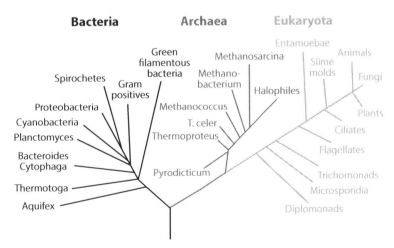

Figure 5.12. Phylogenetic tree

This type of diagram is useful for showing relationships in genetics, but not necessarily actual physical similarity. It should be easy to see that although animals and fungi might share their genotype, they definitely have almost no similar phenotypic characteristics.

The diagram is also relative in nature, meaning that no absolute geologic time scale can be assigned to the branches. We know from the fossil record and DNA evidence which species are more closely related than others are; this allows us to construct the tree. However, other than a rough estimation on when the branching actually occurred, we cannot put exact numbers on the ages of the species.

Taxonomy

TAXONOMY is the science of grouping species into correct taxa, or related groups. Groups descend in nature of similarity. For example, the kingdom group is less similar than the genus group. The current classification of species is:

Organisms are identified by their genus and species names. For example, humans are *Homo sapiens* and grizzly bears are *Ursus arctos*.

- domain
- kingdom
- phylum
- class
- order
- family
- genus
- species

According to this organization, two species from the same phylum are more related than two species from the same order. A good mnemonic to remember this organization scheme is: *Dear King Phillip Cried Out For Good Soup!*

Morphological Similarities Between Species

Many organisms share phenotypic similarities; these may or may not be due to shared ancestry. A **HOMOLOGOUS STRUCTURE** is a phenotype structure that is similar due to genetic relatedness, as in one species evolved from another, or two species both evolved from a common ancestor. A good example of a homologous structure is the thumb. In the fossil record and from present day analysis, the thumb bone is seen in nearly all mammalian species. This is because they were all derived from a common ancestor.

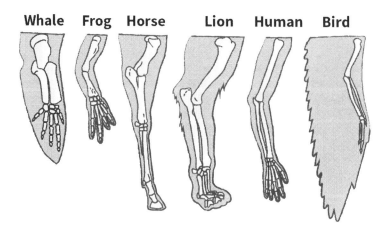

Figure 5.13. Homologous structures

An ANALOGOUS STRUCTURE is one not based on DNA similarity or shared ancestry. A good example of an analogous structure is the comparison between a bird wing and a bat wing. Upon looking at the bone structure, there are some similarities, but the two species have a completely different genetic history, having evolved independently by convergent evolution. As a result, it would be incorrect to conclude that birds and bats are closely related.

Examples

1. Which of the following is an example of an analogous structure?

   A) the fact that salmon and tuna both have gills

   B) the ability of multiple types of plants to grow in a rainforest

   C) the ability of both birds and butterflies to fly

   D) the many different species of elephants that exist

2. Which two species will likely share the greatest percentage of their genomes?

   A) those in the same family

   B) those in the same order

   C) those in the same kingdom

   D) those in the same class

3. A student proposes the idea that the modern day sparrow is a descent of the genus Archaeopteryx, an ancient bird. Which of the following findings would help support this hypothesis?

   A) The finding that Archaeopteryx and sparrows had the same diet.

   B) The finding that Archaeopteryx and sparrows lived in the same region.

   C) The finding that Archaeopteryx and sparrows were both able to fly.

   D) The finding that Archaeopteryx and sparrows share bone structure homology.

   Answers: 1. C) 2. A) 3. D)

BACTERIA

BACTERIA and ARCHAEA are a large subset of species that are mostly unicellular. Unlike the kingdoms Plantae and Animalia, nearly all of these species are single-celled prokaryotes, which are unicellular organisms that are quite small, usually less than 10 μm in diameter. (The smallest eukaryotic cells are usually larger than 10μm.)

Like plants, prokaryotes have a cell wall. However, unlike plants, the cell wall structural material is peptidoglycan, which is a polymer created by a mixture of cross-linked proteins and sugar. The cell wall supporting material in plants is called cellulose, which is made entirely from glucose, a sugar. The presence of the cell wall allows prokaryotes to be separated into two classes: gram-positive and gram-negative.

GRAM-POSITIVE bacteria contain peptidoglycan in their cell walls, and they turn purple-red when dyed with gram stain (a solution of crystal violet and iodine). Archaea cell walls contain a cross-linked polysaccharide, but do not have any peptidoglycan. As a result, they are GRAM-NEGATIVE.

As prokaryotes, none of the bacteria or Archaea species contain nuclear membranes. All of the DNA is freely arranged within the cytosol in a structure called the NUCLEOID. In addition to the chromosomal DNA contained inside the nucleoid, the cells also contain plasmids, which are ring-shaped DNA sequences that contain an active gene.

Example

Which of the following is a key difference between organisms in the domains Archaea and Bacteria?

A) Archaea cells do not contain peptidoglycan in their cell wall.

B) Archaea cells do not contain phospholipids in their cell membrane.

C) Archaea cells do not use RNA.

D) Archaea cells do not use ribosomes to produce amino acid chains.

Answer: A)

VIRUSES

A VIRUS is a special form of organism designed to be infectious. Its name is derived from the Latin word for poison. Viruses are interesting organisms that do not contain organelles or other structures usually found in living creatures. For this reason, the question of whether viruses are alive has been a subject of serious debate.

What is the Definition of Life?

Scientists debate many different definitions of life, but in general, there is agreement on the following characteristics:

1. Growth: A living organism must be able to grow, usually by converting some external material into its own mass.

2. Stimulus response: A living organism must be able to react to stimuli in its environment, such as light, other organisms, or toxins.

3. Energy use: A living organism must be able to use energy and convert energy into different forms, either as heat or as a stored energy compound.

4. Homeostasis: A living organism must be able to maintain its own organism conditions within a certain level.

5. Reproduction: Living organisms must be able to reproduce.

6. Mutation: The genetic code of living organisms must be able to change between generations.

7. Autonomous motion: Living organisms must be able to move, even if it is just a short distance.

Under these requirements, the majority of scientists do not consider viruses to be alive. This is because they do not have a metabolism of their own and cannot reproduce by themselves: they require a host.

Virus Structure and Lifecycle

A virus' structure is simple: it consists of a protein coat, known as a CAPSID, which surrounds a nucleic acid, which can be either DNA or RNA. The capsid is a tough layer of protein that is resistant to heat, moisture, and other environmental variables. It protects the genetic information inside the virus, and usually has some sort of receptor or protein that allows the virus to inject its DNA to a host organism.

Viruses can infect many types of cells, including animal somatic cells, plant cells, and bacteria. Because the capsid of a virus reacts with particular receptors on the cell's membrane, viruses usually require a specific type of host cell. For example, HIV infects human immune cells, and the cauliflower mosaic virus mostly infects members of the Brassicaceae family. A virus that infects bacteria is called a BACTERIOPHAGE.

Viruses are obligate parasites (meaning they cannot complete their life cycle outside a host) and inject their DNA or RNA into other organisms in order to reproduce. In most cases, a virus will enter a host and use the host cell's energy and resources to reproduce, and then lyse the host cell, releasing more virus cells. This is known as the LYTIC CYCLE. The lytic cycle of a typical virus is detailed below:

1. Attachment: the virus bonds to the host cell using proteins on the capsid.

2. Entry: the proteins inject DNA into the host cell.

3. Synthesis and reproduction: the DNA is replicated using the host cell's machinery.

4. Assembly: new viruses are assembled from the reproduced parts in the cell.

5. Lysis and release: the virus destroys the host cell, lysing the cell membrane and releasing the newly created virus cells.

Some viruses contain RNA genomes rather than DNA. Among these viruses is the human immunodeficiency virus, or HIV. These viruses inject RNA, and the RNA can be translated into proteins or enzymes directly after infection. In order for this method of transmission to work, the virus must carry some RNA reverse transcriptase. This protein is able to translate RNA back into DNA, so that the host organism can utilize it.

Although viruses are not "alive" per se, they are capable of evolving very quickly due to their short life cycle and their ability to use a host genome. Many viruses are capable of assimilating other pieces of DNA into their own genome, often creating a new virus. For example, what people refer to as influenza, or the flu, is actually a group of viruses that continue to change and evolve; this is why new vaccines are introduced each year.

⚠ Vaccines contain harmless versions of infectious agents that activate the body's immune system without causing illness.

Examples

1. Viruses and prokaryotes both differ from eukaryotes in that they do not have a nuclear membrane. What is one manner in which viruses are distinguished from prokaryotes?

   A) Viruses contain RNA, and prokaryotes do not.

   B) Prokaryotes have ribosomes, whereas viruses do not.

   C) Prokaryotes can form a protein shell, whereas viruses cannot.

   D) Viruses are harmful to humans, whereas prokaryotes are not.

2. Which of the following statements about viruses is not true?

   A) Viruses are only able to reproduce after infecting a host cell.

   B) Because they are obligate parasites, viruses do not evolve.

   C) Some viruses contain RNA instead of DNA inside their capsid.

   D) Bacteriophages are viruses that infect bacteria.

   Answers: 1. B) 2. B)

PLANTS

Plants make up the largest percentage of organic matter on the planet. Without plants, which are autotrophs, the majority of other living organisms could not exist. Plants act as a necessary source of both oxygen and nutrients for the organisms that consume them.

A plant is composed of three basic units: the roots, stems, and leaves. The **ROOTS** of plants usually reside in the soil and are responsible for absorbing water and minerals from the soil. There are two types of roots: a taproot, which is a central, thick root (think of a carrot), and lateral roots, which are smaller roots that branch out from the main root. Some root tubers, such as potatoes and carrots, are able to elongate and store significant amounts of nutrients.

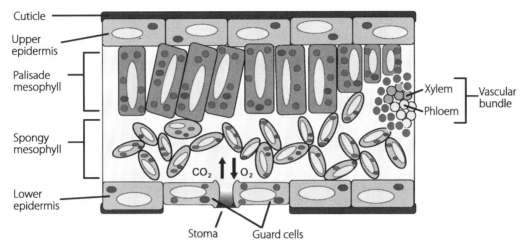

Figure 5.14. Structure of a leaf

The **STEM** of the plant provides structural stability and also moves water and nutrients from the roots to the other parts of the plant. The **LEAVES** of the plant are high in surface area and contain the majority of the plant's chlorophyll. They absorb sunlight and perform photosynthesis.

Plants are composed of three main types of cells:

- The **PARENCHYMA** cells have thin, flexible cell walls and have a large vacuole in the middle of the cell used for storage. These types of cells perform many functions, including many metabolic reactions. Root tissue, the interior of leaves, and most fruit tissue is made from parenchyma cells.

- The **COLLENCHYMA** cells are seen in parts of the stem and support the plant as it is growing. These cells remain flexible even as they get older.

- The **SCLERENCHYMA** cells are the most rigid of the cells. These cell types contain high amounts of lignin and cellulose in the secondary cell wall, making it an indigestible structural component of the plant.

The Vascular Tissue System

VASCULAR TISSUE is able to transport sugar and water to other parts of the plant. Plants contain two types of vascular tissue: xylem and phloem. **XYLEM** is commonly known as woody tissue, and is very stiff. It consists of a series of hollow cell structures that move water from the roots up to the leaves or flowers. **Phloem** is a living tissue near the outside of the stem of the plant which transports sugars.

In plants, the movement of water from the roots to the top of the plant is an important and difficult process. Diffusion is effective over short distances, but in order to move water to the top of a twenty-meter tall tree, additional forces are needed. In plants, the bulk flow of water from the roots is regulated by several mechanisms. These include the capillary action of water moving up the xylem, the transpiration of water from the leaves at the top of the tree, osmotic pressure in the roots, and active transport in the plant.

Plant Growth

Plant growth takes place at **meristems**, which are groups of undifferentiated, quickly dividing cells. The roots grow starting at the **root apical meristem**, where new root cells are created and capped by a harder layer of tissue known as the **root cap**. Shoot growth occurs at the **shoot apical meristem**, and flowers grow from **floral meristems**.

The growth at these meristems elongates the plants and is known as **primary growth**. Plant stems will also expand outward in a process called **secondary growth**. The majority of this growth occurs in the **cambium**, a layer of high growth cells on the outer edge of the stem. These cells increase the diameter of the stem, and create the wood and bark in woody plants.

Leaves

The **epidermis** is the outer layer of leaf cells, and is surrounded by the **cuticle**, a waxy layer that aids the plant in retaining moisture and preventing evaporation from the leaf. The epidermis also contains structures called **stomata** (singular: stoma). These openings in the leaf structure allow carbon dioxide and oxygen to be exchanged for photosynthesis.

The **mesophyll** consists of parenchyma cells that contain large amounts of chlorophyll and are specialized for photosynthesis. In the middle of the leaf are the two types of mesophyll: the palisade and spongy mesophyll. The **palisade mesophyll** has layers of parallel cells and is located on the upper portion of the leaf. The **spongy mesophyll** is a collection of loosely organized cells that have many spaces in which carbon dioxide and oxygen are able to penetrate.

Plant Reproduction

Plants have a wide variety of reproductive strategies and life cycles. Some plants are able to reproduce asexually by producing genetically identical clones, but the majority of plants reproduce sexually. These plants produce seeds from female and male gametes, known respectively as eggs and pollen.

Seed-producing plants are broken down into two groups: gymniosperms and angiosperms. **GYMNOSPERMS**, which include conifers, Ginkgos, and cycads, produce "naked" seeds that grow in cones or on the surface of leaves. **ANGIOSPERMS**, or flowering plants, produce seeds that are surrounded by a fruit which provides protection and can help with seed dispersal.

The reproductive organs of angiosperms are contained in flowers. The **PETALS** of the flowers are usually colorful appendages that attract pollinators and protect the reproductive organs. At the base of the flower are the **SEPALS,** protective leaf-like structures. The male and/or female reproductive organs are contained within the petals.

The female organs include the **OVARY**, which contains egg-producing ovules. The **STYLE** is a long, slender stalk that connects the ovary to the **STIGMA**, which collects pollen. Together the ovary, style, and stigma are called the **PISTOL** (and sometimes the carpel).

The male organs include the **ANTHER**, which contains the pollen, and the **FILAMENT**, which holds the anther. Together, the anther and filament comprise the **STAMEN**. The male gametophytes are known as **POLLEN**, and are housed inside the anther. Inside each anther are microsporangia, which contain the cells that undergo meiosis to produce pollen.

Flowers often have colors, scents, or shapes that have evolved to attract a specific pollinator. For example, bees can see ultraviolet (UV) light, so many flowers have UV patterns in their petals that humans cannot see.

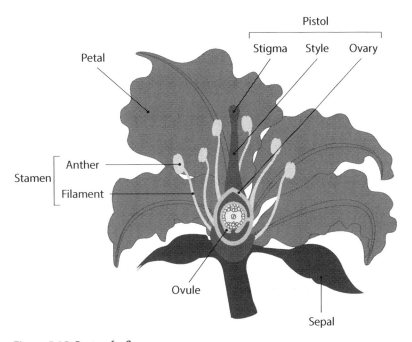

Figure 5.15. Parts of a flower

POLLINATION occurs when there is a transfer of pollen from the anther of one flower to the ovaries of another flower. Pollination can occur through many means, including wind, water, or animals.

After pollination occurs, a pollen tube starts to grow down from the stigma to the ovaries. Upon reaching the ovaries, the pollen tube will discharge two sperm cells into the embryo sac. One sperm cell will be able to fertilize the egg, creating the zygote. The other sperm is involved in the formation of the ENDOSPERM, which grows into a nutritious layer that surrounds the zygote. Examples of the endosperm include the grain of wheat and the white meat of a coconut.

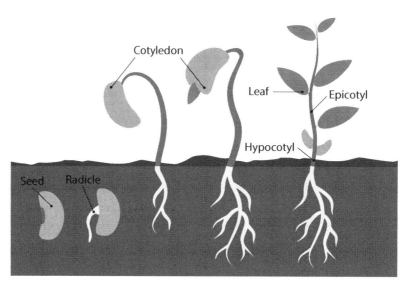

Figure 5.16. Seed germination

The embryo develops a short while after the endosperm. After it has matured, the seed will have several parts, including the epicotyl, the hypocotyl, the radicle, and the cotyledon.

Examples

1. Stomata allow for the passage of all of the following except

   A) carbohydrates

   B) carbon dioxide

   C) oxygen

   D) water

2. In plants, the formation of a seed includes the creation of an endosperm. Which of the following is not true about the endosperm?

   A) It can have a triploid (3n) chromosome number.

   B) The endosperm in many plants contains fats and nutrients for the growing embryo.

   C) The endosperm is created solely from maternal tissue.

   D) The endosperm begins formation after a pollen grain contacts the maternal cell.

3. Which of the following phenomena is not a mechanism by which trees move water from the roots to the leaves?

   A) transpiration

   B) osmotic pressure

   C) capillary action

   D) sublimation

4. Both gymnosperms and angiosperms produce which of the following?

   A) seeds

   B) fruits

   C) petals

   D) endosperm

Answers: 1. A) 2. C) 3. D) 4. A)

PHOTOSYNTHESIS

DURING PHOTOSYNTHESIS, light energy is absorbed by plants and converted via photosynthesis into sugars. This process is the energy source for nearly all the biomass on Earth. The term is derived from *photo*, meaning light, and *synthesis*, meaning construction. Organisms that are able to produce their own sustenance in this manner are known as AUTOTROPHS.

Photosynthesis takes place in CHLOROPLASTS, which are small organelles in plant tissue that contain CHLOROPHYLL, a green pigment that allows plants to capture the energy from light. Chloroplasts are contained inside the mesophyll of the plant leaf (the section sandwiched between the top and bottom layers of the leaf). Inside the chloroplast are two primary structures: the STROMA, which is the envelope of the chloroplast, and the THYLAKOIDS, which are stacks of sacs that contain the chlorophyll.

The Chemistry of Photosynthesis

The overall chemical reaction of photosynthesis is as follows:

$$6\,CO_2 + 6\,H_2O + \text{Light energy} \rightarrow C_6H_{12}O_6 \text{ (Glucose)} + 6\,O_2$$

The photosynthesis reaction uses carbon dioxide and water, in addition to energy from sunlight, to produce glucose and oxygen. In this reaction, the carbon from carbon dioxide ends up in the glucose molecule. Half of the oxygen from carbon dioxide ends up in the glucose, and the other half ends up in the produced water. All of the oxygen from the water molecules on the reactant side of the equation ends up in the oxygen produced.

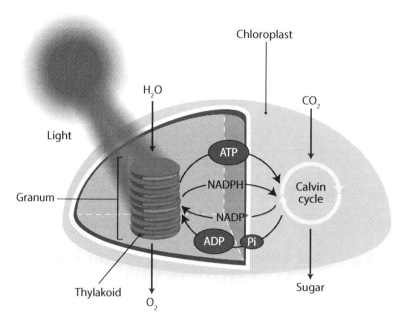

Figure 5.17. Photosynthesis

Similar to aerobic respiration, photosynthesis is an oxidation-reduction process, and relies on the transfer of electrons to be effective. These reactions take place in two phases. The first is the light reactions, in which the energy from the sun is captured and translated into high-energy electrons. The second is in the Calvin cycle, where this energy is used in conjunction with carbon dioxide and water to produce a glucose molecule.

Light Reactions

The **LIGHT REACTIONS** occur in the chloroplast. They take light from the sun, which is best absorbed by chlorophyll between the wavelengths of 420 nanometers to 460 nanometers, and convert it into active electrons.

The movement of electrons in chlorophyll occurs in two systems: **PHOTOSYSTEM I** and **PHOTOSYSTEM II**. These systems work together to funnel high-energy electrons down to a terminal electron acceptor. The passage of electrons along the system is aided by molecules called quinones. At the end of the chain, the enzyme NADP+ reductase adds an electron to an NADP+ molecule, creating the energy storage molecule NADPH. The basic steps of the light reactions are as follows:

1. Light strikes PS II, energizing an electron.
2. The electron is transferred to a primary electron acceptor in P680, a compound in the chlorophyll.
3. An enzyme splits water, supplying two H+ ions and an oxygen atom. The H+ ions form a gradient across the lumen layer in the thylakoid membrane.

4. The energized electrons pass to PSI via a chain of quinone structures.

5. The transport of electrons helps to drive the gradient of H+ ions even further onto one side of the thylakoid membrane.

6. The enzyme NADP+ reductase takes the active electrons and catalyzes the formation of NADPH. Two electrons are needed for one molecule of NADPH.

The Calvin Cycle

Now that the energy molecules of NADPH have been produced by the light-fixing reactions, they can be used to fix carbon dioxide and turn it into glucose. The **CALVIN CYCLE** is somewhat similar to the citric acid cycle, in that there is an intermediate compound (oxalo-acetate in the TCA cycle) recycled after every round of synthesis. The Calvin cycle produces a sugar precursor, known as glyceralde-hyde 3-phosphate (G3P). This 3-carbon molecule requires three cycles of the Calvin cycle for construction with each cycle fixing one molecule of carbon dioxide. Two molecules of G3P are required to create one 6-carbon glucose molecule.

The steps of the Calvin cycle are as follows:

1. Three CO_2 molecules are used by RuBisCo (Ribulose-1, 5-bisphosphate carboxylase/oxygenase), an enzyme, to produce six molecules of 3-phosphoglycerate.

2. 6-ATP is then used to convert the 3-phosphoglycerate into six molecules of 1, 3-bisphosphoglycerate, an activated compound.

3. 6-NADPH is then used to convert the 1, 3-bisphos-phoglycerate into six molecules of glyceraldehyde 3-phosphate. At this point, one molecule of the G3P is exported for conversion to glucose or other materials, and five molecules of G3P continue in the cycle.

4. The five molecules of G3P, in addition to three ATP, are used to regenerate the three molecules of ribulose bisphosphate that catalyze the CO_2 fixation reaction.

Note that this is a energy-intensive process. In order to make one G3P molecule, a plant has to expend nine units of ATP and six units of NADPH. These energy molecules are generated from light reactions that occur in the chloroplast.

C3 vs. C4 Plants

There are two types of carbon fixing plants, referred to as C3 or C4 plants because of the number of carbons that the fixed molecule contains. The majority of plants are C3 and fix carbon into G3P.

C4 plants are rarer, and are seen in only about 20 different plant families. Instead of fixing carbon into glyceraldehyde 3-phosphate, these plants fix carbon into a 4-carbon molecule known as oxaloacetate, which becomes malate that is then transformed into pyruvate for the production of sugar or ATP.

The major difference between these plants is the manner in which they PHOTORESPIRATE. In order to get an adequate amount of carbon dioxide, plants need to have stomata open, which allows air to enter the leaf. This is typical in most C3 plants. However, in hot environments, such as the desert, having stomata open during the day, when the light fixing reactions take place, can be lethal. Thus, C4 plants use a different enzyme, called PEP carboxylase, that can fix carbon dioxide even in very low concentrations. This eliminates the need to have stomata open during the day and reduces the amount of water lost due to photorespiration.

Examples

1. Which of the following is the primary feature distinguishing C3 from C4 plants?

   A) C3 plants use the Krebs cycle and C4 plants use the Citric Acid cycle.

   B) C3 plants produce a 3-carbon glucose precursor whereas C4 plants produce a 4-carbon glucose precursor.

   C) C4 plants are able to tolerate extreme cold temperatures but C3 plants cannot.

   D) C4 plants produce four molecules of ATP per round of the citric acid cycle whereas C3 plants only produce three molecules of ATP per round of the citric acid cycle.

2. The thylakoid membrane structures, found only in organisms with chlorophyll, are the sites that

   A) produce ATP from sugar, much like mitochondria.

   B) trap energy from the sun in the form of NADH and ATP.

   C) provide an active site for the enzyme RuBisCo to fix carbon dioxide.

   D) act as a structural platform from which the plant cell wall is generated.

3. Which of the following is correct regarding the relationship between photosystem I and II?

   A) Electrons are trapped by photosystem I, and proceed to photosystem II.

   B) Photosystem I and II both trap electrons, but only photosystem II produces ATP.

   C) Photosystem II traps energy from the sun to excite electrons, which are then provided to photosystem I.

   D) Photosystem I is located in the cytosol, whereas photosystem II is located in the chloroplasts.

4. A scientist provides a growing sunflower plant with CO_2 that has been made with heavy oxygen, an isotope of normal oxygen that has a weight of 18 AMUs, rather than 16. After the carbon dioxide has been metabolized, where will the heavy oxygen show up?

A) in water secreted by the plant

B) in glucose created by the plant

C) in pyruvate created by the plant

D) in oxygen produced by the plant

Answers: 1. B) 2. B) 3. C) 4. B)

ECOLOGY

Ecology is the study of the relationships between organisms and their environment, including both the **BIOTIC** components, which are alive, and the **ABIOTIC** components, which are not alive.

Population Ecology

A **POPULATION** is a group of individuals of the same species. (As discussed above, a species is any group of organisms who can interbreed and produce fertile hybrids.) This field of study focuses on how populations grow and interact with the enviornment.

Ecologists have developed a number of mathemeatical models that describe how populations may grow. In theory, a population would show geometric (generational) or logarithmic (continuous) growth. In practice, population size is constrained by the enviroment and the resources available. A population's **CARRYING CAPACITY** (K) is the number of individuals the environment can support.

Species can be placed into two broad categories based on their life histories. Species that produce large amounts of offspring with low parental investment and high mortality rates are known as **R-SELECTED** species. Examples of such species include rodents and insects. Conversely, some species produce fewer offspring but invest more in each, resulting in a lower mortality rate among the young. These species, which includes humans, are **K-SELECTED**.

Community Ecology

A **COMMUNITY** is comprised of populations of many species occupying the same geographic area. Much of community ecology focuses on the many types of interactions between species.

- **COMPETITION** occurs when species compete for the same resources.
- **PREDATION** occurs when one individual (the predator) consumes another (the prey) for sustenance.
- **MUTUALISM** is an interaction between species in which both benefit.

Would the following species be described as r-selected or K-selected?
- mice
- elephants
- whales
- mosquitos
- wheat

The species within a community consume each other for energy and nutrients; these interactions are mapped out in a FOOD WEB. In a food web, it's possibly to see which TROPHIC LEVEL a particular species occupies. Primary producers (plants) occupy the first trophic level, herbivores make up the second level, and predators comprise the remaining trophic levels.

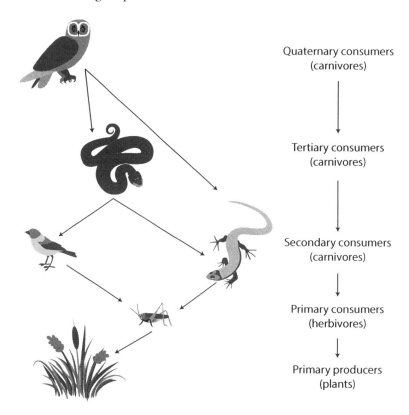

Quaternary consumers
(carnivores)

Tertiary consumers
(carnivores)

Secondary consumers
(carnivores)

Primary consumers
(herbivores)

Primary producers
(plants)

Figure 5.18. Food web

Ecosystems

An ECOSYSTEM includes all the biotic and abiotic components in a particular geographic area. Ecosystems are typically defined by their climate, which is the average temperature and precipitation in the area.

- A TROPICAL RAINFOREST is typically moist and warm, with average temperatures year round of 25° – 29° Celsius, and receiving 150 – 200 centimeters of precipitation every year. Tropical forests have a large number of species and are the most species-dense of all the ecosystems.

- DESERTS are characterized by extreme temperatures and low rainfall. Daytime temperatures can exceed 45° Celsius, and nighttime temperatures can fall below 30° Celsius. Average precipitation is less than 30 centimeters per year.

- The SAVANNA is best characterized as grassland with moderate precipitation. Rainfall is usually between 30 – 50 centimeters every year, and temperatures range between 24° – 29° Celsius.

- CHAPARRAL is an ecosystem characterized by shrubs and low trees. A temperate ecosystem, it features rocky soil and low, rolling hills.

- TEMPERATE GRASSLANDS typically receive 40 – 60 centimeters of seasonal precipitation every year. There are well-defined seasons, with temperatures in the summer rising above 30° Celsius, and temperatures in the winter falling below 0° Celsius.

- CONIFEROUS FORESTS are the most common type of forest. They are characterized by moderately cold temperatures, with an average year-round temperature around 15° Celsius. They feature plentiful coniferous trees, such as pine, hemlock, and spruce.

- BROADLEAF FORESTS, containing many deciduous trees, are characterized by moderate temperatures. They receive 70 – 150 centimeters of precipitation annually.

- The TUNDRA is one of the world's largest land area ecosystems, covering 20% of the world's existing land mass. It is quite cold, with temperatures usually no higher than 10° Celsius, even in the summer.

- WETLANDS, or swamps, are areas of land permeated with shallow water. They are among the most productive habitats in the world and support a high level of biodiversity.

- ESTUARIES are regions that flow from the river into the sea. They are characterized by low beds of silt and sand. Many invertebrate crustaceans live in this zone.

- FRESHWATER ECOSYSTEMS include lakes, streams, and rivers. These bodies of water have a low salt concentration and support a wide variety of wildlife.

- MARINE ECOSYSTEMS, which include oceans, coral reefs, and tidal zones are bodies of water characterized by their high salt content. They cover 71 percent of the Earth's surface.

6

CHEMISTRY

THE ATOM

The **ATOM** is the basic building block of all physical matter. It is composed of three subatomic particles: protons, electrons, and neutrons. A **PROTON** is a positively charged subatomic particle with a mass of approximately 1.007 atomic mass units. The number of protons in an atom determines which **ELEMENT** it is. For example, an atom with 1 proton is hydrogen, and an atom with 12 protons is carbon.

A **NEUTRON** is a non-charged subatomic particle with a mass of approximately 1.008 atomic mass units. The number of neutrons in an atom does not affect its chemical properties, but will influence its rate of radioactivity. Both protons and neutrons are found in the center, or **NUCLEUS**, of the atom.

Lastly, an **ELECTRON** is a negatively charged subatomic particle with a mass of approximately 0.00055 atomic mass units. The number of electrons in an atom, in conjunction with the protons, determines the atom's charge. In addition, the number of electrons in the valence shell of an atom affects its reactivity. Electrons move in a cloud that surrounds the nucleus.

The modern concept of the atom, which provided the basis for all of chemistry, was first laid out in John Dalton's **ATOMIC THEORY**, which was developed in 1808. Atomic theory states that:

1. An element is composed of atoms, which are extremely small, indivisible particles. Although we now know that atoms are composed of smaller units such as protons, electrons, and neutrons, it is still recognized that atoms are the basic building block of matter.

2. Each individual element has a set of properties that are distinct and different from that of other elements.

3. Atoms cannot be created, destroyed, or transformed through physical changes. We now know that atoms can be created or destroyed, although this requires a massive amount of energy. Furthermore, radioactive elements can be transformed into other elements.

4. Compounds are defined by a specific ratio of atoms that are combined with one another, and the relative numbers and types of atoms are constant in any given compound.

Previous Models of the Atom

When the field of chemistry was young, people proposed many different models of the structure of an atom.

DALTON'S MODEL (EARLY 1800S)

Dalton was the first to propose some aspects of atomic theory, including atomic weights and a general shape. According to Dalton's model of the atom, each atom was a single, indivisible unit that was solid. Simply put, an atom was something like a very small marble, and a solid was something composed of many of these marbles.

Dalton's model was disproved in the early twentieth century when the proton and neutron were discovered by Ernest Rutherford. Rutherford found that a hydrogen atom could be extracted from a nitrogen atom by collision, and that it had a positive charge. This showed that an atom was composed of smaller, positively charged pieces, and was not a unified whole.

RUTHERFORD'S MODEL (1911)

Rutherford proposed that an atom was a core of heavier particles (protons and neutrons) surrounded by a layer of electrons. In this model, the electrons were evenly dispersed around the core of the atom.

In Rutherford's model, physics would predict that the evenly dispersed electrons would slowly lose energy while orbiting the nucleus. As a result, if Rutherford's model were true, all electrons would eventually collapse into the nucleus.

BOHR'S THEORY

To fix this problem with the model, Niels Bohr proposed that electrons can only orbit the nucleus in certain energy stages, or orbits, that are a set distance from the nucleus. The electrons orbiting closer to the nucleus have the highest energy, and shells have lower energy moving away from the nucleus. He further proposed that it is possible to change the energy state of electrons through the emission or addition of electromagnetic waves. The idea of electron shells was thus introduced by Bohr's theory, and Bohr's model is still used today, (with some modifications).

Atomic Structure

The atom consists of a nucleus of protons and neutrons surrounded by a shell, or multiple shells, of electrons. The nucleus is very dense and contains the majority of mass in the atom. The actual size of the atom, due to the large electron shell, is much larger than the nucleus.

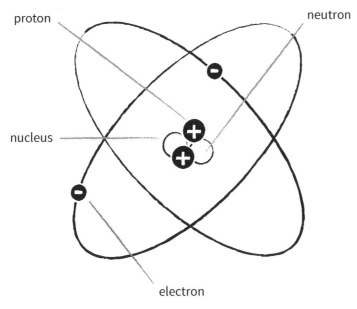

Figure 6.1. Atomic structure

Electrons surround the nucleus in clouds called ORBITALS; each orbital has a particular shape and holds a particular number of electrons. There are four orbital shapes: *s* orbitals hold 2 electrons, *p* orbitals hold 6 electrons, *d* orbitals hold 10 electrons, and *f* orbitals hold 14 electrons. The size and distance of the orbital from the nucleus is described by an integer value (1, 2, ...).

The location of an electron can be described with an integer number and orbital letter, for example the single electron in hydrogen is in orbital 1s. The number of electrons in each orbital is written as a superscript. For example, the two electrons in helium are described as $2s^2$. With some exceptions, electrons fill orbitals in a specific order (see Figure 6.2). This order can also be found using the periodic table (more on this on the following page).

CONTINUE

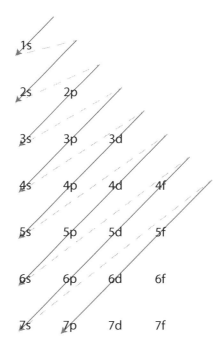

$$1s^2 2s^2 2p^6 3s^2 3p^6 4s^2 3d^{10} 4p^6 5s^2 \ldots$$

Figure 6.2. Electron orbitals

Valence Shell Reactivity

The reactivity of each individual atom is determined by the number of electrons in its electron shells, of which the most important is the outermost, or **VALENCE**, shell. Typically, the closer an atom is to reaching a full valence shell, the more reactive it is. Elements that have a single electron in a shell (such as sodium: last orbital $3s^1$) or need only a single electron to fill a shell (such as chlorine: last orbital $2p^5$) are the most reactive.

There are some elements that are not reactive at all. These are the noble gases, which possess a full valence shell. Thus, they have no free electrons with which to react. In chemistry, there are no common reactions that occur with a noble gas.

Examples

1. Which of these is the correct electron configuration for gold?

   A) $[Xe]\ 6s^2\ 5d^9$

   B) $[Xe]\ 5d^9\ 6s^2$

   C) $[Xe]\ 4f^{14}\ 5d^{10}\ 6s^1$

   D) $[Xe]\ 6s^2\ 5d^{10}\ 4f^{13}$

2. The electron configuration for phosphorus is:

A) $1s^22s^22p^63s^23p^3$

B) $1s^22s^22p^63s^23p^6$

C) $1s^22p^63s^23p^3$

D) $1s^22s^22p^23s^23p^34s^24p^3$

3. Which subatomic particles are found in the nucleus of an atom?

I.	protons
II.	electrons
III.	neutrons

A) I only

B) II only

C) I and III

D) I, II, and III

Answers: 1. C) 2. A) 3. C)

THE PERIODIC TABLE OF ELEMENTS

The **PERIODIC TABLE** is a table used to organize and characterize the various elements. The table was first proposed by Dimitri Mendeleev in 1869, and a similar organization system is still used today. In the table, each column is called a **GROUP** and each row is called a **PERIOD**. Elements in the same column have similar electron configurations and the same number of electrons in their valence shells.

Figure 6.3. Periodic table

Reading the Periodic Table

Each cell in the table includes the symbol for the element, which is a letter or set of letters. For example, C for carbon and Fe for iron. The number at the top of each cell in the table is the ATOMIC NUMBER. This represents the number of protons in the element. The number below the element symbol is the ATOMIC MASS, which represents the total mass of the element (atomic mass – atomic number = number of neutrons).

Because atoms of the same element can have different numbers of neutrons, elements have no single standard atomic mass. Instead, the atomic mass is the weighted average of all commonly found species of the element. For this reason, it is almost never a whole number. For example, a small amount of carbon actually has an atomic mass of 13, possessing 7 neutrons instead of the usual 6, giving carbon an atomic mass of 12.011. Atoms of the same element with different numbers of neutrons are called ISOTOPES.

Trends in the Periodic Table

Some element properties can be predicted based on the placement of the element on the periodic table.

- Elements in groups 1 and 2 are the alkali and the alkali earth metals, which are very reactive.
- Elements in group 17 are the halogens, which are very reactive.
- Elements in group 18 are the noble gases, which are very unreactive.
- Elements along the "staircase" (marked in gray in the periodic table in Figure 9.3) consisting of boron, silicon, etc., are semi-metallic. They have some properties of metals, and some properties of non-metals.
- The atomic radius of an element increases from the top left to the bottom right.
- ELECTRONEGATIVITY, which is a measure of how strongly an atom attracts electrons, increases roughly from lower left to the top right.
- IONIZATION ENERGY, which is a measure of how much energy is required to remove an electron from an atom, increases from lower left to top right.

Properties of Elements

Below are the important properties of various groups of elements.

GROUP 1 (THE ALKALI METALS)

The elements in group 1 are all silvery metals that are soft and can be easily crushed or cut. They all possess a single valence electron, which makes them very reactive. The presence of just a single valence

Many elemental symbols are derived from the Latin names for elements. For example, gold's symbol is Au from its Latin name Aurum.

You don't need to memorize all of these properties, but be able to recognize the general similarities of a group's chemical properties.

electron means that there is a high likelihood of losing the electron, resulting in a +1 cation. Because these metals are so reactive, they are not usually found in their pure form. Bonds that involve Group 1 metals are always bonds that have high ionic character.

GROUP 2 (THE ALKALI EARTH METALS)

The elements in group 2 are also silvery metals that are soft. These metals contain two valence electrons, which fill the S-shell, so these elements are not as reactive as those in group 1. However, they still have a high tendency to lose these electrons, and form a +2 cation. Normally, group 2 elements are found in this +2 oxidation state. Bonds that involve group 2 metals are almost always bonds that have high ionic character.

GROUPS 3 – 12 (THE TRANSITION METALS)

The elements from groups 3 to 12 are called the transition metals, and are all capable of conducting electricity (some better than others). They are called transition metals in part due to their capability to possess multiple oxidation states. Because of the presence of the D-shell of electrons in these metals, they may have anywhere from a +1 to a +6 oxidation state, resulting in the formation of many different compounds and bonds. Transition metals are moderately reactive, malleable, and can conduct electricity due to the capability of gaining and losing many electrons in their outer electron shell.

GROUPS 13 AND 14 (SEMI-METALLIC)

The elements in groups 13 and 14 are semi-metallic. They have moderate conductivity, and are very soft. Elements in group 13 have three valence electrons and elements in group 14 have four, allowing for five and four bonds respectively.

GROUP 15

This group is characterized by a shift from the top of this group (gases) to the bottom (semi-metallic). This group has five valence electrons and can form three bonds. The semi-metallic elements, such as arsenic and antimony, are relatively reactive.

GROUP 16

This group is also characterized by a shift from gases at the top of the group to semi-metallic at the bottom. This group has six valence electrons and is quite reactive. The need to obtain only two more electrons to fill the valence shell means that these elements are electronegative and typically form an anion with a charge of -2. As a result, these elements are reactive and tend to bond with the alkali or alkali earth metals.

GROUP 17 (HALOGENS)

The halogens are all gases and all contain seven electrons in their valence shell. They are extremely reactive, much like the alkali metals. Due to their reactivity and gaseous form at room temperature, they are often hazardous to humans. Inhaling chlorine or fluorine, for example, is usually deadly. The halogens will react in order to obtain a single additional electron to fill their valence shell and typically have a charge of -1.

GROUP 18 (THE NOBLE GASES)

The noble gases already contain a full valence shell. Because their electron orbitals are already full, the noble gases are largely unreactive, except for a few rare exceptions. The heavier noble gases (xenon and radon) can sometimes react with other species under high temperature and pressure conditions. The noble gases have no net charge.

Examples

1. Which of the following is not true of the alkali metals?

   A) They are more likely to be oxidized than reduced.

   B) They typically form +1 monatomic cations.

   C) Large amounts of energy are required to remove their first electron.

   D) They are highly reactive.

2. Which of the following statements is not true regarding the halogens in the periodic table?

   A) All of the halogens are extremely reactive.

   B) The halogen elements require 1 more electron to fill their valence shell.

   C) Halogen elements usually form ionic bonds with other elements.

   D) All of the halogens are very electronegative, except for astatine and iodine.

3. Which of the following elements has the highest first ionization energy?

   A) sodium

   B) sulfur

   C) carbon

   D) argon

   Answers: 1. C) 2. D) 3. C)

CHEMICAL BONDING

Molecules and Compounds

Atoms can exist on their own or bound together. When two or more atoms are held together by chemical bonds, they form a MOLECULE. If the molecule contains more than one type of atom, it is a **COMPOUND**. Molecules and compounds form the smallest unit of a substance—for example, if water (H_2O) is broken down into hydrogen and oxygen atoms, it no longer has the unique properties of water. Molecules and compounds always have the same ratio of elements. Water, for example, always has two hydrogens for every one oxygen.

Intramolecular Forces

A chemical bond is a force that holds two atoms together. There are two primary types of bolds: ionic and covalent.

In an **IONIC BOND**, one atom has lost electrons to the other, which results in a positive charge on one atom and a negative charge on the other atom. The bond is then a result of the electrostatic interaction between these positive and negative charges. For example, in the compound sodium chloride, sodium has lost an electron to chlorine, resulting in a positive charge on sodium and a negative charge on chlorine.

In a **COVALENT BOND**, electrons are shared between two atoms; neither atom completely loses or gains an electron. This can be in the form of one pair of shared electrons (a single bond), two pairs (a double bond), or three pairs of electrons shared (triple bond). In diatomic oxygen gas, for example, the two oxygen molecules share two sets of electrons.

Covalent bonds are often depicted using Lewis diagrams, in which an electron is represented by a dot and a shared pair of electrons is represented by a line.

Figure 6.4. Lewis diagram of a covalent bond

Electrons within a covalent bond aren't always shared equally. More electronegative atoms, which exert a strong pull on the electrons, will hold onto the electrons longer than less electronegative atoms. For example, oxygen is more electronegative than hydrogen, so in H_2O (water) both oxygens have a slight negative charge, and the hydrogen has a slight positive charge. This imbalance is called **POLARITY**, and the small charge a **DIPOLE**.

Note that there is a commonality between the two types of bonding. In both ionic and covalent bonding types, the bond results in each atom having a full valence shell of electrons. When bonding, atoms seek to find the most stable electron configuration. In the majority of cases, this means filling the valence shell of the atom either through the addition or removal of electrons.

Intermolecular Forces

What causes water to stick together, forming a liquid at room temperature but a solid at lower temperatures? Why do we need more heat and energy to increase the temperature of water compared to other substances? The answer is INTERMOLECULAR FORCES: attractive or repulsive forces that occur between molecules. These are different from ionic and covalent bonds, which occur within a molecule.

There are two main types of intermolecular forces that you need to know for the test: Dipole-dipole interactions, and Van der Waals forces. In a DIPOLE-DIPOLE INTERACTION, the small charge on the atoms in a polar molecule interact with the charge on other polar molecules. When a hydrogen is bonded to a very electronegative atom, the resulting interaction is called HYDROGEN BONDING. This force can be seen between the oxygen and hydrogen atoms in water and is responsible for many of water's distinctive properties. Hydrogen bonds are the strongest of the intermolecular forces.

VAN DER WAALS FORCES are the sum of small force interactions between molecules that are a result of forces that **are not** covalent, ionic, or hydrogen bonding in nature. There are several distinct Van der Waals forces, but the most important is the LONDON DISPERSION FORCE, which arises from temporary dipoles created by the normal movement of electrons.

Chemical and Physical Properties

Substances, whether they are composed of individual atoms or molecules, all have unique properties that are grouped into two categories: physical and chemical. A change in a PHYSICAL PROPERTY does not result in a change in the chemical composition of a reactant, but only the physical structure. For example, a change of state is a physical reaction. A change in a CHEMICAL PROPERTY is one in which the molecular structure or composition of the compound has been changed. Physical and chemical properties are often influenced by intra- and intermolecular forces. For example, substances with strong hydrogen bonds will have higher boiling points.

Examples

1. Which of these statements is not true of covalent bonds?

   A) They include two overlapping atomic orbitals.

   B) The net formal charge on the resulting compound must be zero.

   C) They allow bonded atoms to achieve electron configurations comparable to those of noble gases.

   D) They may include more than one pair of shared electrons.

2. Which of the following molecules does not have an ionic bond?

A) $FeCl_2$

B) H_3PO_4

C) KOH

D) C_2H_6

3. In organic biomolecules such as proteins and DNA, interactions between the constituent pieces of the chain contribute substantially to the molecule's secondary structure. While these bonds are fairly strong, they frequently break to permit the molecule to bend and flex. The described interactions are most likely caused by:

A) hydrogen bonding

B) ionic bonding

C) covalent bonding

D) van der Waals forces

Answers: 1. C) 2. D) 3. C)

NAMING MOLECULES

A CHEMICAL FORMULA (sometimes called a molecular formula) describes the chemical composition of a compound or molecule using elemental symbols and integers to represent the number of each atom. There are two methods for writing a chemical formula. The first is the simplest, and just states the ratio of elements in a compound. For example, the compound acetic acid has the formula $C_2H_4O_2$, which means that a single molecule of acetic acid has 2 carbons, 4 hydrogens, and 2 oxygen atoms.

However, this chemical formula does not describe the structure of the compound. For this, it's necessary to use FUNCTIONAL GROUP NOTATION. When writing a chemical formula using functional group notation, the letters are moved around in the formula to reflect the correct order of the elements in the compound. In functional group notation, acetic acid is written as CH_3COOH. From this formula, it's clear that the first carbon in the molecule is attached to three hydrogen, and then to the next carbon, which is attached to the O-O-H chain.

Molecules can also be described using their EMPIRICAL FORMULA, which is just the molecule's chemical formula reduced to its simplest ratio. The empirical formula for acetic acid is CH_2O.

Chemical Names: Ionic Compounds

Ionic compounds are formed from one or more CATIONS (with a positive charge) and one or more ANIONS (with a negative charge). The naming rules for ionic compounds are as follows:

1. The cation is written first, followed by the anion. The cation has no suffix added. The anion has a suffix of –ide in the majority of cases (such as sodium chloride).

2. The stoichiometry of the molecule, as indicated by the subscripts, must produce a molecule that has no net charge. For example, $NaCl_2^-$, sodium dichloride, is not a valid compound.

3. The compound should be an empirical formula, meaning it should have the lowest subscripts possible. For example Na_2Cl_2 is not correct.

4. A polyatomic anion such as SO_4^{2-} does not have parentheses unless there are multiples of the anion. For example, $Na_2(SO_4)$ is not correct. However, $Al_2(SO_4)_3$ is correct because there are three sulfate anions.

Chemical Names: Covalent Compounds

The naming of covalent compounds is similar to ionic naming. In the naming of covalent compounds, the following rules apply:

1. The first element is named, along with a prefix indicating the number of atoms of that element in the molecular formula.

2. The second element is named, along with an appropriate suffix.

3. The first element, if having a value of 1, does not use the prefix mono-.

CH_4 = carbon tetrahydride
CO_2 = carbon dioxide

Table 6.1. Naming prefixes

NUMBER	PREFIX
1	mono
2	di
3	tri
4	tetra
5	penta
6	hexa
7	hepta
8	octa
9	nona

Examples

1. Which of these is not a properly named chemical by ionic nomenclature?

   A) potassium acetate

   B) lithium hydroxide

   C) lead nitrate

   D) calcium sulfite

2. Which of the following is the correct formula for chromium (III) oxide?

A) Cr_3O

B) CrO_3

C) Cr_3O_2

D) Cr_2O_3

3. What is the correct name for Na_2SO_4?

A) disodium sulfite

B) disodium sulfur oxide

C) sodium sulfate

D) sodium (II) sulfate

Answers: 1. C) 2. D) 3. C)

STATES OF MATTER

A STATE is a description of the physical characteristics of a material. There are four states: solid, liquid, gas, and plasma.

- A SOLID is a dense phase characterized by close bonds between all molecules in the solid; they have a definite shape and volume.

- A LIQUID is a fluid phase characterized by loose bonds between molecules in the liquid; they have an indefinite shape but a definite volume.

- A GAS is a very disperse phase characterized by the lack of, or very weak bonds, between molecules; gases have both an indefinite shape and volume.

- The PLASMA phase occurs when a substance has been heated and pressurized past its critical point, resulting in a new phase that has liquid and gas properties.

A substance will change phase depending on the temperature and pressure. As temperature increases, the phase will progress from solid to liquid to gas. As pressure increases, the opposite is true, and the phase will progress from gas to liquid to solid.

These phase changes have specific names, as shown below. Note that reciprocal changes will involve the same amount of energy, but moving from a less to a more energetic state uses energy while moving from a more to less energetic state will release energy.

- evaporation: liquid to gas (uses energy); occurs at boiling point

- condensation: gas to liquid (releases energy); occurs at boiling point

- melting: solid to liquid (uses energy); occurs at freezing point

- freezing: liquid to solid (releases energy); occurs at freezing point
- sublimation: solid to gas (uses energy)
- deposition: gas to solid (releases energy)

PHASE DIAGRAMS are used to show the relationships between phases, temperature, and pressure for a particular substance. In the phase diagram there are two points that are interesting to note. At the TRIPLE POINT, all three phases exist together, and at the CRITICAL POINT, the substance enters the plasma phase.

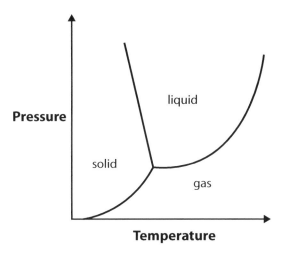

Figure 6.5. Phase diagram

Boiling Point and Freezing Point

The boiling point and freezing point of a molecule are related to its structure. There are three important factors that contribute to boiling and freezing points:

1. Strength of intermolecular forces: the greater the intermolecular force, the greater the boiling point of the substance will be.

2. Molecule size: as the molecule becomes larger, the boiling point of the molecule typically increases.

3. Molecule branching: as more branch points are present in the molecule, the molecule's boiling point will increase.

Let's look at an example. Methane has a molecular weight of 16 grams per mole, and water has a molecular weight of 18 grams per mole. Neither molecule is branched. As a result, factors 2 and 3 (as listed above), are not relevant. However, water has a boiling point of 100°C while methane has a boiling point of –164°C.

This large difference is a result of intermolecular forces. Water is a highly polar molecule that has strong intermolecular forces. On the other hand, methane is an uncharged, non-polar molecule with next to no intermolecular forces. Thus, the energy required to break the bonds between water molecules, and cause the phase change from liquid to vapor, is much greater than that for the methane molecule.

The Gas Laws

The interactions between each atom and molecule in a gas are extremely weak, and for this reason, gases have a low density compared to liquids and solids. However, due to their increased activity, the internal energy of a molecule in the gaseous phase is higher than that of a molecule in the liquid or solid phase.

When discussing gases, it's important to differentiate between real gases and ideal gases. **REAL GASES** are what we experience in the real world. These gases are compressible, have intermolecular interactions, and may react. An **IDEAL GAS** is an idealized version of a gas that simplifies calculations in chemistry. An ideal gas is assumed to follow these rules:

Standard temperature and pressure (STP) is 0°C (298 K) and 1 atm (101.35 kPA).

- Each gas molecule occupies a very small volume (close to zero) compared to the overall volume of the container.

- All collisions between gas molecules are perfectly elastic.

- There are no attractive or repulsive forces acting on the gas molecules.

- The gas molecules are in constant motion and move completely randomly.

A gas under these conditions will follow a number of laws that describe the relationship between pressure (P), volume (V), temperature (T), moles (n), and a value called the ideal gas constant (R). The value of the ideal gas constant will change depending on the units used for the other variables.

- Ideal gas law: $PV = nRT$

- Charles' Law: $\dfrac{V_1}{T_1} = \dfrac{V_2}{T_2}$

- Boyle's law: $P_1 V_1 = P_2 V_2$

- Avogadro's Law: $\dfrac{V_1}{n_1} = \dfrac{V_2}{n_2}$

Table 6.2. The ideal gas constant

R VALUE	UNITS
8.314	J/(mol·K)
0.08205	(L·atm)/(mol·K)
1.987	cal/(mol·K)

→

CONTINUE

Examples

1. What is the correct term for the energy required for a solid to become a liquid?

    A) latent heat of vaporization

    B) latent heat of fusion

    C) latent heat of fission

    D) latent heat of condensation

2. Which of the following is not a state of matter?

    A) plasma

    B) liquid

    C) solid

    D) crystal

3. Which of the following is likely to have the highest number of molecules?

    A) 1 liter of water vapor

    B) 1 liter of water

    C) 0.5 liter of ice

    D) 0.5 liter of an ice-water mixture

4. Which of the following is not true of a liquid?

    A) A liquid fills the volume of the container holding it.

    B) A liquid is fluid and can change shape.

    C) A liquid is always warmer than a solid.

    D) Molecules in a liquid can have attractive interactions.

5. The freezing point of a compound is the same as the:

    A) boiling point of the compound

    B) melting point of the compound

    C) triple point of the compound

    D) critical point of the compound

6. When the pressure is increased on a sample of gas with a constant temperature, its volume:

    A) stays the same

    B) increases

    C) decreases

    D) oscillates

7. A scientist has 1 mole of a sample of gas at 274°C and 1 atm of pressure. How much volume will it occupy? ($R = 0.0821$ L·atm/K·mol)

A) 18.5 liters

B) 19.9 liters

C) 22.4 liters

D) 25.2 liters

Answers: 1. B) 2. D) 3. B) 4. A) 5. B) 6. C) 7. C)

ACIDS AND BASES

In general, an **ACID** can be defined as a substance that produces hydrogen ions (H⁺) in solution, while a **BASE** produces hydroxide ions (OH). Acidic solutions, which include common liquids like orange juice and vinegar, share a set of distinct characteristics: they have a sour taste and react strongly with metals. Bases, such as bleach and detergents, will taste bitter and have a slippery texture.

There are a number of different technical definitions for acids and bases, including the Arrhenius, Bronsted-Lowry, and Lewis acid definitions.

- The **ARRHENIUS** definition: An acid is a substance that produces H+ hydrogen ions in aqueous solution. A base is a substance that produces hydroxide ions OH– in aqueous solution.
- The **BRONSTED-LOWRY** definition: An acid is anything that donates a proton H+, and a base is anything that accepts a proton H+.
- The **LEWIS** definition: An acid is anything able to accept a pair of electrons, and a base is anything that can donate a pair of electrons.

Measuring the Strength of Acids and Bases

The **pH** of a solution is a measure of the acidity or basicity of the solution. It's found by taking the negative log of the concentration of hydrogen ions, making pH an exponential scale. The pH scale runs from 0 to 14 with a low pH being more acidic and a high pH more basic. A pH of 7 is that of water with no dissolved ions, and is considered neutral.

$pH = -\log[H+]$

→
CONTINUE

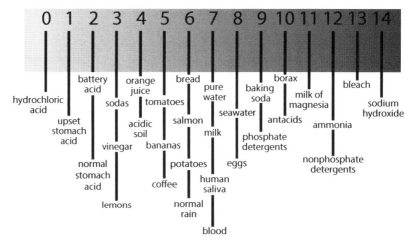

Figure 6.6. pH scale

Strong acids and bases will dissolve completely in solution, while weak acids and bases will only partially dissolve. Thus, strong acids and bases will have high or low pH values, respectively, and weak acids and bases will have pH values closer to 7.

Table 6.3. Strong and weak acids

STRONG ACIDS	WEAK ACIDS
Hydrobromic acid (HBr)	Acetic acid ($C_2H_4O_2$)
Hydrochloric acid (HCl)	Formic acid (HCOOH)
Sulfuric acid (H_2SO_4)	Butryic acid ($C_4H_8O_2$)

Acid Base Reactions

Acids and bases react with each other in solution to produce a salt and water, a process called **NEUTRALIZATION**. As a result of this reaction, if an equal amount of strong acid is mixed with an equal amount of strong base, the pH will remain at 7. For example, mixing hydrochloric acid and sodium hydroxide yields sodium chloride (a salt) and water, as shown below:

$$HCl(aq) + Na(OH)(aq) \rightarrow H_2O + NaCl(aq)$$

Examples

1. One of the characteristic properties of an acid is that it increases the concentration of:

   A) hydrogen ions

   B) hydroxyl ions

   C) hydroxide ions

   D) oxide ions

2. A solution with a pH of 12 is:

A) very acidic

B) neutral

C) very basic

D) slightly acidic

3. Proper blood pH level for humans is:

A) 7.0

B) 7.2

C) 7.6

D) 7.4

Answers: 1. A) 2. C) 3. D)

SOLUTIONS

In chemistry, the term MIXTURE describes a set of two or more substances that have been mixed together but are not chemically joined together. In a HOMOGENOUS mixture, the substances are evenly distributed; in a HETEROGENEOUS mixture, the substances are not evenly distributed.

A SOLUTION is a specific type of homogenous mixture in which all substances share the same basic properties and generally act as a single substance. In a solution, a SOLUTE is dissolved in a SOLVENT. For example, in salt water, salt is the solute and water is the solvent. The opposite process, in which a compound comes out of the solution, is called PRECIPITATION.

The CONCENTRATION of a solution—the amount of solute versus the amount of solvent—can be measured in a number of ways. Usually it's given as a ratio of solute to solvent in the relevant units. Some of these include:

- weight per volume (e.g., grams per liter)
- volume per volume (e.g., milliliter per liter)
- weight per weight (e.g., milligrams per gram)
- moles per volume (e.g., moles per liter)—also called MOLARITY
- moles per weight (e.g., moles per kilogram)—also called MOLALITY

Solubility

Solubility is a measure of how much solute will dissolve into a solvent. When a solution contains the maximum amount of solute possible, it is called a SATURATED SOLUTION. A solution with less solute is UNSATURATED, and a solution with more solute than can normally be dissolved in that solvent is SUPERSATURATED.

✓

Are the following mixtures homogenous or heterogeneous?
- lemonade
- concrete
- air
- trail mix
- salt water

There are many factors that can affect the solubility of a compound, including temperature and pressure. Another factor affecting solubility is the COMMON ION EFFECT, which occurs in solutions with two compounds that share a common ion. When the two compounds are mixed into a solvent, the presence of the common ion reduces the solubility of each compound. For example, NaCl and $MgCl_2$ share the common ion of chlorine. When they are mixed in a solution, the maximum saturation of the chlorine ion in water will be reached before the saturation of either sodium or magnesium is reached. This causes a reduction in the overall solubility.

Examples

1. In a carbonated soda, carbon dioxide is dissolved in water. In this solution, water is the

    A) common ion

    B) solvent

    C) solute

    D) precipitant

2. How much ethanol should be added to 2.5 L of water to produce a solution with a molarity of 5 M?

    A) 2 mol

    B) 2.5 mol

    C) 7.5 mol

    D) 12.5 mol

    Answers: 1. B) 2. D)

REACTIONS

In a CHEMICAL REACTION, one set of chemical substances, called the REACTANTS, are transformed into another set of chemical substances called the PRODUCTS. This transformation is described in a chemical equation with the reactants on the left and products on the right. In the equation below, methane (CH_4) reacts with oxygen (O_2) to produce carbon dioxide (CO_2) and water (H_2O).

$$CH_4 + 2O_2 \rightarrow CO_2 + 2H_2O$$

When a reaction runs to COMPLETION, all the reactants have been used up in the reaction. If one reactant limits the use of the other reactants (i.e., if one reactant is used up before the others), it's called the LIMITING REACTANT. The YIELD is the amount of product produced by the reaction.

Balancing Equations

The integer values placed before the chemical symbols are the COEFFICIENTS that describe how many molecules of that substance are involved in the reaction. These values are important because in a chemical reaction, there is a conservation of mass. The inputs, or reactant mass, must equal the outputs, or products. For example, the reaction shown on the previous page includes one carbon, four hydrogen, and four oxygen on either side of the arrow.

In order to **BALANCE AN EQUATION**, you'll need to add the coefficients necessary to match the atoms of each element on both sides. In the reaction below, the numbers of bromine (Br) and nitrate ions (NO_3^-) do not match up:

$$CaBr_2 + NaNO_3 \rightarrow Ca(NO_3)_2 + NaBr$$

To balance the equation, start by adding a coefficient of 2 to the products to balance the bromine:

$$CaBr_2 + NaNO_3 \rightarrow Ca(NO_3)_2 + 2NaBr$$

There are now 2 sodium ions on the right, so another 2 need to be added on the left to balance it:

$$CaBr_2 + 2NaNO_3 \rightarrow Ca(NO_3)_2 + 2NaBr$$

Notice that adding this 2 also balances the nitrate ions, so the equation is now complete.

Types of Reactions

There are five main types of chemical reactions.

- In a **SYNTHESIS** reaction, two or more reactants will form a single product. $A + B \rightarrow C$

- In a **DECOMPOSITION** reaction, a single reactant will decompose into two products. Decomposition reactions typically require an input of energy. $A \rightarrow B + C$

- In a **SINGLE DISPLACEMENT** reaction, one reactant will dissociate, and its complement ion will react with another species in solution. $AB + C \rightarrow A + BC$

- In a **DOUBLE DISPLACEMENT** reaction, two reactants will dissociate and exchange complement ions. $AB + CD \rightarrow AC + BD$

- In a **COMBUSTION** reaction, a fuel (alkane or carbohydrate are typical) will react with oxygen to form carbon dioxide and water. $C_xH_yO_z + O_2 \rightarrow CO_2 + H_2O$

Oxidation and Reduction

An oxidation and reduction reaction (often called a redox reaction) is one in which there is an exchange of electrons. The species that loses electrons is **OXIDIZED**, and the species that gains electrons is **REDUCED**. The species that loses electrons is also called the **REDUCING AGENT**, and the species that gains electrons the **OXIDIZING AGENT**.

The movement of electrons in a redox reaction is analyzed by assigning each atom in the reaction an **OXIDATION NUMBER** (or state) that corresponds roughly to that atom's charge. (The actual meaning

OIL RIG
Oxidation
Involves
Loss
Reduction
Involves
Gain

of the oxidation number is much more complicated.) Once all the atoms in a reaction have been assigned an oxidation number, it's possible to see which elements have gained electrons and which elements have lost electrons. The basic rules for assigning oxidation numbers are given in the table below.

Table 6.4. Assigning oxidation numbers

SPECIES	EXAMPLE	OXIDATION NUMBER
Elements in their free state and naturally occurring diatomic elements	$Zn(s)$, O_2	0
Monoatomic ions	Cl^-	−1
Oxygen in compounds	H_2O	−2
Hydrogen in compounds	HCl	+1
Alkali metals in a compound	Na	+1
Alkaline earth metals in a compound	Mg	+2

RULES		
The oxidation numbers on the atoms in a neutral compound sum to zero.	NaOH	Na: +1; O: −2; H: +1 $1 + -2 + 1 = 0$
The oxidation numbers of the atoms in an ion sum to the charge on that ion.	SO_3^{-2}	S: +4; O: −2 $4 + (-2)(3) = -2$

Reaction Stoichiometry

STOICHIOMETRY is the use of the relative amounts of reagents and products in a reaction to find quantities of those reagents and products. Stoichiometry can be used to find a number of variables, including the quantities of products and reagents involved in a reaction, and to identity the limiting reagent (the reagent that gets used up first).

An important unit to know when doing stoichiometry is the MOLE, which is defined the amount of a substance that contains 6.02×10^{23} particles (either individual atoms or molecules). On the periodic table, the atomic mass of an element is also the number of grams per mole of that element; these values can be used in stoichiometry to convert between moles and grams.

For example, in the single displacement reaction shown below, 1 mole of magnesium chloride is needed for every 2 moles of sodium to complete the reaction. This reaction creates 1 mole of magnesium and 2 moles of sodium chloride.

$$MgCl_2 + 2Na \rightarrow Mg + 2NaCl$$

So, if 50 grams of sodium are used up the reaction, stoichiometry can be used to find the number of grams of magnesium that are produced:

$$\frac{50 \text{ g Na}}{1} \times \frac{1 \text{ mol Na}}{23 \text{ g Na}} \times \frac{1 \text{ mol Mg}}{2 \text{ mol Na}} \times \frac{24.3 \text{ g Mg}}{1 \text{ mol Mg}} = 26.4 \text{ g Mg}$$

Examples

1. In a furnace, natural gas (methane) is burned to produce heat to keep a house warm. What sort of reaction is this?

   A) acid base reaction

   B) combustion reaction

   C) single displacement reaction

   D) synthesis reaction

2. If 4 moles of methane are used in the reaction below, how many moles of water will be produced?

   $CH_4 + 2O_2 \rightarrow CO_2 + 2H_2O$

   A) 2

   B) 8

   C) 12

   D) 16

3. Which of the following is a substance or compound that is entering into a reaction?

   A) mole

   B) reactant

   C) product

   D) yield

4. Sulfur trioxide (SO_3) is produced when sulfur is burned. Which of the following is the correct general reaction for this process?

   A) sulfur + nitrogen → sulfur trioxide

   B) sulfur + oxygen → sulfur dioxide

   C) sulfur dioxide + oxygen → sulfur trioxide

   D) sulfur + oxygen → sulfur trioxide

5. In a balanced equation,

   A) the mass of the reactants equals the mass of the products.

   B) the number of moles of reactants equals the number of moles of the products.

   C) the size of each molecule in the reaction remains the same.

   D) the number of moles of each element in the reaction remains the same.

6. Balance the following equation:

A) $2KClO_3 \rightarrow KCl + 3O_2$

B) $KClO_3 \rightarrow KCl + 3O_2$

C) $2KClO_3 \rightarrow 2KCl + 3O_2$

D) $6KClO_3 \rightarrow 6KCl + 3O_2$

Answers: 1. B) 2. B) 3. B) 4. D) 5. D) 6. C)

CHEMICAL EQUILIBRIUM

CHEMICAL EQUILIBRIUM is a state reached in reversible reactions in which the rate of forward reaction equals the rate of reverse reaction. Once equilibrium has been reached, it will appear as though the reaction has stopped because there is no noticeable change in the creation of products. However, this isn't true: at chemical equilibrium, reactions are still occurring, just at an equal rate.

Le Chatelier's Principle

LE CHATELIER'S PRINCIPLE states that a chemical reaction at equilibrium will respond to changes in concentration, pressure, volume, or temperature by shifting to reestablish equilibrium. This new equilibrium will favor either the reactants or the products relative to the original equilibrium.

An increase in the concentration of a reactant or product will shift the equilibrium to the other side (e.g., adding a reactant will result in the production of more products to offset the addition). Decreasing the concentration of a reactant or product will shift the reaction toward that side of the reaction (e.g., removing reactant will result in the production of more reactants and a corresponding decrease in the concentration of the products).

In a reaction involving gases, changes in pressure and volume can shift the equilibrium; the direction of the shift will depend on the number of moles of reactants and products. Decreasing the pressure (or increasing the volume) will result in a shift toward the side of the equation with more moles. Increasing the pressure (or decreasing the volume) will result in a shift toward the side of the equation with fewer moles.

Shifts in chemical equilibriums due to changes in temperature are determined by whether the equation is endothermic (uses energy) or exothermic (gives off energy). Increasing the temperature will favor the products in endothermic reactions and the reactants in exothermic reactions. The opposite is true when decreasing the temperature of a system.

Examples

1. According to Le Chatelier's principle, if hydrochloric acid (HCl) is removed from the reaction below, what will happen?

   $BaCl_2$ (aq) + H_2SO_4 (aq) → $BaSO_4$ (s) + 2HCl (aq)

   A) The reaction will shift to the left, and more reactants will be formed.

   B) The reaction will shift to the right, and more products will be formed.

   C) The reaction will not be able to reestablish equilibrium.

   D) The reaction will stop.

2. Which of the following statements about chemical equilibrium is true?

   A) Chemical equilibrium cannot be reestablished if the concentration of reactants is changed.

   B) In chemical equilibrium, all the reactants have been turned into products.

   C) Chemical equilibriums cannot be reached by reversible reactions.

   D) In chemical equilibrium, forward and reverse reactions are occurring at the same rate.

   Answers: 1. B) 2. D)

CHEMICAL KINETICS

Collision Theory

COLLISION THEORY refers to the idea that a chemical reaction cannot occur until two molecules which may react collide with one another. In a solid, although molecules are all touching one another, there is not much movement. As a result, chemical reactions in solid phase have a low reaction rate, or none at all. A solid usually only reacts when its surface comes into contact with a liquid or gas.

In liquids or gases, molecules are able to move freely, which allows greater interaction and an increased chance that two capable molecules will react. For this reason, the majority of chemical reactions occur in the liquid phase or the gas phase. However, even if two molecules collide that could react, most of the time they do not. In order for a reaction to take place, the reaction must have a minimum amount of energy, a quantity known as the reaction's ACTIVATION ENERGY.

Reaction Rates

Different reactions will occur at different rates. This REACTION RATE is determined by a number of factors, including the concentration of reactants, particle surface area, and temperature. Generally, increasing any of these variables will increase the reaction rate by providing more opportunities for particles to collide.

- Increasing the concentration of reactants introduces more particles to the system, meaning they are more likely to collide.
- Increasing particle surface area makes it more likely particles will come in contact with each other.
- Increasing the temperature increases the velocity of the particles, making them more likely to collide.

Catalysts

There are some substances, called **CATALYSTS**, that are able to reduce the activation energy of a reaction, which subsequently will increase the reaction rate. A chemical catalyst is commonly a metal or other elemental compound with many electrons in their valence shell; they assist in the stabilization of reaction intermediates. Common chemical catalysts include platinum, palladium, nickel, or cobalt.

A biological catalyst is known as an **ENZYME**. Common enzymes include cellulase, amylase, or DNA polymerase. Biological catalysts typically function by bringing two reactants close together. Many enzymes also have active sites in their protein chains that function similarly to a chemical catalyst, and assist in stabilizing reaction intermediates.

There are two types of catalysts subdivided by their phase: homogenous and heterogeneous. A **HOMOGENOUS CATALYST** is in the same phase as the reactants. Most enzymes are homogenous, and are soluble in the same phase as the reactants.

A **HETEROGENEOUS CATALYST** is not in the same phase as the reactants. An example of a heterogeneous catalyst is the platinum found in the catalytic converter in the exhaust stream of cars. The catalyst is in the solid phase, and the reactants are in the gas phase.

Examples

1. A reaction with a high activation energy will:
   A) require energy to begin
   B) require a catalyst to begin
   C) produce energy
   D) produce enzymes

2. A company is trying to make ammonia from the reaction of nitrogen (N_2) and hydrogen (H_2), but the reaction is progressing very slowly. Which of the following would be effective in increasing the reaction rate?

A) increasing the temperature

B) increasing the pressure

C) adding a catalyst

D) all of the above

Answers: 1. A) 2. D)

LAWS OF THERMODYNAMICS

THERMODYNAMICS is the study of energy in a system and its relationship to chemical reactions. The use of thermodynamics can help explain the rate at which a reaction will occur and whether a reaction will occur at all. There are three basic laws of thermodynamics:

The FIRST LAW OF THERMODYNAMICS states that the internal energy of a system (U) is equal to the heat in the system (Q) minus the work performed by the system (W): $U = Q - W$. This law also confirms the conservation of energy (that energy can neither be created nor destroyed).

This law is probably the most important for chemistry; it helps explain energy shifts in a reaction. For example, if the internal energy of reactants is greater than the internal energy of the products, energy must be released during the course of the reaction, either in the form of heat or work.

The SECOND LAW OF THERMODYNAMICS states that the entropy of a system increases with time and with action. In layman's terms, this law states that any action results in an increase of entropy, a property that describes disorder. The THIRD LAW OF THERMODYNAMICS states that the entropy of a substance approaches zero as the temperature approaches absolute zero (0 Kelvin).

Endothermic and Exothermic Reactions

There are three types of reactions: endothermic, exothermic, and isothermic reactions. An ENDOTHERMIC reaction requires heat in order to proceed while an EXOTHERMIC reaction releases heat during the course of the reaction. An ISOTHERMIC reaction has no net input or output of energy.

$\longrightarrow$
CONTINUE

Examples

1. In chemistry class, a student mixes two unknown chemicals in a beaker. He notices that the beaker becomes hot to the touch. What type of reaction must be taking place in the beaker?

    A) exothermic

    B) endothermic

    C) combustion

    D) single replacement

2. Which of these processes is exothermic?

    A) freezing water

    B) baking a cake

    C) melting iron

    D) breaking up a gaseous diatom

Answers: 1. A) 2. A)

NUCLEAR CHEMISTRY AND RADIOACTIVITY

The nuclei of some elements are unstable and will emit radioactive particles or energy in order to stabilize; together these emissions of particles and energy are called RADIOACTIVE DECAY or RADIATION. The three types of radiation that will be covered on the test include alpha, beta, and gamma radiation.

ALPHA PARTICLES consist of two protons and two neutrons (i.e., a helium nucleus). They are written as $_0^2He$. In beta decay, high energy electrons or positrons are emitted from the nucleus. BETA PARTICLES are written as $_{-1}^0\beta$ (for electrons) and $_{+1}^0\beta$ (for positrons). Lastly, GAMMA RADIATION is a high frequency (and thus high energy) electromagnetic radiation written as $_0^0\gamma$. All three types of radiation can cause serious health issues ranging from nausea to cancer; both alpha and beta particles are relatively large and thus can be stopped by simple protective barriers. Gamma radiation, however, can travel through most substances, including concrete; lead is usually needed to provide protection from gamma rays.

Half-Life

The time it takes for half a sample of a radioactive substance to decay is called the substance's HALF-LIFE ($t_\frac{1}{2}$). A sample of lead-210 has a half-life of 22.2 years, meaning a 100 gram sample of lead-210 would be reduced to 50 grams after 22.2 years; 25 grams after 44.4 years; 12.5 grams after 66.6 years; and so on.

Examples

1. Uranium 233 has a half-life of about 70 years. If an area is contaminated with this compound, how long will it take to reach less than 5% of its original concentration? Round to the nearest number.

A) 3 half lives

B) 4 half lives

C) 5 half lives

D) 6 half lives

2. In the nuclear reaction shown below, what is the missing product?

$^{11}_{5}B \rightarrow$ product $+ ^{4}_{2}He$

A) $^{9}_{5}B$

B) $^{7}_{5}Li$

C) $^{7}_{3}Li$

D) $^{9}_{3}B$

Answers: 1. C) 2. C)

7

ANATOMY AND PHYSIOLOGY

Anatomy and physiology are the studies of body parts and body systems. This section will cover all necessary medical terms, prefixes, suffixes, and terminology as well as the anatomy and physiology of each body system.

TERMINOLOGY

Table 7.1. Directional terms

TERM	DEFINITION
superior	toward the head, or toward the upper body region
inferior	toward the lower body region
anterior (ventral)	on the belly or front side of the body
posterior (dorsal)	on the buttocks or back side of the body
proximal	near the trunk or middle part of the body
distal	furthest away from the point of reference
medial	close to the midline of the body
lateral	away from the midline of the body

Table 7.2. Prefixes and suffixes

PREFIX	DEFINITION	SUFFIX	DEFINITION
epi–	on/upon	–coccus	spherical bacterium
hyper–	over	–ia	condition
hypo–	under	–ectomy	removal
intra–	within	–malacia	softening
para–	beside	–tomy	to cut
per–	through	–rrhea	discharge
peri–	surrounding	–plasty	surgical repair
sub–	under	–opsy	view of

These prefixes can help you on the Reading and English Language Usage portions of the test.

Table 7.3. Cavities

CAVITY	CONTAINS
cranial	the brain
spinal	contains the spinal cord, and extends from the brainstem in the cranial cavity to the end of the spinal cord
thoracic	contains the lungs, heart, and large blood vessels, and is separated from the abdomen by the diaphragm
abdominal	contains the stomach, intestines, liver, gallbladder, pancreas, spleen, and kidneys, and is separated from the thoracic cavity by the diaphragm
pelvic	contains the urinary bladder, urinary structures, and reproductive organs

THE CIRCULATORY SYSTEM

The CIRCULATORY SYSTEM circulates nutrients, gases, wastes, and other substances throughout the body. This system includes the blood, which carries these substances; the heart, which powers the movement of blood; and the blood vessels, which carry the blood.

The Heart

The whole system relies on the HEART, a cone-shaped muscular organ that is no bigger than a closed fist. The heart must pump the blood low in oxygen to the lungs; once the blood is in the lungs, it is oxygenated and returned to the heart. The heart then pumps the oxygenated blood through the whole body.

The heart is located inside the rib cage. It can be found approximately between the second and the sixth rib from the bottom of the rib cage. The heart does not sit on the body's midline. Rather, two-thirds of it is located on the left side of the body. The narrower part of the heart is called the apex, and it points downwards and to the left of the body; the broader part of the heart is called the base, and it points upwards.

The cavity that holds the heart is called the PERICARDIAL CAVITY. It is filled with serous fluid produced by the pericardium, which is the lining of the pericardial cavity. The serous fluid acts as a lubricant for the heart. It also keeps the heart in place and empties the space around the heart.

The heart wall has three layers:

- **EPICARDIUM**: the outermost layer of the heart, and is one of the two layers of the pericardium.
- **MYOCARDIUM**: the middle layer of the heart that contains the cardiac muscular tissue. It performs the function of pumping what is necessary for the

circulation of blood. It is the most massive part of the heart.

- ■ **ENDOCARDIUM**: the smooth innermost layer that keeps the blood from sticking to the inside of the heart.

The heart wall is uneven because some parts of the heart—like the atria—don't need a lot of muscle power to perform their duties. Other parts, like the ventricles, require a thicker muscle to pump the blood.

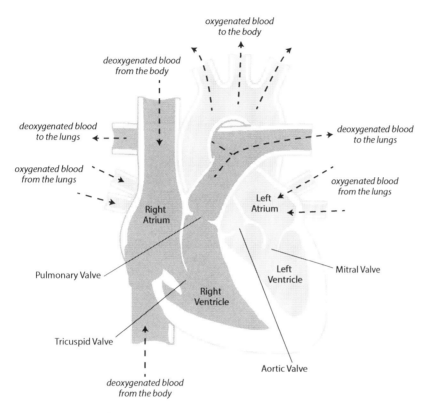

Figure 7.1. Heart diagram

There are four **CHAMBERS** in the heart: the right and left atria, and the right and left ventricles. The **ATRIA** (plural for atrium) are smaller than the ventricles, and they have thin walls, as their function is to receive blood from the lungs and the body and pump it to the ventricles. The **VENTRICLES** have to pump the blood to the lungs and the rest of the body, so they are larger and have a thicker wall. The left half of the heart, which is responsible for pumping the blood through the body, has a thicker wall than the right half which pumps the deoxygenated blood to the lungs.

The heart has one-way valves allowing the blood to flow in only one direction. The valves that keep the blood from going back into the atria from the ventricles are called the **ATRIOVENTRICULAR VALVES**, and the valves that keep the blood from going back into the ventricles from the arteries are called the **SEMILUNAR VALVES**.

The pumping function of the heart is made possible by two groups of cells that set the heart's pace and keep it well-coordinated: the sinoatrial and the atrioventricular node. The SINOATRIAL NODE sets the pace and signals the atria to contract; the ATRIOVENTRICULAR NODE picks up the signal from the sinoatrial node, and this signal tells the ventricles to contract.

The Blood Vessels

The BLOOD VESSELS carry the blood from the heart throughout the body and then back. They vary in size depending on the amount of the blood that needs to flow through them. The hollow part in the middle, called the LUMEN, is where the blood actually flows. The vessels are lined with endothelium, which is made out of the same type of cells as the endocardium and serves the same purpose—to keep the blood from sticking to the walls and clotting.

ARTERIES are blood vessels that transport the blood away from the heart. They work under a lot more pressure than the other types of blood vessels; hence, they have a thicker, more muscular wall, which is also highly elastic. The smaller arteries are usually more muscular, while the larger are more elastic.

The largest artery in the body is called the AORTA. It ascends from the left ventricle of the heart, arches to the back left, and descends behind the heart. Narrower arteries that branch off of main arteries and carry blood to the capillaries are called ARTERIOLES. The descending part of the aorta carries blood to the lower parts of the body, except for the lungs. The lungs get blood through the PULMONARY ARTERY that comes out of the right ventricle.

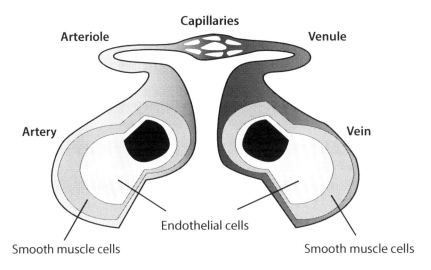

Figure 7.2. Artery and vein diagram

The arching part of the aorta (called the AORTIC ARCH) branches into three arteries: the brachiocephalic artery, the left common artery, and the left subclavian artery. The BRACHIOCEPHALIC ARTERY carries blood to the brain and head. The brachiocephalic artery divides into the right subclavian artery, which brings the blood to the right arm. The **LEFT COMMON CAROTID ARTERY** carries blood to the brain; the **LEFT SUBCLAVIAN ARTERY** carries blood to the left arm.

VEINS are blood vessels that bring the blood from the body back to the heart. As they don't work under the same pressure as the arteries, they are much thinner and not as muscular or elastic. The veins also have a number of one-way valves that stop the blood from going back through them.

Veins use inertia, muscle work, and gravity to get the blood to the heart. Thin veins that connect to the capillaries are called **VENULES**. The lungs have their own set of veins: the **LEFT** and **RIGHT SUPERIOR** and **INFERIOR PULMONARY VEINS**. These vessels enter the heart through the left atrium.

The two main veins are called the superior vena cava and the inferior vena cava. The **SUPERIOR VENA CAVA** ascends from the right atrium and connects to the head and neck, delivering the blood supply to these structures. The superior vena cava also connects to the arms via both subclavian and brachiocephalic veins. The **INFERIOR VENA CAVA** descends from the right atrium, carrying the blood from the lumbar veins, gonadal veins, hepatic veins, phrenic veins, and renal veins.

CAPILLARIES are the smallest blood vessels, and the most populous in the body. They can be found in almost every tissue. They connect to arterioles on one end and the venules on the other end. Also, capillaries carry the blood very close to the cells and thus enable cells to exchange gases, nutrients, and cellular waste. The walls of capillaries have to be very thin for this exchange to happen.

The Blood

BLOOD is the medium for the transport of substances throughout the body. There are four to five liters of this liquid connective tissue in the human body. Blood is comprised of red blood cells, hemoglobin, white blood cells, platelets, and plasma.

CONTINUE

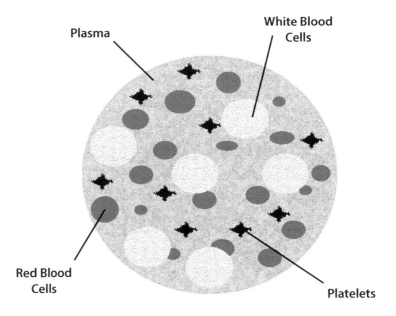

Figure 7.3. Blood

Also called ERYTHROCYTES, RED BLOOD CELLS (RBCs) are produced inside the red bone marrow and transport oxygen. HEMO-GLOBIN (HGB) is a red pigment found in the red blood cells, and it is rich in iron and proteins, which both allow these cells to transport the oxygen. RBCs also have a biconcave shape, which means they are round and thinner in the middle. This shape gives them a larger surface area, making them more effective.

WHITE BLOOD CELLS (WBCs), also called LEUKOCYTES, are important for the human immune system. There are two classes of white blood cells: granular and agranular leukocytes. GRANULAR LEUKOCYTES are divided into three types: the neutrophils that digest bacteria, the eosinophils that digest viruses, and the basophils that release histamine. AGRANULAR LEUKOCYTES are divided into two classes: the lymphocytes, which fight off viral infections and produce antibodies for fighting pathogen-induced infection, and the monocytes, which play a role in removing pathogens and dead cells from wounds.

PLATELETS, also called THROMBOCYTES, are vital for blood clotting. They are formed in the red bone marrow and serve many functions in the body. Finally, PLASMA is the liquid part of blood, and it forms 55 percent of the total blood volume. Plasma consists of up to 90 percent water, as well as proteins, including antibodies and albumins. Other substances circulating in the blood plasma include glucose, nutrients, cell waste, and various gases.

The Cardiac Cycle

The heart works by shifting between two states: systole and diastole. In **SYSTOLE**, the cardiac muscles are contracting and moving blood from any given chamber. During **DIASTOLE**, the muscles are relaxing and the chamber is expanding to fill with blood. The systole and diastole are responsible for the pressure in the major arteries. This is the **BLOOD PRESSURE** that is measured in a regular exam. The two values are systolic and diastolic pressures respectively, with the former being larger than the latter.

A **CARDIAC CYCLE** is the series of events that occur during one heartbeat. These events include:

- Atrial systole: The first phase of the cardiac cycle is atrial systole. With this, the blood is pushed by the atria through the valves into ventricles, which are in diastole during that event.

- Ventricular systole: After atrial systole, ventricular systole occurs. This pushes the blood from the ventricles to the organs, which occurs while the atria are in diastole.

- Relaxation phase: After ventricular systole, there is a pause called the relaxation phase. During this, all the chambers are in diastole, and the blood enters the atria through the veins.

- Refilling phase: When atria are at about 75 percent of their capacity, the cycle starts again. With the refilling phase, the atria are fully filled before atrial systole occurs again.

THE HEART VALVES
Try Pulling My Aorta
- Tricuspid
- Pulmonary
- Mitral
- Aorta

Atrial Diastole	Atrial Systole	Ventricular Systole	Ventricular Diastole
All heart muscle in relaxation	Atria in contraction	Ventricles in contraction	All heart muscle in relaxation
All heart valves are closed	AV valves are open	Semilunar valves are open	All heart valves are closed
Blood returning to atria	Blood to ventricles	Blood passing to the arteries	Blood returning to atria

Figure 7.4. Cardiac cycle

Oxygenating the Blood

There are four steps to blood cell oxygenation:

1. The poorly oxygenated blood comes into the right atrium through the superior and inferior vena cava.

2. The blood is then passed to the right ventricle, which sends it through the pulmonary artery into the lungs where oxygenation occurs.

3. The oxygen-rich blood then comes to the left atrium through the pulmonary veins, and gets moved from the left atrium to the left ventricle.

4. By way of blood pressure, the blood is then sent from the left ventricle through the aorta and the aortic arch into the arteries in the whole body.

After leaving the left ventricle, the blood passes from the arteries to the arterioles and on to the capillaries, where the exchange of gases, nutrients, wastes, and hormones occur. The blood then passes into venules, and gets back to the heart through the veins. A healthy resting heart can pump around five liters per minute through this cycle.

The veins of the stomach and intestines don't carry the blood directly to the heart. Rather, they divert it to the liver first, through the hepatic portal vein, so that the liver can store sugar, remove toxins, and process the products of digestion. The blood then goes to the heart through the inferior vena cava.

Examples

1. At what rate does a healthy heart pump blood while resting?

   A) around 3 liters per minute

   B) around 5 liters per minute

   C) around 8 liters per minute

   D) around 10 liters per minute

2. Which of the layers of the wall of the heart contains cardiac muscles?

   A) myocardium

   B) epicardium

   C) endocardium

   D) all layers of the heart

3. The heart chamber with the thickest wall is:

   A) the left atrium

   B) the right ventricle

   C) the right atrium

   D) the left ventricle

4. The blood from the left ventricle goes to:

A) the right ventricle

B) the vena cava

C) the aorta and aortic arch

D) the lungs

5. The blood vessels that carry the blood from the heart are called:

A) veins

B) venules

C) capillaries

D) arteries

Answers: 1. B) 2. A) 3. D) 4. C) 5. D)

THE RESPIRATORY SYSTEM

The human body needs oxygen in order to function. The system that is responsible for intake of this gas is called the **RESPIRATORY SYSTEM**. It's also in charge of removing carbon dioxide from the body, which is equally important. The respiratory system can be divided into two sections: the upper respiratory tract and the lower respiratory tract.

Figure 7.5. Respiratory tract

CONTINUE

The Upper Respiratory Tract

The **UPPER RESPIRATORY TRACT** consists of the nose, nasal cavity, olfactory membranes, mouth, pharynx, epiglottis, and the larynx.

The **NOSE** is the primary body part for air intake and removing carbon dioxide. The nose itself is made out of bone, cartilage, muscle, and skin, and it serves as a protector of the hollow space behind it called the **NASAL CAVITY**. The nasal cavity is covered with hair and mucus, which together serve an important function—they stop contaminants from the outside. Common contaminants include dust, mold, and other particles. The nasal cavity prevents the contaminants from entering further into the respiratory system; it also warms and moisturizes air.

The nose and the nasal cavity also contain **OLFACTORY MEMBRANES**, which are small organs responsible for our sense of smell. They are located on the top of the nasal cavity, just under the bridge of the nose.

We can also breathe through the **MOUTH**, although it is not the primary breathing opening. The mouth doesn't perform as well when it comes to the three functions of the primary opening (filtering, moisturizing, and warming of air). However, the mouth does have advantages over the nose when it comes to breathing, including its larger size and proximity to the lungs.

The next part of the respiratory system is the **THROAT**, which is also called the **PHARYNX**. The pharynx is a smooth, muscular structure lined with mucus and divided into three regions: the nasopharynx, the oropharynx, and the laryngopharynx.

Air comes in through the nose and then passes through the **NASOPHARYNX**, which is also where the Eustachian tubes from the middle ears connect with the pharynx. The air then enters the **ORO-PHARYNX**, which is where air from the mouth enters the pharynx; this is the same passageway used for transporting food when eating. Both air and food also pass through the **LARYNGOPHARYNX**, where these substances are diverted into different systems.

The **EPIGLOTTIS** is responsible for ensuring that air enters the trachea and food enters the esophagus. The epiglottis is a flap made of elastic cartilage, which covers the opening of one passageway to allow the air or food to go into the other one. When you breathe, the epiglottis covers the opening of the esophagus, and when you swallow, it protects the opening of the trachea.

The **LARYNX** is the part of the airway that sits between the pharynx and the trachea. It is also called the voice box, because it contains mucus membrane folds (vocal folds) that vibrate when air passes through them to produce sounds. The larynx is made out of three cartilage structures: the epiglottis, the thyroid cartilage (also called the Adam's apple), and the cricoid cartilage, a ring-shaped structure that keeps the larynx open.

The Lower Respiratory Tract

The LOWER RESPIRATORY TRACT consists of the trachea, bronchi, lungs, and the muscles that help with breathing.

The lower respiratory tract begins with the TRACHEA, also known as the windpipe. The trachea is the part of the respiratory system between the larynx and the bronchi. As its name suggests, the windpipe resembles a pipe, and it's really flexible so it can follow various head and neck movements. The trachea is made out of fibrous and elastic tissues, smooth muscle, and about twenty cartilage rings.

The interior of the windpipe is lined with mucus-producing cells called GOBLET CELLS, as well as cells that have small fringes that resemble hair. These hair-like structures, called CILIA, allow air to pass through the windpipe, where it is further filtered by the mucus. The fringes also help to move mucus up the airways and out, keeping the air passage free.

Connecting to the trachea are the BRONCHI. The PRIMARY BRONCHI, consisting of many C-shaped cartilage rings, branch into the secondary bronchi. Two extend from the left primary bronchi, and three branch from the right, corresponding to the number of lobes in the lungs.

The SECONDARY BRONCHI contain less cartilage and have more space between the rings. The same goes for the TERTIARY BRONCHI, which are extensions of the secondary bronchi as they divide throughout the lobes of the lungs. Like the trachea, the bronchi are lined with epithelium that contains goblet cells and cilia.

BRONCHIOLES branch from the tertiary bronchi. They contain no cartilage at all; rather, they are made of smooth muscle and elastic fiber tissue, which allows them to be quite small yet still able to change their diameter. For example, when the body needs more oxygen, they expand, and when there is a danger of pollutants entering the lungs, they constrict.

Bronchioles end with TERMINAL BRONCHIOLES, which connect them with ALVEOLI, which is where the gas exchange happens. Alveoli are small cavities located in alveolar sacs and surrounded by capillaries. The inner surface of alveoli is coated with ALVEOLAR FLUID, which plays a vital role in keeping the alveoli moist, the lungs elastic, and the thin wall of the alveoli stable. The wall of the alveoli is made out of alveolar cells and the connective tissue that forms the respiratory membrane where it comes into contact with the wall of the capillaries.

The LUNGS themselves are two spongy organs that contain the bronchi, bronchioles, alveoli, and blood vessels. The lungs are contained in the rib cage, and are surrounded by the pleura, a double-layered membrane consisting of the outer PARIETAL PLEURA and the inner VISCERAL PLEURA. Between the layers of the pleura is a hollow space called the PLEURAL CAVITY, which allows the lungs to expand.

The lungs are wider at the bottom, which is referred to as the BASE, and they are narrower at the top part, which is called the APEX. The lungs are divided into LOBES, with the larger lung (the right one) consisting of three lobes, and the smaller lung (the left lung) consisting of two lobes.

Respiration

The muscles that play a major role in respiration are the diaphragm and the intercostal muscles. The DIAPHRAGM is a structure made of skeletal muscle, and it is located under the lungs, forming the floor of the thorax. The INTERCOSTAL MUSCLES are located between the ribs. The INTERNAL INTERCOSTAL MUSCLES help with breathing out (expiration) by depressing the ribs and compressing the thoracic cavity; the EXTERNAL INTERCOSTAL MUSCLES help with breathing in (inspiration).

Breathing in and out is also called PULMONARY VENTILATION. The two types of pulmonary ventilation are inhalation and exhalation.

During INHALATION (also called inspiration), the diaphragm contracts and moves a few inches towards the stomach, making more space for the lungs to expand, and this movement pulls the air into the lungs. The external intercostal muscles also contract to expand the rib cage, and pull more air into the lungs. The lungs are now at a lower pressure than the atmosphere, (called negative pressure), which causes air to come into the lungs until the pressure inside the lungs and the atmospheric pressure are the same.

During EXHALATION (in expiration), the diaphragm and the external intercostal muscles relax, and the internal intercostal muscles contract. This causes the thoracic cavity to become smaller, and the pressure in the lungs to climb higher than the atmospheric pressure, which moves air out of the lungs.

Types of Breathing

In shallow breathing, around 0.5 liters of air is circulated, a capacity called TIDAL VOLUME. During deep breathing, a larger amount of air is moved, usually three to five liters, a volume known as VITAL CAPACITY. The abdominal, as well as other muscles, are also involved in breathing in and out during deep breathing.

EUPNEA is a term for the breathing our body does when resting, which consists of mostly shallow breaths with an occasional deep breath. The lungs are never completely without air—around a liter of air is always present in the lungs.

Examples

1. The primary opening for breathing in and out is:

   A) the nose

   B) the mouth

   C) the skin pores

   D) the pharynx

2. The air that we breathe in through the mouth enters the throat at the:

   A) nasopharynx

   B) oropharynx

   C) laryngopharynx

   D) larynx

3. For air to go to the lungs, the epiglottis needs to close the:

   A) bronchi

   B) pharynx

   C) larynx

   D) esophagus

4. How many lobes does the left lung have?

   A) 1

   B) 2

   C) 3

   D) 4

5. Bronchioles branch from the:

   A) primary bronchi

   B) secondary bronchi

   C) tertiary bronchi

   D) quaternary bronchi

   Answers: 1. A) 2. B) 3. D) 4. B) 5. C)

THE SKELETAL SYSTEM

There are a number of roles the skeletal system plays in the body. The bones and joints that make up the skeletal system are responsible for:

- providing support and protection
- allowing movement

- blood cell genesis
- storing fat, iron, and calcium
- guiding the growth of the entire body

Generally, the skeleton can be divided into two parts: the axial skeleton and the appendicular skeleton. The AXIAL SKELETON consists of eighty bones placed along the body's midline axis and grouped into the skull, ribs, sternum, and vertebral column. The APPENDICULAR SKELETON consists of 126 bones grouped into the upper and lower limbs and the pelvic and pectoral girdles. These bones anchor muscles and allow for movement.

Bone Components

On the cellular level, the bone consists of two distinctively different parts: the matrix and living bone cells. The BONE MATRIX is the non-living part of the bone, which is made out of water, collagen, protein, calcium phosphate, and calcium carbonate crystals. The LIVING BONE CELLS (OSTEOCYTES) are found at the edges of the bones and throughout the bone matrix in small cavities. Bone cells play a vital part in the growth, development, and repair of bones, and can be used for the minerals they store.

Looking at a cross section of a bone, you can see that it is made out of layers. These include the PERIOSTEUM, which is the topmost layer of the bone, acting as a layer of connective tissue. The periosteum contains collagen fibers that anchor the tendons and the muscles; it also holds the stem and the osteoblast cells that are necessary for growth and repair of the bones. Nervous tissue, nerve endings, and blood vessels are also present in the periosteum.

Under the periosteum is a layer of COMPACT BONE, which gives the bone its strength. Made out of mineral salts and collagen fibers, it also contains many cavities where osteocytes can be found. Under the compact bone is a layer where the bone tissue grows in columns called TRABECULAE. The bone tissue forms space that contains the red bone marrow. The trabeculae provide structural strength, even while keeping the bones light.

Hematopoiesis and Calcification

Inside the red bone marrow, which is located in the medullar cavity of the bones, a process called HEMATOPOIESIS occurs. In the process, white and red blood cells are made from stem cells. The amount of the red bone marrow declines at the end of puberty, as a significant part of it is replaced by the yellow bone marrow.

When we are born, we have 300 bones. As we grow, the structure of the bones changes. In CALCIFICATION, bones transform from mostly hyaline cartilage and connective tissue to osseous tissue. They also fuse together, which is why adults have 206 instead of 300 bones.

The Five Types of Bones

The LONG BONES make up the major bones of the limbs. They are longer than they are wide, and they are responsible for most of our height. The long bones can be divided in two regions: the EPIPHYSES, located at the ends of the bone, and DIAPHYSIS, located in the middle. The middle of the diaphysis contains a hollow medullary cavity, which serves as a storage for bone marrow.

The SHORT BONES are roughly as long as they are wide, and are generally cube-shaped or round. Short bones in the body include the carpal bones of the wrist and tarsal bones of the foot. The FLAT BONES do not have the medullary cavity because they are thin and usually thinner on one end region. Flat bones in the body include the ribs, the hip bones, as well as the frontal, the parietal, and the occipital bones of the skull. The IRREGULAR BONES are those bones that do not fit the criteria to be the long, the short, or the flat bones. The vertebrae and the sacrum, among others, are irregular bones.

There are only two SESAMOID BONES that are actually counted as proper bones: the patella and the pisiform bone. Sesamoid bones are formed inside the tendons located across the joints, and apart from the two mentioned, they are not present in all people.

The Skull

Made out of twenty-two bones, the SKULL protects the brain and the sense organs for vision, hearing, smell, taste and balance. The skull has only one movable joint that connects it with the mandible—the jaw bone, which is the only movable bone of the skull. The other twenty-one are fused together.

The upper part of the skull is known as the CRANIUM, which is the part that protects the brain, while the lower and frontal parts of the skull form the facial bones. Located just under the mandible, and not a part of the skull, is the HYOID BONE. The hyoid is the only bone in the body that is not attached to any other bone. It helps keep the trachea open and is where the tongue muscles are anchored.

Other bones closely connected to, but not part of the skull, are the AUDITORY OSSICLES: the malleus, incus, and stapes. These bones play an important role in hearing.

The Vertebral Column

The VERTEBRAL COLUMN, or the spine, begins at the base of the skull and stretches through the trunk down the middle of the back to the coccyx; it provides support for the weight of the upper body and protects the spinal cord. It is made up of twenty-four vertebrae, plus the SACRUM and the COCCYX (the tailbone). These twenty-four vertebrae are divided into three groups:

- the **CERVICAL**, or the neck vertebrae (seven bones)
- the **THORACIC**, or the chest vertebrae (twelve bones)
- the **LUMBAR**, or the lower back vertebrae (five bones)

Furthermore, each vertebra has its own name, which is derived from the first letter of the group to which it belongs (for example, *L* for lumbar vertebrae). The letter is placed first, followed by a number (the first of the lumbar vertebrae is thus called *L1*).

Figure 7.6 Vertebral column

The Ribs and the Sternum

The ribs and the sternum are the bones that form the rib cage of the thoracic region. The **STERNUM**, also known as the breastbone, is a thin bone that goes along the midline of the thoracic region. Most of the ribs are connected to this bone via the **COSTAL CARTILAGE**, a thin band of cartilage.

The human skeleton has twelve **RIBS**. On the back side, they are attached to the thoracic vertebrae. On the front, the first seven of them attach directly to the sternum, the next three attach to the cartilage between the seventh rib and the sternum, and the remaining two do not attach to the sternum at all. Rather, they protect the kidneys, not the lungs and heart. The first seven ribs are known as the true ribs, and the rest are known as false ribs. Together, these bones form the **THORACIC CAGE**, which supports and protects the heart and lungs.

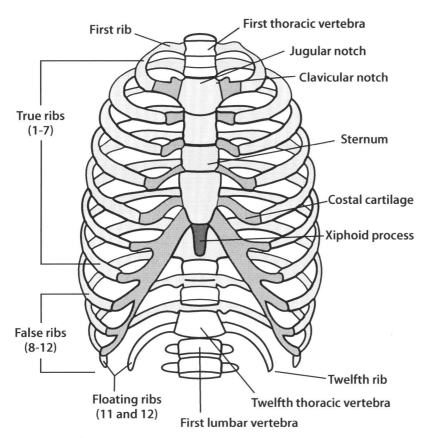

First rib

First thoracic vertebra

Jugular notch

Clavicular notch

True ribs (1-7)

Sternum

Costal cartilage

Xiphoid process

False ribs (8-12)

Twelfth rib

Floating ribs (11 and 12)

Twelfth thoracic vertebra

First lumbar vertebra

Figure 7.7. Ribs

The Appendicular Skeleton

The upper limbs, which belong to the **APPENDICULAR SKELETON**, are connected with the axial skeleton by the **PECTORAL GIRDLE**. The pectoral girdle is formed from the left and right **CLAVICLE** and **SCAPULA**. The scapula and the **HUMERUS**, the bones of the upper arm, form the ball and socket of the shoulder joint. The upper limbs also include the **ULNA**, which forms the elbow joint with the humerus, and the **RADIUS**, which allows the turning movement at the wrist.

The **WRIST JOINT** is formed out of the forearm bones and the eight **CARPAL** bones, which themselves are connected with the five **METACARPALS**. Together, these structures form the bones of the hand. The metacarpals connect with the fingers, each made out of three bones called **PHALANGES**, except the thumb which only has two phalanges.

The lower limbs are connected to the axial skeleton by the **PELVIC GIRDLE**, which includes the left and right hip bones. The hip joint is formed by the hip bone and the **FEMUR**, which is the largest bone in the body. On its other end, the femur forms the knee joint with the **PATELLA** (the kneecap) and the **TIBIA**, which is one of the bones of the lower leg.

Of the two lower leg bones, the **TIBIA** is the larger, and it carries the weight of the body. The **FIBULA**, the other leg bone, serves mostly to anchor the muscle. Together, these two bones form the ankle joint with a foot bone called the TALUS. The talus is one of seven tarsal bones which form the back part of the foot and the heel. They connect to the five long METATARSALS, which form the foot itself and connect to the toes. Each toe is made out of three phalanges, except the big toe, which has only two phalanges.

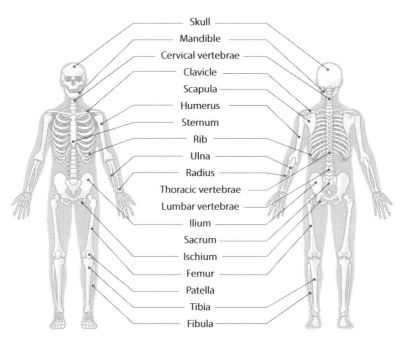

Figure 7.8. Skeletal system

The Joints

The JOINTS, also known as articulations, are where the bones come into contact with each other, with cartilage, or with teeth. There are three types of joints: synovial, fibrous, and cartilaginous joints.

The SYNOVIAL JOINTS feature a small gap between the bones that is filled with synovial fluid, which lubricates the joint. They are the most common joints in the body, and they allow the most movement. FIBROUS JOINTS, found where bones fit tightly together, permit little to no movement. These joints also hold teeth in their sockets. In a CARTILAGINOUS JOINT, two bones are held together by cartilage; these joints allow more movement than fibrous joints but less than synovial ones.

Examples

1. How many bones do adults have?

   A) 201

   B) 206

   C) 222

   D) 300

2. Stem cells can be found in the:

A) red bone marrow

B) periosteum

C) compact bones

D) cartilaginous joints

3. The long bones are the main bones of the:

A) limbs

B) thoracic cage

C) scull

D) vertebral column

4. The jawbone is called the:

A) mandible

B) cranium

C) hyoid

D) ulna

5. The second vertebra in the chest region is called:

A) L2

B) L3

C) T2

D) T3

Answers: 1. B) 2. A) 3. A) 4. A) 5. C)

THE MUSCULAR SYSTEM

Movement is the main function of the MUSCULAR SYSTEM; muscles are found attached to the bones in our bodies and allow us to move our limbs. They also work in the heart, blood vessels, and digestive organs, where they facilitate movement of substances through the body. In addition to movement, muscles also help support the body's posture and create heat. There are three types of muscle: visceral, cardiac, and skeletal.

Visceral Muscle

VISCERAL MUSCLE is the weakest type of muscle. It can be found in the stomach, intestines, and blood vessels, where it helps contract and move substances through them. We cannot consciously control visceral muscle—it is controlled by the unconscious part of the brain. That's why it's sometimes referred to as *involuntary muscle*.

Visceral muscle is also called SMOOTH MUSCLE because of its appearance under the microscope. The cells of the visceral muscle form a smooth surface, unlike the other two types of muscle.

Cardiac Muscle

CARDIAC MUSCLE is only found in the heart; it makes the heart contract and pump blood through the body. Like visceral muscle, cardiac muscle cannot be voluntarily controlled. Unlike visceral muscle, however, the cardiac muscle is quite strong.

Cardiac muscle is composed of individual muscle cells called CARDIOMYOCYTES that are joined together by INTERCALATED DISCS. These discs allow the cells in cardiac muscle to contract in sync. When observed under a microscope, light and dark stripes are visible in the muscle: this pattern is caused by the arrangement of proteins.

Skeletal Muscle

The last type of muscle is SKELETAL MUSCLE, which is the only type of muscle that contracts and relaxes by voluntary action. Skeletal muscle is attached to the bone by tendons. Tendons are formed out of connective tissue rich in collagen fibers.

Skeletal muscle is made out of cells that are lumped together to form fiber structures. These fibers are covered by a cell membrane called the SARCOLEMMA, which serves as a conductor for electrochemical signals that tell the muscle to contract or expand. The TRANSVERSE TUBES, which are connected to the sarcolemma, transfer the signals deeper into the middle of the muscle fiber.

CALCIUM IONS, which are necessary for muscle contraction, are stored in the SARCOPLASMIC RETICULUM. The fibers are also rich in MITOCHONDRIA, which act as power stations fueled by sugars and providing the energy necessary for the muscle to work. Muscle fibers are mostly made out of MYOFIBRILS, which do the actual contracting. Myofibrils are made out of protein fibers arranged into small subunits called SARCOMERES.

Skeletal muscle can be divided into two types, according to the way it produces and uses energy. TYPE I fibers contract slowly and are used for stamina and posture. They produce energy from sugar using aerobic respiration, making them resistant to fatigue. TYPE II muscle fibers contract more quickly. Type IIA fibers are found in the legs, and are weaker and show more endurance than Type IIB fibers, which are found mostly in the arms.

Skeletal muscles work by contracting. This shortens the length in their middle part, called the muscle belly, which in turn pulls one bone closer to another. The bone that remains stationary is called the ORIGIN. The other bone, the one that is actually moving towards the other, is called the INSERTION.

Skeletal muscles usually work in groups. The muscle mainly responsible for the action is called the AGONIST, and it's always paired with another muscle that does the opposite action, called the ANTAGONIST. If the two were to contract together at the same time, they would cancel each other out and produce no movement. Other muscles that support the agonist include **SYNERGISTS**, which are found near the agonist, attach to the same bones, stabilize the movement, and reduce unnecessary movement. **FIXATORS** are other support muscles that keep the origin stable.

There are several different ways to name the more than 600 skeletal muscles found in the human body. Muscles can be named according to:

- the region of the body in which they're located (e.g., transverse abdominis)
- number of origins (e.g., biceps)
- bones to which they are attached (e.g., occipitofrontalis)
- function (e.g., flexor)
- relative size (e.g., gluteus maximus)

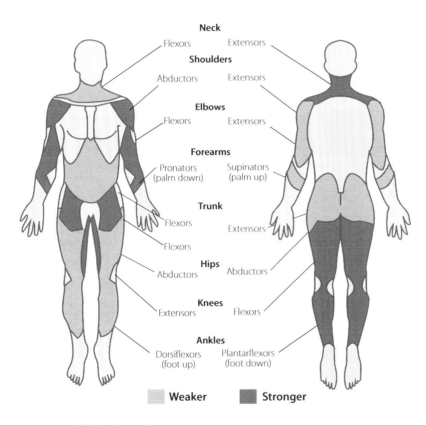

Figure 7.9. Skeletal muscles

Motor Neurons and Contractions

The neurons that control muscles are called **MOTOR NEURONS**. Motor neurons control a number of muscle cells that together are called the **MOTOR UNIT**. The number of cells in the motor unit is larger in big muscles that need more strength, like those in the arms and legs. In small muscles where precision is more important than strength, like the muscles in fingers and around the eyes, the number of cells in motor units is smaller.

When signaled by motor neurons, muscles can contract in several different ways:

- Isotonic muscle contractions produce movement.
- Isometric muscle contractions maintain posture and stillness.
- Muscle tone is naturally occurring constant semi-contraction of the muscle.
- Twitch contraction is a short contraction caused by a single, short nerve impulse.
- Temporal summation is a phenomenon in which a few short impulses delivered over time build up the muscle contraction in strength and duration.
- Tetanus is a state of constant contraction caused by many rapid short impulses.

Muscle Metabolism

There are two ways muscles get energy: through aerobic respiration, which is most effective, and through LACTIC ACID FERMENTATION, which is a type of anaerobic respiration. The latter is less effective and it only happens when blood cannot get into the muscle due to very strong or prolonged contraction.

In both these methods, the goal is to produce ADENOSINE TRI-PHOSPHATE (ATP) from glucose. ATP is the most important energy molecule for our bodies. During its conversion to ADENOSINE DI-PHOSPHATE (ADP), energy is released.

Muscles also use other molecules to help in the production of energy. MYOGLOBIN stores oxygen, allowing muscles to use aerobic respiration even when there is no blood coming into the muscles. CREATINE PHOSPHATE creates ATP by giving its phosphate group to the energy-depleted adenosine di-phosphate. Lastly, muscles use GLYCOGEN, a large molecule made out of several glucose molecules, which helps muscles make ATP.

When it runs out of energy, a muscle goes into a state called MUSCLE FATIGUE. This means it contains little to no oxygen, ATP, or glucose, and that it has high levels of lactic acid and ADP. When a muscle is fatigued, it needs more oxygen to replace the oxygen used up from myoglobin sources, and to rebuild its other energy supplies.

Examples

1. Which type of muscle is found in the blood vessels?

   A) cardiac muscle

   B) skeletal muscle

   C) visceral muscle

   D) Type IIA

2. Cardiac muscle is:

A) involuntary muscle

B) voluntary muscle

C) both

D) neither

3. Tendons always attach skeletal muscle to bone:

A) along the entire length of the bone

B) at one end only

C) at both ends

D) on at least one end

4. Myofibrils:

A) store sugars

B) are found only in smooth muscle

C) make up the sarcolemma

D) cause muscle contractions

5. Which is the strongest type of skeletal muscle?

A) Type I

B) Type II A

C) Type II B

D) Type III

Answers: 1. C) 2. A) 3. D) 4. D) 5. C)

THE NERVOUS SYSTEM

The **NERVOUS SYSTEM** consists of the brain, the spinal cord, the nerves, and the sensory organs. This system is responsible for gathering, processing, and reacting to information from both inside and outside of the body. It is divided into two parts: the central nervous system and the peripheral nervous system. The **CENTRAL NERVOUS SYSTEM** (**CNS**) is made of the brain and spinal cord and is responsible for processing and storing information, as well as deciding on the appropriate action and issuing commands.

The **PERIPHERAL NERVOUS SYSTEM** (**PNS**) is responsible for gathering information, transporting it to the CNS, and then transporting commands from the CNS to the appropriate organs. Sensory organs and nerves do the gathering and transporting of information, while the efferent nerves transport the commands.

Nervous System Cells

The nervous system is mostly made out of nervous tissue, which in turn consists of two classes of cells: neurons and neuralgia. **NEURONS** are the nerve cells. They can be divided into several distinct parts.

The SOMA is the body of the neuron; it contains most of the cellular organelles. DENDRITES are small, treelike structures that extend from the soma. Their main responsibility is to carry information to the soma, and sometimes away from it. Also extending from the soma is the long, thin AXON. There is usually one axon per soma, but the axon can branch out farther. It is responsible for sending information from the soma, rarely to it. Lastly, the places where two neurons meet, or where they meet other types of cells, are called SYNAPSES.

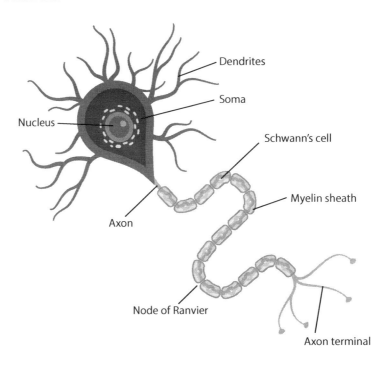

Figure 7.10. Neuron

Neurons can be divided into three classes. EFFERENT NEURONS are motor neurons responsible for transmitting signals from the CNS to the effectors in the body, while AFFERENT NEURONS transmit signals from receptors in the body to the CNS. The third type of neuron—INTERNEURONS—form complex networks in the CNS. They integrate the signals received from the afferent neurons, and control the body by sending signals through the efferent neurons.

Together, these three types of neurons perform the three main tasks of the nervous system:

1. Efferent neurons (also called motor neurons) signal effector cells in muscles and glands to react to stimuli.

2. Afferent neurons (also called sensory neurons) take in information from inside and outside the body through the sensory organs and receptors.

3. Interneurons transmit information to the CNS where it is evaluated, compared to previously stored information, stored or discarded, and used to make a decision (a process called integration).

Neuroglia are the maintenance cells for neurons. Neurons are so specialized that they almost never reproduce. Therefore, they need the neuroglial cells, a number of which surround every neuron, to protect and feed them. Neuroglia are also called the GLIAL CELLS.

Protecting the Central Nervous System (CNS)

The **CNS** consists of the brain and spinal cord. Both are placed within cavities in protective skeletal structures: the brain is housed in the cranial cavity of the skull, and the spinal cord is enclosed in the vertebral cavity in the spine.

Since the organs that form the CNS are vital to our survival, they are also protected by two other important structures: the meninges and the cerebrospinal fluid. The MENINGES are a protective covering of the CNS made up of three distinct layers. The first is the DURA MATER, which, as its name suggests, is the most durable, outer part of the meninges. It is made out of collagen fibers—rich and thick connective tissue, and it forms a space for the cerebrospinal fluid around the CNS.

Next is the ARACHNOID MATER, which is the thin lining on the inner side of the dura mater. It forms many tiny fibers that connect the dura mater with the next layer, the PIA MATER, which is separated from the arachnoid mater by the SUBARACHNOID SPACE. The pia mater directly covers the surface of the brain and spinal cord, and it provides sustenance to the nervous tissue through its many blood vessels.

The subarachnoid space is filled with CEREBROSPINAL FLUID (CSF), a clear fluid formed from blood plasma. CSF can also be found in the ventricles (the hollow spaces in the brain) and in the central canal (a cavity found in the middle of the spinal cord).

As the CNS floats in the cerebrospinal fluid, it appears lighter than it really is. This is especially important for the brain, because the fluid keeps it from being crushed by its own weight. The floating also protects the brain and the spinal cord from shock—like sudden movements and trauma. Additionally, the CSF contains the necessary chemical substance for the normal functioning of the nervous tissue, and it serves to remove the cellular waste from the neurons.

The Brain

The nervous tissue that makes up the brain is divided into two classes. The GRAY MATTER, which consists mostly of interneurons that are unmyelinated, is the tissue where the actual processing of signals happens. It is also where the connections between neurons are made. The WHITE MATTER, which consists mostly of myelinated neurons, is the tissue that conducts signals to, from, and between the gray matter regions.

The brain can be divided into three distinct parts: the prosencephalon (forebrain), the mesencephalon (midbrain), and the rhombencephalon (hindbrain).

The PROSENCEPHALON is further broken down into two more regions: the cerebrum and the diencephalon. The outermost and the largest part of the brain, the CEREBRUM is divided through the middle by the longitudinal fissure into the left and the right hemisphere, each of which is further divided into four lobes: the frontal, parietal, temporal, and occipital.

The surface of the cerebrum, called the CEREBRAL CORTEX, is made out of gray matter with characteristic grooves (SULCI) and bulges (GYRI). The cerebral cortex is where the actual processing happens in the cerebrum: it's responsible for the higher brain functions like thinking and using language. Under the cerebral cortex, there is a layer of white matter, which connects the regions of the cerebrum with one another, and the cerebrum itself with the rest of the body. It contains a special band of white matter that connects the two hemispheres, which is called the CORPUS CALLOSUM. The regions located under the white matter are divided into two groups: the basal nuclei, which help control and regulate the movement of muscles, and the limbic system, which plays a role in memory, emotions, and survival.

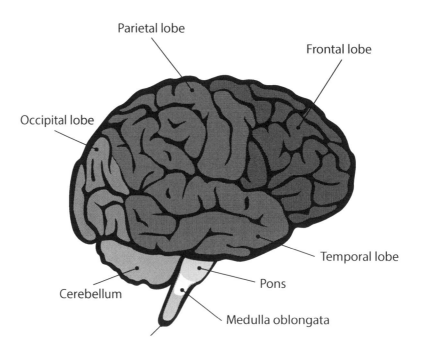

Figure 7.11. The brain

The DIENCEPHALON is a structure formed by the thalamus, hypothalamus, and the pineal gland. Made out of two gray matter masses, the THALAMUS is located around the third ventricle of the brain. Its role is to route the sensory signals to the correct parts of the cerebral cortex. Under the thalamus is the HYPOTHALAMUS, which plays a role in regulating hunger, thirst, blood pressure and body temperature changes, as well as heart rate and the production of hormones. The PINEAL GLAND is located beneath the hypothalamus (and is directly controlled by it) and produces the hormone melatonin, which plays a vital role in sleep.

The MESENCEPHALON is the topmost part of the brain stem. It is divided into two regions. The first is the TECTUM, which plays a role in reflex reactions to visual and auditory information. Second is the CEREBRAL PEDUNCLES, which connect the cerebrum and thalamus with the lower parts of the brain stem and the spinal cord. It also contains the SUBSTANTIA NIGRA, which is involved in muscle movement, reward-seeking, and learning.

The RHOMBENCEPHALON consists of the brain stem and the cerebellum. The brain stem is further broken down into the medulla oblongata and the pons. The MEDULLA OBLONGATA connects the spinal cord with the pons. It is mostly made out of white matter, but it also contains gray matter that processes involuntary body functions like blood pressure, level of oxygen in the blood, and reflexes like sneezing, coughing, vomiting, and swallowing. The PONS is located between the medulla oblongata and the midbrain, and in front of the cerebellum. It is in charge of transporting signals to and from the cerebellum, and between the upper regions of the brain, the medulla, and the spinal cord.

The CEREBELLUM looks like a smaller version of the cerebrum—it has two spheres and is wrinkled. Its outer layer, called the CEREBELLAR CORTEX, consists of gray matter, while the inner part, called the ARBOR VITAE, consists of white matter which transports signals between the cerebellum and the rest of the body. The cerebellum's role is to control and coordinate complex muscle activities. It also helps us maintain posture and keep balance.

The Spinal Cord
The SPINAL CORD, located inside the vertebral cavity, is made out of both white and gray matter. It carries signals and processes some reflexes to stimuli. The spinal nerves stretch out from it.

Peripheral Nervous System (PNS)
The nerves that form the **PNS** are made of bundled axons whose role is to carry signals to and from the spinal cord and the brain. A single axon, covered with a layer of connective tissue called the ENDONEURIUM, bundles with other axons to form FASCICLES. These are covered with another sheath of connective tissue called the PERINEURIUM. Groups of fascicles wrapped together in another layer of connective tissue, the EPINEURIUM, form a whole nerve.

There are five types of peripheral nerves. The AFFERENT, EFFERENT and MIXED nerves are formed out of the neurons that share the same name and perform the same roles. The SPINAL NERVES—thirty-one pairs in total—extend from the side of the spinal cord. They exit the spinal cord between the vertebrae, and they carry information to and from the spinal cord and the neck, the arms, the legs, and the trunk. They are grouped and named according to the region they originate from: eight pairs of cervical, twelve pairs of thoracic, five pairs of lumbar, five pairs of sacral, and one pair of coccygeal nerves. Lastly, the CRANIAL NERVES—twelve pairs in total—extend from the lower side of the brain. They are identified by their number, and they connect the brain with the sensory organs, head muscles, neck and shoulder muscles, the heart, and the gastrointestinal track.

The Sense Organs

The sense organs include the specialized sense organs, which are responsible for the specialized senses: hearing, sight, balance, smell, and taste. Sense organs also have sensory receptors for the general senses, which include touch, pain, and temperature. These senses are part of the PNS, and their role is to detect the stimuli and send the signal to the CNS when the detection occurs.

The Divisions of the Peripheral Nervous System

The PNS is divided into two parts based on our ability to exert conscious control. The part of the PNS we can consciously control is the SOMATIC NERVOUS SYSTEM (SNS), which stimulates the skeletal muscles. The AUTONOMIC NERVOUS SYSTEM (ANS) cannot be consciously controlled; it stimulates the visceral and cardiac muscle, as well as the glandular tissue.

The ANS itself is further divided into the sympathetic, parasympathetic, and enteric nervous systems. The SYMPATHETIC NERVOUS SYSTEM forms the fight or flight reaction to stimuli like emotion, danger, and exercise. It increases respiration and heart rate, decreases digestion, and releases stress hormones. The PARASYMPATHETIC NERVOUS SYSTEM is responsible for stimulating activities that occur when the body is at rest, including digestion and sexual arousal.

Lastly, the ENTERIC NERVOUS SYSTEM is responsible for the digestive system and its processes. This system works mostly independently from the CNS, although it can be regulated through the sympathetic and parasympathetic systems.

Examples

1. Which of the following forms the CNS with the brain?
    A) the peripheral nerves
    B) the sensory organs
    C) the spinal cord
    D) the cerebral cortex

2. The part of the neuron that is mainly responsible for transporting information from the cell is called the:

A) soma

B) axon

C) dendrites

D) sulci

3. The neurons that signal muscles to contract are called:

A) neuroglia

B) afferent neurons

C) interneurons

D) efferent neurons

4. Cerebrospinal fluid can be found in all of the following except:

A) arachnoid mater

B) the central canal

C) the ventricles

D) the subarachnoid space

5. The hypothalamus is located in the:

A) mesencephalon

B) rhombencephalon

C) prosencephalon

D) pineal gland

Answers: 1. C) 2. B) 3. D) 4. A) 5. C)

THE DIGESTIVE SYSTEM

The **DIGESTIVE SYSTEM** is a system of organs in the body that is responsible for the intake and processing of food and the removal of food waste products. The digestive system ensures that the body has the necessary nutrients and the energy it needs to function.

The digestive system includes the **GASTROINTESTINAL (GI) TRACT**, which is formed by the organs through which the food passes on its way through the body:

1. oral cavity
2. pharynx
3. esophagus
4. stomach
5. small intestines
6. large intestines

Throughout the digestive system there are also organs that have a role in processing food, even though food doesn't pass through them directly. These include the teeth, tongue, salivary glands, liver, gallbladder, and pancreas.

Figure 7.12. Digestive system

Questions about the order of the organs in the digestive tract are common on the HESI A².

The Mouth

The digestive system begins with the **MOUTH**. Also known as the oral cavity, the mouth contains other organs that play a role in digestion. The **TEETH** are small organs that cut and grind food. They are located on the edges of the mouth, are made out of dentin, which is a substance that resembles bone, and are covered by enamel. The teeth are very hard organs, and each of them has its own blood vessels and nerves, which are located in the matter that fills the tooth, called the pulp.

Also in the mouth is the **TONGUE**, which is a muscle located behind the teeth. The tongue contains the taste buds and moves food around the mouth as it is being processed by the teeth. It then moves food towards the pharynx when it's time to swallow. The **SALIVARY GLANDS**, located around the mouth, produce saliva. There are three pairs of salivary glands, and the saliva they produce lubricates and digests carbohydrates.

The Pharynx

The **PHARYNX** is a tube that enables the passage of food and air further into the body. This structure performs two functions. The pharynx needs the help of the epiglottis, which allows food to pass to the esophagus by covering the opening of the larynx, a structure that carries air into the lungs. When you need to breathe in, the esophagus is closed, so the air passes only into the larynx.

The Esophagus

The ESOPHAGUS begins at the pharynx and continues to carry food all the way to the stomach. The esophagus is a muscular tube, and the muscles in its wall help to push food down. During vomiting, it pushes food up.

The esophagus has two rings of muscle, called SPHINCTERS. These sphincters close at the top and the bottom ends of the esophagus when food is not passing through it. Heartburn occurs when the bottom sphincter cannot close entirely and allows the contents of the stomach to enter the esophagus.

The Stomach

The stomach is a round organ located on the left side of the body just beneath the diaphragm. It is divided into four different regions. The CARDIA connects the stomach to the esophagus, transitioning from the tube-like shape of the esophagus into the sack shape of the rest of the stomach. The cardia is also where the lower sphincter of the esophagus is located.

The BODY of the stomach is its largest part, and the FUNDUS is located above the body. The last part of the stomach is the PYLORUS, a funnel-shaped region located beneath the body of the stomach. It controls the passage of partially digested food further down the GI tract through the PYLORIC SPHINCTER.

The stomach is made out of four layers of tissue. The innermost layer, the MUCOSA, contains a smooth muscle and the mucus membrane that secretes digestive enzymes and hydrochloric acid. The cells that secrete these products are located within the small pores called the GASTRIC PITS. The mucus membrane also secretes mucus to protect the stomach from its own digestive enzymes.

The SUBMUCOSA is located around the mucosa and is made of connective tissue; it contains nerves and blood vessels. The MUSCULARIS layer enables the movement of the stomach; it's made up of three layers of smooth muscle. This layer enables the movement of the stomach. The outermost layer of the stomach is the serosa. It secretes SEROUS FLUID that keeps the stomach wet and reduces friction between the stomach and the surrounding organs.

The Small Intestine

The SMALL INTESTINE continues from the stomach and takes up most of the space in the abdomen. It's attached to the wall of the abdomen and measures around twenty-two feet long.

The small intestine can be divided into three parts. The DUODENUM is the part of the small intestine that receives the food and chemicals from the stomach. The JEJUNUM, which continues from the duodenum, is where most of the nutrients are absorbed

THE INTESTINAL TRACT
Dow Jones Industrial **C**limbing **A**verage **C**losing **S**tock **R**eport
- Duodenum
- Jejunum
- Ileum
- Cecum
- Appendix
- Colon
- Sigmoid colon
- Rectum

into the blood. Lastly, the ILEUM, which continues from the jejunum, is where the rest of the nutrients are absorbed.

Absorption in the small intestine is helped by the VILLI, which are small protrusions that increase the surface area available for absorption. The villi are made out of smaller microvilli.

The Liver and Gallbladder

The LIVER is not a part of the GI tract. However, it performs roles that are vital for digestion and life itself. The liver is located just beneath the diaphragm and is the largest organ in the body after the skin. It's triangular in shape, and extends across the whole width of the abdomen.

The liver is divided into four lobes: the left lobe, the right lobe, the caudate lobe (which wraps around the inferior vena cava), and the quadrate lobe (which wraps around the gallbladder). The liver is connected to the peritoneum by the coronary, left, right, and falciform ligaments.

The liver is responsible for a number of functions, including detoxification of the blood, storage of nutrients, and production of components of blood plasma. Its role in digestion is to produce BILE, a fluid that aids in the digestion of fats. After its production, bile is carried through the bile ducts to the GALLBLADDER, a small, muscular, pear-shaped organ that stores and releases bile.

The Pancreas

The PANCREAS is another organ that is not part of the GI tract but which plays a role in digestion. It's located below and to the left of the stomach. The pancreas secretes both the enzymes that digest food and the hormones insulin and glucagon, which control blood sugar levels.

The pancreas is what is known as a HETEROCRINE GLAND, which means it contains both endocrine tissue, which produces insulin and glucagon that move directly into the bloodstream, and exocrine tissue, which produces digestive enzymes that pass into the small intestine. These enzymes include:

- pancreatic amylase that breaks large polysaccharides into smaller sugars
- trypsin, chymotrypsin, and carboxypeptidase that break down proteins into amino acid subunits
- pancreatic lipase that breaks down large fat molecules into fatty acids and monoglycerides
- ribonuclease and deoxyribonuclease that digest nucleic acids

The Large Intestine

The LARGE INTESTINE continues from the small intestine and loops around it. No digestion actually takes place in the large intestine. Rather, it absorbs water and some leftover vitamins. The large intestine carries waste (feces) to the RECTUM, where it's stored until it's expelled through the ANUS.

Examples

1. Food passes through all of the following organs except:

   A) stomach

   B) large intestine

   C) esophagus

   D) liver

2. How many pair(s) of salivary glands are in the human body?

   A) 1

   B) 2

   C) 3

   D) 4

3. The esophagus performs all of the following functions except:

   A) connecting the pharynx to the stomach

   B) preventing stomach acid from reaching the pharynx

   C) pushing food into the stomach

   D) moving food from the stomach to the small intestine

4. Which layer of the stomach contains blood vessels and nerves?

   A) the mucosa

   B) the submucosa

   C) the serosa

   D) the cardia

5. Bile is stored in the:

   A) liver

   B) duodenum

   C) gallbladder

   D) pancreas

   Answers: 1. D) 2. C) 3. D) 4. B) 5. C)

CONTINUE

THE ENDOCRINE SYSTEM

The **ENDOCRINE SYSTEM** consists of many **GLANDS** that produce and secrete hormones, which send signals to molecules that are traveling through the bloodstream. **HORMONES** allow cells, tissues, and organs to communicate with each other, and they play a role in almost all bodily functions, including growth, sleeping, digestion, response to stress, and sexual functioning. The glands of the endocrine system are scattered throughout the body, and each has a specific role to play.

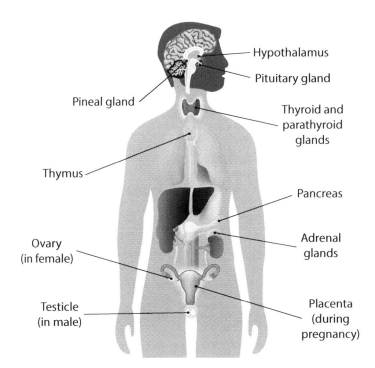

Figure 7.13. Endocrine system

- The **PITUITARY GLAND** hangs from the base of your brain and produces the hormone which controls growth and some aspects of sexual functioning (hormones: growth hormone, thyroid-stimulating hormone, oxytocin, follicle-stimulating hormone).

- The **HYPOTHALAMUS** is also located in the brain. Its main function is to control the pituitary gland, and many of the hormones it releases stimulate the pituitary gland to in turn release hormones itself (hormones: dopamine, thyrotropin-releasing hormone, growth-hormone-releasing hormone).

- The **PINEAL GLAND**, located in the brain, releases melatonin, a hormone that induces drowsiness and lowers body temperature (hormone: melatonin).

- The **THYROID GLAND** is found in the neck just below the Adam's apple. It controls protein production and the body's use of energy (hormones: T_3 and thyroxine).

The thyroid is regulated by the thyroid-stimulating hormone, which is released by the pituitary gland.

- The **PARATHYROID GLANDS** are located behind the thyroid. They produce parathyroid hormone, which regulates calcium and phosphate levels in the body (hormones: parathyroid hormone).

- The **PANCREAS,** discussed above, is located behind the stomach and releases hormones that regulate digestion and blood-sugar levels (hormones: insulin, glucagon, somatostatin).

- The **ADRENAL GLANDS** sit atop the kidneys. The adrenal glands have two regions that produce two sets of hormones: the adrenal cortex releases corticosteroids and androgens while the adrenal medulla regulates the fight-or-flight response (hormones: cortisol, testosterone, adrenaline, noradrenaline, dopamine).

- The **TESTES** are glands found in males; they regulate maturation of sex organs and the development of secondary sex characteristics like muscle mass and growth of axillary hair (hormones: testosterone, estradiol).

- The **OVARIES** are glands found in females; they regulate the menstrual cycle, pregnancy, and secondary sex characteristics like enlargement of breasts and the widening of the hips (hormones: progesterone, estrogen).

Examples

1. Which gland(s) indirectly controls growth by acting on the pituitary?

A) hypothalamus

B) thyroid

C) adrenal glands

D) parathyroid glands

2. Which hormone is primarily responsible for the development of male secondary sexual characteristics?

A) melatonin

B) follicle-stimulating hormone

C) estrogen

D) testosterone

CONTINUE

3. A patient experiencing symptoms such as kidney stones and arthritis due to a calcium imbalance probably has a disorder of which gland?

A) hypothalamus

B) thyroid

C) parathyroid

D) adrenal glands

Answers: 1. A) 2. D) 3. C)

THE REPRODUCTIVE SYSTEM

Reproductive systems are the groups of organs that enable the successful reproduction of a species. In humans, fertilization is internal, with sperm being transferred from the male to the female during copulation.

The Male Reproductive System

The male reproductive system consists of the organs that produce and ejaculate SPERM, the male gamete. Sperm are produced in the TESTES, which are housed in the SCROTUM, which is located under the penis. During sexual arousal, the VAS DEFERENS carry sperm to the URETHRA, the tube which runs through the PENIS and carries semen (and urine) out of the body. Also emptying into the urethra is the PROSTATE GLAND, which produces a nutrient-filled fluid that protects sperm and makes up the majority of SEMEN. Before ejaculation, the COWPER'S GLAND produces a thin, alkaline fluid that flushes any remaining urine from the urethra and makes up a small portion of the semen.

THE PATH OF SPERM

SEVEn UP

- Seminiferous tubes
- Epididymis
- Vas deferens
- Ejaculatory duct
- Urethra
- Penis

The Female Reproductive System

Sexual reproduction in animals occurs in cycles that depend on the production of an OVULE, or egg, by the female of the species. In humans, the reproductive cycle occurs approximately once a month, when an egg is released from the female's ovaries.

The female reproductive organs, or gonads, are called OVARIES. Each ovary has a follicle that contains OOCYTES, or undeveloped eggs. The surrounding cells in the ovary help to protect and nourish the oocyte until it is needed. During the menstrual cycle, one or more oocytes will mature into an egg with help from the CORPUS LUTEUM, a mass of follicular tissue that provides nutrients to the egg and secretes estradiol and progesterone.

Once it has matured, the egg will be released into the FALLOPIAN TUBE where fertilization will take place if sperm are present. The egg will then travel into the UTERUS. Unfertilized eggs are shed along with the uterine lining during MENSTRUATION. Fertilized eggs, known as ZYGOTES, implant in the lining of the uterus where they continue to develop.

Embryo Fertilization and Development

After fertilization, the cell will start to divide and, after four to five days, become a ball of cells known as a BLASTOCYST. The blastocyst is then implanted into the ENDOMETRIUM of the uterus. After the blastocyst has been implanted into the endometrium, the placenta develops. The PLACENTA is a temporary organ that attaches the embryo to the mother; it provides nutrients to the fetus, carries waste away from the fetus, protects the fetus from infection, and produces hormones that support pregnancy. The placenta develops from cells called the TROPHOBLAST, which come from the outer layer of the blastocyst.

In humans, the gestation period of the EMBRYO (also called the FETUS), is 266 days or roughly 8.8 months. The human development cycle in the womb is divided into three trimesters. In the first trimester, the organs responsible for the embryo's growth develop. This includes the placenta and umbilical cord. During this time, ORGANOGENESIS occurs, and the various stem cells from the blastocyst differentiate into the organs of the body. The organs are not fully developed at this point, but they do exist.

In the second trimester, the fetus experiences rapid growth, up to about twenty-five to thirty centimeters in length. At this point, it is usually apparent that the woman is pregnant, as the uterus grows and extends, and the woman's belly becomes slightly distended. In the third trimester, the fetus finishes developing. The baby exits the uterus through the CERVIX and leaves the body through the VAGINA.

Examples

1. All of the following contribute material to semen except:

   A) the prostate

   B) Cowper's gland

   C) the penis

   D) the testes

2. Fertilization typically takes place in the:

   A) fallopian tubes

   B) ovaries

   C) uterus

   D) cervix

$\longrightarrow$

CONTINUE

3. Which of the following statements about the placenta is not true?

A) The placenta serves as part of the endocrine system because it releases hormones.

B) The placenta provides nutrients to the fetus.

C) The placenta develops from the outer layer of cells on the blastocyst.

D) The placenta is expelled during the menstrual cycle if fertilization does not take place.

Answers: 1. C) 2. A) 3. D)

8

PHYSICS

Physics is the science of matter and energy and the interaction between the two. Physics is grouped into fields such as acoustics (the study of sound), optics (the study of light), mechanics (the study of motion), and electromagnetism (the study of electric and magnetic fields).

MECHANICS

Motion

$$d = \frac{1}{2}at^2 + v_i t \ (d = vt \text{ when } a = 0)$$

$$v_f = v_i + at$$

$$v_f^2 = v_i^2 + 2ad$$

m = mass
d = displacement
v = velocity
a = acceleration
t = time

Newtonian mechanics is the study of masses in motion using five main variables. **MASS** (m), as discussed above, is the amount of matter in an object; it is measured in kilograms (kg). **DISPLACEMENT** (d) is a measure of how far an object has moved from its starting point, usually given in meters (m). **VELOCITY** is the distance covered by an object over a given period of **TIME**, usually given in meters per second (m/s). Finally, the change in velocity over time is called **ACCELERATION** (a) and is measured in meters per second squared (m/s^2).

Velocity and displacement are both **VECTORS,** meaning they have a magnitude (e.g., 4 m/s) and a direction (e.g., 45°). **SCALARS,** on the other hand, have only a magnitude. **DISTANCE** is a scalar: it describes how far something has traveled. So, if you run 1000 meters around a track and end up back where you started, your displacement is 0 meters, but the distance you covered was 1000 meters. **SPEED** is also a scalar; it is the distance traveled over the time the trip took.

The motion of objects with uniform acceleration is described by a set of equations that define the relationships between distance, velocity, time, distance, and acceleration. These equations can be used to solve for any of these five variables. When the object is moving in a single dimension, problems can be solved using the following steps:

1. Identify the variables given in the problem and the variable to be solved for.
2. Choose the equation that includes the variables from Step 1.
3. Plug the values from the problem into the equation and solve.

When the object is moving in two dimensions, it's necessary to separate the variables into their horizontal and vertical components because only variables in a single dimension can be used within the same equation. Often, it's necessary to solve for a variable in one dimension and use that value to solve for a variable in the second dimension.

Examples

1. How far will a car moving with a constant velocity of 40 mi/hr travel in 15 minutes?

   A) 2.7 miles

   B) 10 miles

   C) 40 miles

   D) 600 miles

2. A ball is dropped from a building with a height of 20 m. If there is no air resistance, how long will it take the ball to reach the ground ($g = 9.8$ m/s^2)?

   A) 2 s

   B) 4 s

   C) 5 s

   D) 10 s

   Answers: 1. B) 2. A)

Momentum

$$p = mv$$

$$J = \Delta P$$

$$m_{1_i} v_{1_i} + m_{2_i} v_{2_i} = m_{1_f} v_{1_f} + m_{2_f} v_{2_f} \text{ (elastic collision)}$$

$$m_1 v_{1_i} + m_2 v_{2_i} = (m_1 + m_2) v_f \text{ (inelastic collision)}$$

Multiplying an object's mass by its velocity gives a quantity called MOMENTUM (p), which is measured in kilogram meters per second

p = momentum
J = impulse

((kg·m)/s). Momentum is always conserved, meaning when objects collide, the sum of their momentums before the collision will be the same as the sum after (although their kinetic energy may not remain the same). Because momentum is derived from velocity, it is a vector. The change in momentum is called IMPULSE (J); it's measured in Newton seconds (N·s).

Examples

1. What is the momentum of an object of 1.5 kg mass moving with a velocity of magnitude 10 m/s?

   A) 1.5 (kg·m)/s

   B) 15 (kg·m)/s

   C) 150 (kg·m)/s

   D) 1500 (kg·m)/s

2. Two objects are traveling in the same direction at different speeds. Object 1 moves at 5 m/s and has a mass of 1 kg. Object 2 moves at a 2 m/s and has a mass of 0.5 kg. If object 1 collides with object 2 and they stick together, what will be the final velocity of the two objects?

   A) 2.5 m/s

   B) 3 m/s

   C) 4 m/s

   D) 7 m/s

   Answers: 1. B) 2. C)

FORCES

$$G = 6.67408 \times 10^{-11} \text{ m}^3 \text{ kg}^{-1} \text{ s}^{-2}$$

$$g = 9.8 \text{ m/s}^2$$

$$F_g = mg \text{ (for falling objects)}$$

$$F_g = \frac{Gm_1m_2}{r_2} \text{ (for the gravitational force between two masses)}$$

$$F = ma$$

$$F_f = \mu_k F_N$$

Obviously, objects need a reason to get moving: they don't just start accelerating on their own. The "push" that starts or stops an object's motion is called a FORCE (F) and is measured in Newtons (N). Examples of forces include GRAVITY (created by mass of objects), FRICTION (created by the movement of two surfaces in contact with each other), TENSION (created by hanging a mass from a string or chain), and ELECTRICAL FORCE (created by charged particles). A force that creates circular motion is called a CENTRIPETAL FORCE.

Gravitational force is proportional to the masses of two objects and the distance between the center of mass of the two objects, not the distance between the surfaces.

Note that all of these forces are vectors with a magnitude and direction. Gravity, for example, always points down toward the earth, and friction always points in the opposite direction of the object's motion. On a FREE BODY DIAGRAM, forces are drawn as vectors, and vectors in the horizontal and vertical directions can be added to find the total force.

Newton's three laws of motion describe how these forces work to create motion:

LAW #1: An object at rest will remain at rest, and an object in motion will continue with the same speed and direction unless acted on by a force. This law is often called "the law of inertia."

LAW #2: Acceleration is produced when a force acts on a mass. The greater the mass of the object being accelerated, the greater the amount of force needed to accelerate the object.

LAW #3: Every action requires an equal and opposite reaction. This means that for every force, there is a reacting force both equal in size and opposite in direction. In other words, whenever an object pushes another object, it gets pushed back in the opposite direction with equal force.

Examples

1. An object is being acted on by only 2 forces as shown below. If the magnitudes of F1 and F2 are equal, which of the following statements must be true?

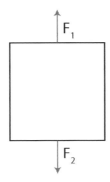

A) The velocity of the object must be zero.

B) The velocity of the object must be constant.

C) The velocity of the object must be increasing.

D) The velocity of the object must be decreasing.

2. An object is pulled across a rough surface with a force of 20 N. If the object moves with a constant velocity and the surface has a coefficient of kinetic friction equal to 0.2, what is the magnitude of the normal force acting on the object?

A) 4 N

B) 10 N

C) 20 N

D) 100 N

Answers: 1. B) 2. D)

CIRCULAR AND ROTATIONAL MOTION

Rotational Motion

$$\theta = \frac{1}{2}\alpha t^2 + \omega_i t$$

$$\omega_f = \omega_i + \alpha t$$

$$\omega_f^2 = \omega_i^2 + 2\alpha\theta$$

θ = angular displacement
ω = angular speed
a = angular acceleration

In addition to moving in a straight line, objects can also rotate. This **ROTATIONAL MOTION** is described using a similar set of variables and equations to those used for linear motion. However, the variables have been converted to represent rotational motion, as shown in the table below.

Table 8.1. Rotational motion

LINEAR VARIABLE	ROTATIONAL VARIABLE
displacement (d)	angular displacement (θ)
velocity (v)	angular speed (ω)
acceleration (a)	angular acceleration (a)

Example

The motor of an engine is rotating about its axis with an angular velocity of 100 rev/minute. After being switched off, it comes to rest in 15s. If the angular deceleration is constant, how many revolutions does the engine make before it comes to rest?

A) 10.5 rev

B) 11.5 rev

C) 12.5 rev

D) 13.5 rev

Answer: C)

CONTINUE

τ = torque

Torque

$$\tau = rF\sin(\theta)$$

TORQUE is a form of work that is applied in a circular motion; it is measured in newton meters (N·m). A wrench, for example, employs torque to apply force to turning a bolt. The specific definition of torque is a force that is applied over a distance and an angle to generate circular motion (as seen below). The amount of torque depends on the radius of the arm (r), the force applied (F), and the angle of the force (θ).

Figure 8.1. Torque

Example

A force of magnitude 10 N is applied at point A to cause a bar to rotate around point B, as shown below. What is the torque produced by the force?

.5 m

A) − 20 N·m

B) − 5 N·m

C) 5 N·m

D) 20 N·m

Answer: B)

Circular Motion

$$a = \frac{v^2}{r}$$

$$F = ma_c = m \times \frac{v^2}{r}$$

CIRCULAR MOTION is the movement of an object around central point. CENTRIPETAL ACCELERATION, which points toward the center of the circle, changes the direction of the object's velocity and keeps the object on a circular path. The force that creates centripetal acceleration can be tension (e.g., swing a weight on a string), friction(e.g., car tires on a turn), or other forces.

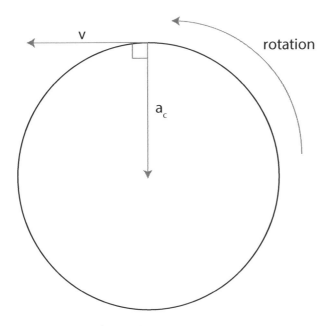

Figure 8.2. Circular motion

Example

An object of mass *m* undergoes uniform circular motion with a speed *v* at a distance *r* from the center of the circle. Which of the following will result in an increase in the centripetal force?

A) A decrease in *r* while maintaining the same speed.

B) An increase in *r* while maintaining the same speed.

C) A decrease in the speed of the mass by a factor of 4 and a decrease in *r* by a factor of 2.

D) An increase in the speed of the mass by a factor of 2 and an increase in *r* by a factor of 4.

Answer: A)

CONTINUE

ENERGY, WORK, AND POWER

Energy

$$KE = \frac{1}{2}mv^2$$

$$PE_g = mgh$$

In simple terms, energy is the capacity to do work; in other words, it's a measurement of how much force a system could apply. Energy is measured in Joules (J), which are $J = kg \cdot m^2/s^2$. There are two main categories of energy. The energy stored within an object due to its relative position is its POTENTIAL ENERGY: that object has the potential to do work. Potential energy can be created in a number of ways, including raising an object off the ground or compressing a spring. KINETIC ENERGY is present when an object is in motion. The sum of an object's kinetic and potential energies is called its MECHANICAL ENERGY.

Energy can be neither created nor destroyed; it can only be converted from one form to another. For example, when a rock is lifted some distance from the ground it has GRAVITATIONAL POTENTIAL ENERGY; when it's released, it begins to move toward the earth and that potential energy becomes kinetic energy. A pendulum is another example: at the height of its swing, the pendulum will have potential energy but no kinetic energy; at the bottom of its swing, it has kinetic energy but no more potential energy.

> ⚠️
> Generally, kinetic energy is the energy of an object in motion, and potential energy is the energy of an object at rest.

Examples

1. The mass of a rider and his cycle combined is 90 kg. What is the increase in kinetic energy if a 90 kg bike increases its speed from 6 km/h to 12 km/h?

   A) 300 J

   B) 350 J

   C) 375 J

   D) 400 J

2. A skier starts from rest at the top of a hill. If the height of the hill is 20 m, what is the speed of the skier at the bottom of the hill? (Assume no air resistance or friction.)

   A) 4 m/s

   B) 20 m/s

   C) 200 m/s

   D) 400 m/s

   Answers: 1. C) 2. B)

Work

$$W = Fd$$

$$P = \frac{W}{t}$$

WORK is defined in physics as a force exerted over a distance; work is also measured in Joules (J). Work has to take place over a distance: if an object is acted upon by a force, but does not move, then no work has been performed. For example, if someone pushes against a wall with 50 N of force, she has not performed any work. However, if she lifted a baseball off of the ground, then she performed work.

Work is a scalar quantity, and cannot be expressed in terms of a vector. However, the force applied to do work is a vector quantity, and thus the net force used to perform work can change depending on the angle at which it is applied.

POWER is force applied over time; it is measured in Watts.

Examples

1. A child pushes a truck across the floor at a velocity of 1 m/s for 5 m using 1 N of force. How much work did the child do?

   A) 0.25 J

   B) 5 J

   C) 2.5 J

   D) 25 J

2. In the same scenario described above, the child pushes the truck for 5 s. How much power did the child deliver to the truck?

   A) 0.05 W

   B) 0.25 W

   C) 0.5 W

   D) 1 W

   Answers: 1. B) 2. D)

THERMODYNAMICS

TEMPERATURE is a measure of the average kinetic energy of the atoms or molecules of a substance. Substances with a higher temperature have more kinetic energy, meaning their molecules are moving at a higher velocity. Lowering the temperature of the substance will slow the speed of the molecules. The SI unit for temperature is Celsius, but it also measured in Fahrenheit and Kelvin.

HEAT is the transfer of energy between substances; it is measured in Joules. When the air warms a block of ice, or a soda gets cold in the fridge, that transfer of energy is heat. Heat always moves from warmer substances to colder ones. Heat can be transferred

q = heat

Fahrenheit and Celsius are reference scales, while Kelvin is an absolute scale.

in several different ways. One is CONDUCTION, which occurs when heat is transferred between neighboring molecules; conduction is what makes a person's hand cold when she holds ice. During CONVECTION, heat is transferred away from an object by the movement of gases or fluids, for example when warm air rises from a radiator.

Heat is not an intrinsic property. It would not be correct to say that an object contains 100 Joules of heat. It would be correct to say that an object has transmitted 100 Joules of heat.

Heat Capacity

$$q = mc\Delta T$$

The HEAT CAPACITY of an object is best defined as its resistance to temperature change. A material with a higher heat capacity will have a lower change in temperature when exposed to a greater amount of heat. For example, water has one of the highest heat capacities of 4.18 J/(g·K), meaning 4.18 Joules are needed to increase the temperature of one gram of water by one degree Kelvin. On the other hand, most metals have low heat capacities. Copper has a heat capacity of just 0.39 J/(g·K). This means that if copper and water are exposed to the same amount of heat, copper will heat up more than 10 times faster than water will.

Example

If 27.53 J of heat are needed to increase the temperature of a 15 g mass by 7.3 K, what is the mass's heat capacity?

A) 0.251 J/(g·K)

B) 1.835 J/(g·K)

C) 3.977 J/(g·K)

D) 13.398 J/(g·K)

Answer: A)

FLUID MECHANICS

Pressure

$$P = \rho g h$$

P = pressure
ρ = density

PRESSURE is the force applied over a specific area; it is measured in Pascal's, atmospheres, or bars. When an object is submersed in a fluid, the weight of the fluid will exert pressure on that object. The magnitude of the pressure depends on the acceleration due to gravity (g), the depth of the object (h), and the fluid's density.

Fluid pressure is affected by depth, not by shape.

The DENSITY (ρ) of a material is defined as its mass per unit volume. For example, water has a density of 1 gram per cubic centimeter, or 1 gram per milliliter. The SPECIFIC DENSITY or specific gravity of a material is defined as its density when compared to water. In this case, water has a set value of 1. Gold has a specific gravity of 19.3, which means that it is 19.3 times denser than water.

Example

Objects A, B, C, and D are submersed in water as shown below. Which of the following statements is true?

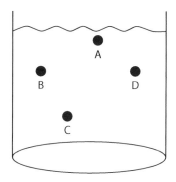

A) The pressure at B is less than the pressure at A.

B) The pressure at A is equal to the pressure at C.

C) The pressure at B and D are equal.

D) The pressure at points A, B, C, and D are equal.

Answer: C)

Buoyancy

BUOYANCY is the ability of an object to float in a fluid that has a greater density than the object. For example, wood might float in water, but a steel marble will not, due to the much higher density of the steel marble compared to the wood.

The buoyant force of an object is a principle first determined by Archimedes, who stated that, "The strength of the buoyant force is equal to the weight of the fluid displaced by the object." Thus, the magnitude of the upward buoyant force on a floating object can be found by calculating the volume of displaced fluid.

Example

When a block is completely submerged in a vessel filled to the top with liquid, the amount of liquid that overflows the vessel—

A) has equal weight to that of the block.

B) has equal volume to that of the block.

C) has the same relative density as that of the block.

D) has the same mass as that of the block.

Answer: B)

CONTINUE

Fluid Flow

$$A_1 v_1 = A_2 v_2$$

$$P_1 + \rho g h_1 + \frac{1}{2}\rho v_1^2 = P_2 + \rho g h_2 + \frac{1}{2}\rho v_2^2$$

When fluid is flowing through a pipe, the area of the pipe and the fluid's velocity have an inverse relationship. Thus, if a pipe gradually becomes thinner, then the water flowing through it will become faster. Based on this understanding, the **Bernoulli Equation** establishes the flow rate of a fluid through a pipe depending on the energy of a fluid flowing through a pipe, the height of the pipe, and the corresponding pressure.

Example

A fluid whose density remains constant is flowing through a tube with radius r_1. It then moves into a section of the tube with a radius r_2. If $r_2 > r_1$, what effect will the increase in radius have?

   A) Decrease the speed of the fluid.

   B) Increase the speed of the fluid.

   C) Increase the volume of fluid that flows past a given point.

   D) Decrease the volume of fluid that flows past a given point.

Answer: A)

WAVES

Types of Waves

A **wave** is a periodic motion that carries energy through space or matter. There are two main types of waves: mechanical and electromagnetic. **Mechanical waves** travel through a physical medium; ripples in a pond and sound waves traveling through the air are both examples of mechanical waves. **Electromagnetic waves** do not require a medium to travel because they consist of oscillating magnetic and electric fields. These waves are classified on the **electromagnetic spectrum** and include visible light, x-rays, and radio waves.

Waves can also be classified by how the particles in the wave vibrate. **Longitudinal waves** cause particles to vibrate parallel to the movement of the wave; **transverse waves** cause particles to vibrate perpendicular to the movement of the wave.

longitudinal wave

transverse wave

Figure 8.3. Types of waves

Example

Which of the following requires a medium to travel?

A) visible light

B) microwaves

C) radio waves

D) sound waves

Answer: D)

Characteristics of Waves

$$v = \lambda f = \frac{\lambda}{T}$$
$$T = \frac{1}{f}$$

The four major characteristics of waves are wavelength, amplitude, period, and frequency. The **WAVELENGTH** (λ) is the distance from the peak of one wave to the next (or from the trough of one wave to the next). The **AMPLITUDE** (A) of a wave is the distance from the top of the wave to the bottom. Both wavelength and amplitude are measured in meters (the SI unit for distance).

The **PERIOD** (T) of a wave is the time it takes the wave to complete one oscillation; it is usually measured in seconds. The **FREQUENCY** (f) of a wave is the number of oscillations that occur per second; it is measured in Hertz (Hz). The period and frequency of a wave are inverses of each other: the shorter the period of a wave, the higher its frequency.

Example

A wave with a speed of 10 m/s is traveling on a string at a frequency of 20 oscillations per second. What is the wave's wavelength?

A) 0.2 m

B) 0.5 m

C) 2 m

D) 200 m

Answer: B)

Properties of Waves

Waves of all kinds exhibit particular behaviors. Waves can interact either to create **CONSTRUCTIVE INTERFERENCE**, where the resulting wave is bigger than either original wave, or **DESTRUCTIVE INTERFERENCE**, which creates a wave that is smaller than either original wave. Waves will also bend when passing through a slit, a process called **DIFFRACTION**. Waves will also **REFRACT**, or bend, when they pass from one medium into another.

Example

What is the maximum possible amplitude of the wave created by the interference of a wave with an amplitude of 0.5 m and a wave with an amplitude of 2 m?

A) 0 m

B) 0.5 m

C) 2.5 m

D) 5 m

Answer: C)

Sound

$I = $ intensity

$I_0 = 1 \times 10^{-12}$ W/m^2 (smallest intensity that can be heard by the human ear)

$$DB = 10\log\left(\frac{I}{I_0}\right)$$

SOUND is comprised of waves that are usually produced by the vibration of an object, such as the strings of an instrument or the human vocal cords. The vibrations cause the air to vibrate as well, which creates a pressure variation in the air, creating a longitudinal wave. When humans hear a sound, it is the detection of the pressure variation by our ear drums. The speed of a sound wave depends on the medium that it is moving through. In air, sound has a speed of about 340 meters per second or 761 miles per hour.

Humans can typically detect sound waves between 20 Hz to 20,000 Hz. Sound waves with a lower frequency have a "lower"

Sound waves travel much faster in water than in air.

pitch to human ears and sound waves with a high frequency have a "high" pitch to human ears.

Sound **INTENSITY** (*I*) is the sound power over a specific area; it's measured in W/m² or decibels (DB). Intensity represents the amount of energy carried by the sound wave; the louder the sound (and larger the amplitude), the greater the intensity. However, sound wave energy is inversely proportional to the distance from which it is heard. Thus, as you move away from a sound source, the intensity of the sound decreases exponentially.

 The decibel scale is a logarithmic scale: it is not linear.

Example

Sound waves will move fastest through which medium?

A) water

B) air

C) a vacuum

D) wood

Answer: D)

PERIODIC MOTION

An oscillation is a **PERIODIC MOTION** that occurs at a specific frequency. Examples of objects that oscillate include pendulum clocks, springs, and the strings in musical instruments.

Springs

$$F = -kx$$

A **SPRING** is a coil of metal or other ductile material that, when compressed or stretched, will return to its original shape if not held by a force. The force required to stretch or compress a spring is related to the distance the spring will be displaced and its spring constant (*k*). The greater the spring constant, the stiffer the spring. The springs which make up the suspension of a car, for example, have very high spring constants, in the range of 3000 – 5000 Newtons per meter, whereas the spring that is used in a ballpoint pen might have a spring constant value of 2 – 3 Newtons per meter.

 x = displacement
k = spring constant

Example

What is the magnitude of the force required to compress a spring 35 cm if the spring has a spring constant of 55 Newtons per meter?

A) 6.74 N

B) 19.25 N

C) 674 N

D) 1925 N

Answer: B)

L = length of pendulum

The mass of the pendulum does not have a significant effect on its period of the swing, as long as there is no air resistance.

Pendulums

$$f = \frac{1}{2\pi}\left(\frac{\sqrt{g}}{L}\right)$$

A PENDULUM is a mass hanging on a string that is swinging back and forth. In a pendulum, as the mass reaches its lowest point, the velocity is the greatest. As it reaches its height on either side, the stored potential energy is the highest, but at its peak the velocity is exactly equal to zero. The frequency of a pendulum is dependent on two things: the gravitational force and the length of the rope.

Examples

Which of the following would increase the frequency of a pendulum?

    A) moving the pendulum to a planet with a higher acceleration due to gravity

    B) making the length of the pendulum longer

    C) adding more mass to the end of the pendulum

    D) increasing the angle of the initial release point

Answer: A)

LIGHT

LIGHT is a form of electromagnetic radiation that makes up a small spectrum of all the electromagnetic waves. Visible light is the wavelength range of 400 to 800 nanometers, and is one of the few types of radiation that is able to penetrate the Earth's atmosphere.

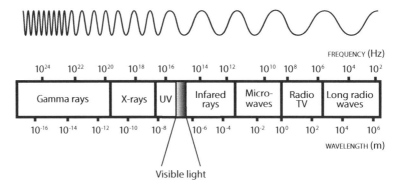

Figure 8.4. Electromagnetic spectrum

Properties of Light

$$n_1 \sin\theta_1 = n_2 \sin\theta_2$$

$$n = \frac{c}{v_s}$$

Light, which is an electromagnetic wave, has a number of special properties because it acts as both a particle and a wave—a phenomenon called the WAVE-PARTICLE DUALITY OF LIGHT. Light will reflect off some materials: the INCIDENT RAY will bounce off a surface, and the incident angle will be equal to the angle of reflection. Light will also bend when it passes from one media to another in a process called **REFRACTION**. The angle of refraction can be found using Snell's law and the material's index of refraction (*n*).

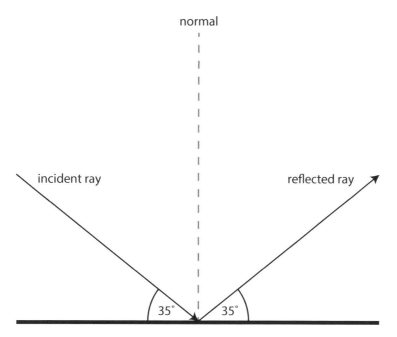

Figure 8.5. Reflection

Light waves can experience both interference and diffraction like any other wave. Because light is made up of discrete packets of energy (called quanta), light also sometimes acts as a particle. For example, when light strikes a metal surface, the packets of energy can eject electrons from atoms in a process called the **PHOTOELECTRIC EFFECT**.

CONTINUE

Example

A ray of light is directed at a reflective surface as shown below.

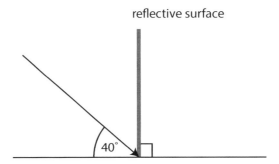

What angle does the reflected ray make with respect to the normal?

A) 0°

B) 40°

C) 50°

D) 90°

Answer: B)

ELECTRICITY

Electric Charge

$$k = 9 \times 10^9 \ \text{N} \times \text{m}_2/\text{C}_2$$

$$F = k\frac{q_1 q_2}{r^2}$$

An electric charge is generated due to the difference in CHARGE (q) potential between protons, which have a +1 charge, and electrons, which have a –1 charge. The charges on a proton or electron are elementary, meaning that they cannot be further subdivided into smaller units. The charge is measured in coulombs (C). A single electron has a charge of –1.6 × 10^{-19} C. One proton has the exact same amount of charge, but of the opposite sign. Electricity is generated by the flow of electrons through a conducting coil, such as copper or steel.

Charged particles are naturally attracted to or repulsed from each other based on their charge. An electron will repel another electron, and a proton will repel another proton. An electron and proton will be attracted to one another. **COULOMB'S LAW** is used to predict the strength of the attractive or repulsive force between two particles. A positive value of force indicates that the particles are being repelled from one another.

⚠️

q = charge

Example

Two particles are separated by a distance of 0.5 m. If one particle has a charge of 1 μC and the other particle has a charge of −2 μC, what is the magnitude of the force between the particles ($k = 9 \times 10^9$ Nm^2/C^2)?

A) 9×10^{-3} N

B) 7.2×10^{-2} N

C) 7.2×10^{10} N

D) 9×10^9 N

Answer: B)

Electric Fields

$$\Delta V = Ed$$

$E = \frac{F}{q}$

Charged particles create an ELECTRIC FIELD (E) in which they will exert an electric force on other charged particles. The strength of an electric field is measured in newtons per coulomb and is proportional to the charge of the particle experiencing the force (i.e., a particle with a higher charge will experience a larger force, and vice versa).

Moving a particle through an electric field will change the potential electrical energy of that particle in an amount proportional to the displacement and force of the electric field. The difference in potential electrical energy between two points is known as VOLTAGE (V), which is measured in volts.

Example

A particle is placed in a uniform electric field of magnitude 1×10^4 N/C. If the particle experiences a force of 0.1 N, what is the magnitude of the charge on the particle?

A) 0.1 μC

B) 1 μC

C) 10 μC

D) 100 μC

Answer: C)

Circuits

$$V = IR$$

$$P = IV = \frac{V^2}{R}$$

I = current
R = resistance
P = power

Current in a circuit can be thought of as analogous to water in a pipe.

In an electric CIRCUIT, a closed loop is formed that is connected to the positive and negative ends of a voltage source. The voltage source provides the charge potential that drives electrons through the circuit to create electricity. The movement of electrons is called CURRENT, which is measured in Amps (A).

A **RESISTOR** is an electrical component that provides resistance to the flow of current through an electric circuit. A resistor is usually composed of a series of materials that are not conducive to electron flow. The units of resistance are Ω. According to Ohm's law, current and resistance are inversely related, and both are proportional to voltage.

Resistors in a circuit can be wired in series or in parallel. In a **SERIES** circuit, the current can only follow one path, while in a **PARALLEL** circuit the current can follow multiple pathways.

Table 8.2. Series and parallel circuits

	SERIES	PARALLEL
Current	$I_1 = I_2 = I_3 = ... = I_n$	$I_t = I_1 + I_2 + ... + I_n$
Voltage	$V_t = V_1 + V_2 + ... + V_n$	$V_1 = V_2 = V_3 = ... = V_n$
Resistance	$R_t = R_1 + R_2 + ... + R_n$	$\frac{1}{R_t} = \frac{1}{R_1} + \frac{1}{R_2} + ... + \frac{1}{R_n}$

Examples

1. What is the current running through a 2 Ω resister in a circuit with a 10 V battery?

   A) 2 A

   B) 5 A

   C) 20 A

   D) 50 A

2. If a circuit wired in series includes five 10 Ω resisters, what is the total resistance of the circuit?

   A) 2 Ω

   B) 10 Ω

   C) 50 Ω

   D) 500 Ω

   Answers: 1. B) 2. C)

MAGNETISM

MAGNETIC FIELDS can be produced by moving electric charges or can be the result of the alignment of subatomic particles in a substance. The SI unit for magnetism is the Tesla, named after the Russian inventor Nikola Tesla. Electricity and magnetism are closely related: moving particles (like electricity) will create magnetic fields. Similarly, magnetic fields will exert a force on moving charged particles, and a moving magnetic field will create an electric current.

All magnets have a north and a south pole. As with charges, like poles repel each other and opposite poles attract each other; the magnitude of this force is directly proportional to the strength of the magnets and inversely proportional to their distance. Magnetic field lines always flow from north to south.

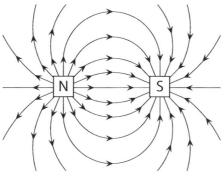

Figure 8.6. Magnetic field lines

Example

The north poles of two magnets are held near each other. At which distance will the magnets experience the most force?

A) 0.1 m

B) 1 m

C) 10 m

D) 100 m

Answer: A)

9

PRACTICE TEST

Mathematics

1. $(43 + 2 - 1) =$
- **A)** 46
- **B)** 44
- **C)** 45
- **D)** 42

2. $(72 - 23 - 6) =$
- **A)** 54
- **B)** 48
- **C)** 43
- **D)** 37

3. A woman's dinner bill comes to $48.30. If she adds a 20% tip, what will she pay in total?
- **A)** $9.66
- **B)** $38.64
- **C)** $68.30
- **D)** $57.96

4. Which of the following is not a rational number?
- **A)** −4
- **B)** 1/5
- **C)** $0.8\overline{33}$
- **D)** $\sqrt{2}$

5. What is 1230.932567 rounded to the nearest hundredth?
- **A)** 1200
- **B)** 1230.9326
- **C)** 1230.93
- **D)** 1230

6. What is the absolute value of −9?
- **A)** −9
- **B)** 9
- **C)** 0
- **D)** −1

7. Add 0.98 + 45.102 + 32.3333 + 31 + 0.00009.
- **A)** 368.573
- **B)** 210.536299
- **C)** 109.41539
- **D)** 99.9975

8. $(9 \div 3) \times (8 \div 4) =$
- **A)** 1
- **B)** 6
- **C)** 72
- **D)** 576

9. $7.95 \div 1.5 =$

    A) 2.4

    B) 5.3

    C) 6.2

    D) 7.3

10. Melissa is ordering fencing to enclose a square area of 5625 square feet. How many feet of fencing does she need?

    A) 75 feet

    B) 150 feet

    C) 300 feet

    D) 5,625 feet

11. If a discount of 25% off the retail price of a desk saves Mark $45, what was the desk's original price?

    A) $135

    B) $160

    C) $180

    D) $210

12. What number is 5% of 2000?

    A) 50

    B) 100

    C) 150

    D) 200

13. A sporting goods store is offering an additional 30% off all clearance items. Angie purchases a pair of running shoes on clearance for $65.00. If the shoes originally cost $85.00, what was her total discount?

    A) 53.5%

    B) 46.5%

    C) 22.9%

    D) 39.2%

14. Molly's headband broke, and her hair is falling in her face. She has 4 pieces of ribbon to choose from. She needs to choose the piece that can go around her 22-inch head. The piece must be at least 4 inches longer than her head so that she can tie a knot, but it cannot be more than 6 inches so that the ends will show through her hair. Which of the following pieces of ribbon will work best?

    A) 2 feet

    B) $2\frac{3}{4}$ feet

    C) $2\frac{5}{8}$ feet

    D) $2\frac{1}{3}$ feet

15. Jane earns $15 per hour babysitting. If she starts out with $275 in her bank account, which of the following equations represents how many hours she'll have to babysit for her account to reach $400?

    A) $-400 = 15h - 275$

    B) $400 = \frac{15}{h} + 275$

    C) $400 = 15h$

    D) $400 = 15h + 275$

16. Anna is buying fruit at the farmers' market. She selects 1.2 kilograms of apples, 800 grams of bananas, and 300 grams of strawberries. The farmer charges her a flat rate of $4 per kilogram. What is the total cost?

    A) $4.40

    B) $5.24

    C) $48.80

    D) $9.20

17. Leslie needs to make a pie and some cupcakes. The pie requires $\frac{3}{8}$ of a cup of sugar; the cupcakes require $\frac{3}{5}$ of a cup of sugar. Leslie has $\frac{15}{16}$ of a cup of sugar. Does she have enough sugar, or how much more does she need?

    A) She has enough sugar.

    B) She needs $\frac{1}{8}$ of a cup of sugar.

    C) She needs $\frac{3}{80}$ of a cup of sugar.

    D) She needs $\frac{4}{19}$ of a cup of sugar.

18. If $|3x+2| = 5$, which of the following options gives us the correct values of x?

A) $\left\{1, \frac{-7}{3}\right\}$

B) $\left\{-1, \frac{7}{3}\right\}$

C) $\{3, 7\}$

D) $\left\{\frac{7}{3}, \frac{3}{7}\right\}$

19. If $\frac{|2k+4|}{8} = 2$, which of the following values of k satisfies this equation?

A) $\{12, 2\}$

B) $\{4, 5\}$

C) $\{3, 6\}$

D) $\{-10, 6\}$

20. If $\frac{2x+7}{9} < 2$, which of the following options is correct?

A) $3x < \frac{21}{3}$

B) $x > -3$

C) $x < \frac{11}{2}$

D) $2x > 1$

21. What is the result when we multiply these given fractions?

$\frac{4}{5} \times \frac{14}{25} \times \frac{125}{7} \times \frac{4}{2} =$

A) 16

B) $\frac{24}{25}$

C) 32

D) 18

22. What is the result when we multiply these given fractions?

$\frac{2}{9} \times \frac{3}{25} \times \frac{125}{6} \times \frac{3}{10} =$

A) $\frac{1}{5}$

B) $\frac{1}{6}$

C) 6

D) $\frac{11}{30}$

23. What is the result when we add these given fractions?

$\frac{1}{5} + \frac{4}{25} =$

A) $\frac{8}{25}$

B) $\frac{5}{29}$

C) $\frac{9}{25}$

D) $\frac{5}{20}$

24. Alan bought a pizza with 8 slices. He ate 3 slices of pizza for lunch and left the remaining pizza for Jenny. What fraction of pizza did Alan leave for Jenny?

A) $\frac{3}{8}$

B) $\frac{1}{2}$

C) $\frac{4}{5}$

D) $\frac{5}{8}$

25. What is the result of the following expression?

$\left(\frac{3}{4} + \frac{1}{5}\right) - \left(\frac{2}{3} + \frac{3}{2}\right) =$

A) $\frac{7}{8}$

B) $\frac{-73}{60}$

C) $\frac{73}{60}$

D) $\frac{-26}{30}$

26. What is the result of the following expression?

$\frac{2}{9} + \left(\frac{5}{6} - \frac{1}{2}\right) =$

A) $\frac{5}{12}$

B) $\frac{7}{9}$

C) $\frac{5}{9}$

D) $\frac{8}{45}$

27. If $3x + 2 > 5$, which of the following options is correct?

A) $x < 1$

B) $x > -1$

C) $x > 1$

D) $x > 3$

28. Which of the following does the roman numeral CLVII equal?

  A) 202

  B) 157

  C) 752

  D) 257

29. Simplify the following expression:
$5\frac{1}{3} - 2\frac{1}{3} =$

  A) $5\frac{1}{3}$

  B) $5\frac{2}{3}$

  C) 5

  D) 3

30. Convert the following into a fraction:
$5.25 + 1.5 =$

  A) $5\frac{3}{4}$

  B) $7\frac{3}{4}$

  C) $6\frac{3}{4}$

  D) $7\frac{1}{4}$

31. Convert 0.28 into a fraction.

  A) $\frac{9}{25}$

  B) $\frac{7}{45}$

  C) $\frac{7}{25}$

  D) $\frac{8}{15}$

32. Convert $\frac{5}{20}$ into decimal form.

  A) 0.55

  B) 0.35

  C) 0.15

  D) 0.25

Use the chart below to answer questions 33 and 34.

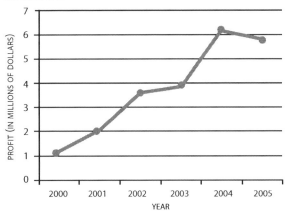

33. Referencing the line graph above, approximately how much did profit increase from 2003 to 2004 in dollars?

  A) 2.3 million

  B) 6.2 million

  C) 3.9 million

  D) 3.2 million

34. Approximately how much more profit was earned in 2001 than in 2000?

  A) 2.2 million

  B) 1 million

  C) 3.5 million

  D) 6.1 million

35. $3 \times (2 \times 4^3) \div 4 =$

  A) 81

  B) 64

  C) 127

  D) 96

36. $(5 \times 3) \times 1 + 5 =$

  A) 20

  B) 21

  C) 90

  D) 13

37. $(5^3 + 7) \times 2 =$

A) 1264

B) 264

C) 139

D) 164

38. Evaluate the expression $\frac{4x}{x-1}$ when $x = 5$.

A) 3

B) 4

C) 5

D) 6

39. Round 707.456 to the nearest tenth.

A) 708.0

B) 710

C) 707.5

D) 700

40. Subtract the following numbers and round to the nearest tenth:

134.679

$-$ 45.548

$\underline{- 67.8807}$

A) 21.3

B) 21.25

C) −58.97

D) −59.0

41. What is the median of the following list of numbers: 4, 5, 7, 9, 10, and 12?

A) 6

B) 7.5

C) 7.8

D) 8

42. Find $0.12 \div 1$.

A) 12

B) 1.2

C) 0.12

D) 0.012

43. $6 \times 0 \times 5 =$

A) 30

B) 11

C) 25

D) 0

44. If a rectangular field has a perimeter of 44 yards and a length of 36 feet, what is the field's width?

A) 30 feet

B) 28 yards

C) 18 feet

D) 42 feet

45. Adam is painting a 4-walled shed. The shed is 5 feet wide, 4 feet deep, and 7 feet high. How much paint will Adam need?

A) 126 ft²

B) 140 ft²

C) 63 ft²

D) 46 ft

46. 35% of what number is 70?

A) 100

B) 110

C) 150

D) 200

47. A car dealer sells an SUV for $39,000, which represents a 25% profit over the cost. What was the actual cost of the SUV to the dealer?

A) $29,250

B) $31,200

C) $32,500

D) $33,800

48. At a bake sale, muffins cost $1.50 each and cookies cost $1 for two. If 11 muffins are sold, and the total money earned is $29.50, how many cookies were sold?

A) 12

B) 13

C) 23

D) 26

49. During a 5-day convention, the number of visitors tripled each day. If the convention started on a Tuesday with 345 visitors, what was the attendance on that Friday?

A) 9,315

B) 1,035

C) 1,725

D) 3,105

50. Simplify: $59.09 - 5.007 - 6.21$.

A) 47.792

B) 47.81

C) 47.873

D) 47.882

51. Jim works for $15.50 per hour at a health care facility. He is supposed to get a $0.75 per hour raise after one year of service. What will be his percent increase in hourly pay?

A) 2.7%

B) 3.3%

C) 133%

D) 4.8%

52. What is the least common multiple of 2, 3, 4, and 5?

A) 30

B) 60

C) 120

D) 40

53. $2 + 3|4n| = 26$. Which of the following correctly gives us the value of n?

A) $\{1, 2\}$

B) $\{-2, 2\}$

C) $\{3, 4\}$

D) $\{-1, -4\}$

54. $|2r + 1| - 10 = 13$. Which of the following values of r satisfies the given equation?

A) $\{12, -2\}$

B) $\{11, -11\}$

C) $\{12, -11\}$

D) $\{-12, 11\}$

55. $\frac{3}{4} \times \frac{4}{5} \times \frac{5}{3} =$

A) 1

B) $\frac{6}{5}$

C) 2

D) $\frac{12}{23}$

The Flu

Influenza (also called the flu) has historically been one of the most common, and deadliest, human infections. While many people who contract the virus will recover, many others will not. Over the past 150 years, tens of millions of people have died from the flu, and millions more have been left with lingering complications such as secondary infections.

Although it's a common disease, the flu is not actually highly infectious, meaning it's relatively difficult to contract. The flu can only be transmitted when individuals come into direct contact with bodily fluids of people infected with the flu or when they are exposed to expelled aerosol particles (which result from coughing and sneezing). Because the viruses can only travel short distances as aerosol particles and will die within a few hours on hard surfaces, the virus can be contained with fairly simple health measures like hand washing and face masks.

However, the spread of the flu can only be contained when people are aware such measures need to be taken. One of the reasons the flu has historically been so deadly is the amount of time between when people become infectious and when they develop symptoms. Viral shedding—the process by which the body releases viruses that have been successfully reproducing during the infection—takes place two days after infection, while symptoms do not usually develop until the third day of infection. Thus, infected individuals have at least twenty-four hours in which they may unknowingly infect others.

1. What is the main idea of the passage?

   A) The flu is a deadly disease that's difficult to control because people become infectious before they show symptoms.

   B) For the flu to be transmitted, individuals must come in contact with bodily fluids from infected individuals.

   C) The spread of the flu is easy to contain because the viruses do not live long either as aerosol particles or on hard surfaces.

   D) The flu has killed tens of millions of people and can often cause deadly secondary infections.

2. Which of the following correctly describes the flu?

   A) The flu is easy to contract and always fatal.

   B) The flu is difficult to contract and always fatal.

   C) The flu is easy to contract and sometimes fatal.

   D) The flu is difficult to contract and sometimes fatal.

3. Why is the flu considered to not be highly infectious?

   A) Many people who get the flu will recover and have no lasting complications, so only a small number of people who become infected will die.

   B) The process of viral shedding takes two days, so infected individuals have enough time to implement simple health measures that stop the spread of the disease.

   C) The flu virus cannot travel far or live for long periods of time outside the human body, so its spread can easily be contained.

   D) Twenty-four hours is a relatively short period of time for the virus to spread among a population.

4. What is the meaning of the word *measures* in the last paragraph?

   A) a plan of action

   B) a standard unit

   C) an adequate amount

   D) a rhythmic movement

5. Which statement is not a detail from the passage?

   A) Tens of millions of people have been killed by the flu virus.

   B) There is typically a twenty-four hour window during which individuals are infectious but not showing flu symptoms.

   C) Viral shedding is the process by which people recover from the flu.

   D) The flu can be transmitted by direct contact with bodily fluids from infected individuals or by exposure to aerosol particles.

6. What can the reader conclude from the previous passage?

   A) Preemptively implementing health measures like hand washing and face masks could help stop the spread of the flu virus.

   B) Doctors are not sure how the flu virus is transmitted, so they are unsure how to stop it from spreading.

   C) The flu is dangerous because it is both deadly and highly infectious.

   D) Individuals stop being infectious three days after they are infected.

Snakes

Skin coloration and markings have an important role to play in the world of snakes. Those intricate diamonds, stripes, and swirls help animals hide from predators and advertise to mates. Perhaps most importantly (for us humans, anyway), the markings can also indicate whether the snake is venomous. While it might seem counterintuitive for a poisonous snake to stand out in bright red or blue, that fancy costume tells any approaching predator that eating him would be a bad idea.

If you see a flashy-looking snake in the woods, though, those markings don't necessarily mean it's poisonous: some snakes have found a way to ward off predators without the actual venom. The California kingsnake, for example, has very similar markings to the venomous coral snake with whom it frequently shares a habitat. However, the kingsnake is actually nonvenomous; it's merely pretending to be dangerous to eat. A predatory hawk or eagle, usually hunting from high in the sky, can't tell the difference between the two species, and so the kingsnake gets passed over and lives another day.

7. What is the author's primary purpose in writing this essay?

   A) To explain how the markings on a snake are related to whether it's venomous.

   B) To teach readers the difference between coral snakes and kingsnakes.

   C) To illustrate why snakes are dangerous.

   D) To demonstrate how animals survive in difficult environments.

8. What can the reader conclude from the passage above?

   A) The kingsnake is dangerous to humans.

   B) The coral snake and the kingsnake are both hunted by the same predators.

   C) It's safe to handle snakes in the woods because you can easily tell whether they're poisonous.

   D) The kingsnake changes its markings when hawks or eagles are close by.

9. What is the best summary of this passage?

   A) Humans can use coloration and markings on snakes to determine whether they're poisonous.

   B) Animals often use coloration and markings to attract mates and warn predators that they're poisonous.

   C) The California kingsnake and coral snake have nearly identical markings.

   D) Venomous snakes often have bright markings, although nonvenomous snakes can also mimic those colors.

10. Which statement is not a detail from the passage?

   A) Predators will avoid eating kingsnakes because their markings are similar to those on coral snakes.

   B) Kingsnakes and coral snakes live in the same habitats.

   C) The coral snake uses its coloration to hide from predators.

   D) The kingsnake is not venomous.

11. What is the meaning of the word *intricate* in the first paragraph?

   A) complex

   B) colorful

   C) purposeful

   D) changeable

12. What is the difference between kingsnakes and coral snakes according to the passage?

   A) Both kingsnakes and coral snakes are nonvenomous, but coral snakes have colorful markings.

   B) Both kingsnakes and coral snakes are venomous, but kingsnakes have colorful markings.

   C) Kingsnakes are nonvenomous while coral snakes are venomous.

   D) Coral snakes are nonvenomous while kingsnakes are venomous.

Taking Temperatures

Taking a person's temperature is one of the most basic and common health care tasks. Everyone from nurses to emergency medical technicians to concerned parents has needed to grab a thermometer and take someone's temperature. But what's the best way to get an accurate reading? The answer depends on the situation.

The most common way people measure body temperature is orally. A simple digital or disposable thermometer is placed under the tongue for a few minutes, and the task is done. There are many situations, however, when measuring temperature orally isn't an option. For example, when a person can't breathe through his nose, he won't be able to keep his mouth closed long enough to get an accurate reading. In these situations, it's often preferable to place the thermometer in the rectum or armpit. Using the rectum also has the added benefit of providing a much more accurate reading other locations cannot provide.

It's also often the case that certain people, like agitated patients or fussy babies, won't be able to sit still long enough for an accurate reading. In these situations, it's best to use a thermometer that works much more quickly, such as one that measures temperature in the ear or at the temporal artery. No matter which method is chosen, however, it's important to check the average temperature for each region, as it can vary by several degrees.

CONTINUE →

13. Which statement is not a detail from the passage?

A) Taking a temperature in the ear or at the temporal artery is more accurate than taking it orally.

B) If an individual cannot breathe through his nose, taking his temperature orally will likely give an inaccurate reading.

C) The standard human body temperature varies depending on whether it's measured in the mouth, rectum, armpit, ear, or temporal artery.

D) The most common way to measure temperature is by placing a thermometer in the mouth.

14. What is the author's primary purpose in writing this essay?

A) To advocate for the use of thermometers that measure temperature in the ear or at the temporal artery.

B) To explain the methods available to measure a person's temperature and the situation where each method is appropriate.

C) To warn readers that the average temperature of the human body varies by region.

D) To discuss how nurses use different types of thermometers depending on the type of patient they are examining.

15. What is the best summary of this passage?

A) It's important that everyone know the best way to take a person's temperature in any given situation.

B) The most common method of taking a person's temperature—orally—isn't appropriate in some situations.

C) The most accurate way to take a temperature is placing a digital thermometer in the rectum.

D) There are many different ways to take a person's temperature, and which is appropriate will depend on the situation.

16. What is the meaning of the word *agitated* in the last paragraph?

A) obviously upset

B) quickly moving

C) violently ill

D) slightly dirty

17. According to the passage, why is it sometimes preferable to take a person's temperature rectally?

A) Rectal readings are more accurate than oral readings.

B) Many people cannot sit still long enough to have their temperatures taken orally.

C) Temperature readings can vary widely between regions of the body.

D) Many people do not have access to quick-acting thermometers.

Credit Scores

Credit scores, which range from 300 to 850, are a single value that summarizes an individual's credit history. Pay your bills late? Your credit score will be lower than someone who gets that electric bill filed on the first of every month. Just paid off your massive student loans? You can expect your credit score to shoot up. The companies that compile credit scores actually keep track of all the loans, credit cards, and bill payments in your name. This massive amount of information is summed up in a credit report, which is then distilled to a single value: your credit score.

Credit scores are used by many institutions that need to evaluate the risk of providing loans, rentals, or services to individuals. Banks use credit scores when deciding whether to hand out loans; they can also use them to determine the terms of the loan itself. Similarly, car dealers, landlords, and credit card companies will likely all access your credit report before agreeing to do business with you. Even your employer can access a modified version of your credit report (although it will not have your actual credit score on it).

When it comes to credit, everyone begins with a clean slate. The first time you access any credit—be it a credit card, student loan, or rental agreement—information begins to accumulate in your credit report. Thus, having no credit score can often be just as bad as having a low one. Lenders want to know that you have a history of borrowing money and paying it back on time. After all, if you've never taken out a loan, how can a bank know that you'll pay back its money? So, having nothing on your credit report can result in low credit limits and high interest rates.

With time, though, credit scores can be raised. With every payment, your credit report improves and banks will be more likely to loan you money. These new loans will in turn raise your score even further (as long as you keep making payments, of course).

In general, you can take a number of basic steps to raise your credit score. First, ensure that payments are made on time. When payments are past due, it not only has a negative impact on your score, but new creditors will be reluctant to lend while you are delinquent on other accounts.

Being smart about taking on debt is another key factor in keeping your credit score high. As someone who is just starting off in the financial world, there will be multiple offers to open accounts, say, for an introductory credit card or short-term loan. You may also find that as your score increases, you will receive offers for larger and larger loans. (Predatory lenders are a scourge on the young as well as the old.) But just because banks are offering you those loans doesn't make them a good idea. Instead, you should only take on debt you know you can pay back in a reasonable amount of time.

Lastly, keep an eye on unpaid student loans, medical bills, and parking tickets, all of which can take a negative toll on your credit score. In fact, your credit score will take a major hit from any bill that's sent to a collection agency, so it's in your best interest to avoid letting bills get to that point. Many organizations will agree to keep bills away from collection agencies if you set up a fee payment system.

18. What is the author's primary purpose in writing this essay?

A) To help readers understand and improve their credit scores.

B) To warn banks about the dangers of lending to people with no credit score.

C) To persuade readers to take out large loans to improve their credit scores.

D) To explain to readers how the process of taking out a bank loan works.

19. According to the passage, which individual is likely to have the highest credit score?

A) Someone who has had medical bills sent to a collection agency.

B) Someone who is in the process of paying back his student loans.

C) Someone who has never borrowed any money but pays his bills on time.

D) Someone who has borrowed a large amount of money and paid it back on time.

20. What is the best summary of this passage?

    A) Individuals with low credit scores will likely have trouble getting credit cards and loans. However, they can improve their credit scores over time.

    B) Having no credit score can often be worse than having a low credit score, so it's important to sign up for credit cards and loans early in life.

    C) Credit scores summarize an individual's credit history and are used by many businesses. They can be improved by making smart financial decisions.

    D) Credit scores can be raised by paying bills on time, taking out reasonably sized loans, and avoiding collection agencies.

21. Which of the following is an opinion stated in the passage?

    A) Credit scores, which range from 300 to 850, are a single value that summarizes an individual's credit history.

    B) Many organizations will agree to keep bills away from collection agencies if you set up a fee payment system.

    C) After all, if you've never taken out a loan, how can a bank know that you'll pay back its money?

    D) Predatory lenders are a scourge on the young as well as the old.

22. What can the reader conclude from the passage?

    A) It's possible to wipe your credit report clean and start over with a blank slate.

    B) People with a large amount of debt can likely get a loan with a low interest rate because they have demonstrated they are trustworthy.

    C) Someone who has borrowed and paid back large sums of money will get a loan with more favorable terms than someone who has never borrowed money before.

    D) A college student with no credit cards or debt likely has a high credit score.

23. Which statement is not a detail from the passage?

    A) In general, you can take a number of basic steps to raise your credit score.

    B) When it comes to credit, everyone begins with a clean slate.

    C) Employers can access your credit score before hiring you.

    D) Predatory lenders are a scourge on the young as well as the old.

24. What is the meaning of the word *distilled* in the first paragraph?

    A) to refine to its essence

    B) to explain at length

    C) to keep records of

    D) to undergo substantial change

Hand Washing

Hand washing is one of our simplest and most powerful weapons against infection. The idea behind hand washing is deceptively simple. Many illnesses are spread when people touch infected surfaces, such as door handles or other people's hands, and then touch their own eyes, mouths, or noses. So, if pathogens can be removed from the hands before they spread, infections can be prevented. When done correctly, hand washing can prevent the spread of many dangerous bacteria and viruses, including those that cause the flu, the common cold, diarrhea, and many acute respiratory illnesses.

The most basic method of hand washing involves only soap and water. Just twenty seconds of scrubbing with soap and a complete rinsing with water is enough to kill and/or wash away many pathogens. The process doesn't even require warm water—studies have shown that cold water is just as effective at reducing the number of microbes on the hands. Antibacterial soaps are also available, although several studies have shown that simple soap and cold water is just as effective.

In recent years, hand sanitizers have become popular as an alternative to hand washing. These gels, liquids, and foams contain a high concentration of alcohol (usually at least 60 percent) that kills most bacteria and fungi; they can also be effective against some, but not all, viruses. There is a downside to hand sanitizer, however. Because the sanitizer isn't rinsed from hands, it only kills pathogens and does nothing to remove organic matter. So, hands "cleaned" with hand sanitizer may still harbor pathogens. Thus, while hand sanitizer can be helpful in situations where soap and clean water isn't available, a simple hand washing is still the best option.

25. What is the meaning of the word *harbor* in the last paragraph?

A) to disguise

B) to hide

C) to wash away

D) to give a home

26. Which of the following is not a fact stated in the passage?

A) Many infections occur because people get pathogens on their hands and then touch their own eyes, mouths, or noses.

B) Antibacterial soaps and warm water are the best way to remove pathogens from hands.

C) Most hand sanitizers have a concentration of at least 60 percent alcohol.

D) Hand sanitizer can be an acceptable alternative to hand washing when soap and water aren't available.

27. What is the best summary of this passage?

A) Many diseases are spread by pathogens that can live on the hands. Hand washing is the best way to remove these pathogens and prevent disease.

B) Simple hand washing can prevent the spread of many common illnesses, including the flu, the common cold, diarrhea, and many acute respiratory illnesses. Hand sanitizer can also kill the pathogens that cause these diseases.

C) Simple hand washing with soap and cold water is an effective way to reduce the spread of disease. Antibacterial soaps and hand sanitizers may also be used but are not significantly more effective.

D) Using hand sanitizer will kill many pathogens but will not remove organic matter. Hand washing with soap and water is a better option when available.

→

CONTINUE

28. Knowing that the temperature of the water does not affect the efficacy of hand washing, one can conclude that water plays an important role in hand washing because it _____.

   A) has antibacterial properties

   B) physically removes pathogens from hands

   C) cools hands to make them inhospitable to dangerous bacteria

   D) is hot enough to kill bacteria

29. What is the author's primary purpose in writing this essay?

   A) to persuade readers of the importance and effectiveness of hand washing with soap and cold water

   B) to dissuade readers from using hand sanitizer

   C) to explain how many common diseases are spread

   D) to describe the many ways hand washing and hand sanitizer provide health benefits

30. What can the reader conclude from the passage above?

   A) Hand washing would do little to limit infections that spread through particles in the air.

   B) Hand washing is not necessary for people who do not touch their eyes, mouths, or noses with their hands.

   C) Hand sanitizer serves no purpose and should not be used as an alternative to hand washing.

   D) Hand sanitizer will likely soon replace hand washing as the preferred method of removing pathogens from hands.

The Jazz Age

In recent decades, jazz has been associated with New Orleans and festivals like Mardi Gras, but in the 1920s, jazz was a booming trend whose influence reached into many aspects of American culture. In fact, the years between World War I and the Great Depression were known as the Jazz Age, a term coined by F. Scott Fitzgerald in his famous novel *The Great Gatsby*. Sometimes also called the Roaring Twenties, this time period saw major urban centers experiencing new economic, cultural, and artistic vitality. In the United States, musicians flocked to cities like New York and Chicago, which would became famous hubs for jazz musicians. Ella Fitzgerald, for example, moved from Virginia to New York City to begin her much-lauded singing career, and jazz pioneer Louis Armstrong got his big break in Chicago.

Jazz music was played by and for a more expressive and freed populace than the United States had previously seen. Women gained the right to vote and were openly seen drinking and dancing to jazz music. This period marked the emergence of the flapper, a woman determined to make a statement about her new role in society. Jazz music also provided the soundtrack for the explosion of African American art and culture now known as the Harlem Renaissance. In addition to Fitzgerald and Armstrong, numerous musicians, including Duke Ellington, Fats Waller, and Bessie Smith, promoted their distinctive and complex music as an integral part of the emerging African American culture.

31. What is the main idea of the passage?

    A) People should associate jazz music with the 1920s, not modern New Orleans.

    B) Jazz music played an important role in many cultural movements of the 1920s.

    C) Many famous jazz musicians began their careers in New York City and Chicago.

    D) African Americans were instrumental in launching jazz into mainstream culture.

32. What can the reader conclude from the passage above?

    A) Jazz music was important to minority groups struggling for social equality in the 1920s.

    B) Duke Ellington, Fats Waller, and Bessie Smith were the most important jazz musicians of the Harlem Renaissance.

    C) Women gained the right to vote with the help of jazz musicians.

    D) Duke Ellington, Fats Waller, and Bessie Smith all supported women's right to vote.

33. What is the author's primary purpose in writing this essay?

    A) to explain the role jazz musicians played in the Harlem Renaissance

    B) to inform the reader about the many important musicians playing jazz in the 1920s

    C) to discuss how jazz influenced important cultural movements in the 1920s

    D) to provide a history of jazz music in the 20th century

34. Which of the following is not a fact stated in the passage?

    A) The years between World War I and the Great Depression were known as the Jazz Age.

    B) Ella Fitzgerald and Louis Armstrong both moved to New York City to start their music careers.

    C) Women danced to jazz music during the 1920s to make a statement about their role in society.

    D) Jazz music was an integral part of the emerging African American culture of the 1920s.

35. What can the reader conclude from the passage above?

    A) F. Scott Fitzgerald supported jazz musicians in New York and Chicago.

    B) Jazz music is no longer as popular as it once was.

    C) Both women and African Americans used jazz music as a way of expressing their newfound freedom.

    D) Flappers and African American musicians worked together to produce jazz music.

CONTINUE

Popcorn

Popcorn is often associated with fun and festivities, both in and out of the home. It's eaten in theaters, usually after being salted and smothered in butter, and in homes, fresh from the microwave. But popcorn isn't just for fun—it's also a multimillion-dollar-a-year industry with a long and fascinating history.

While popcorn might seem like a modern invention, its history actually dates back thousands of years, making it one of the oldest snack foods enjoyed around the world. Popcorn is believed by food historians to be one of the earliest uses of cultivated corn. In 1948, Herbert Dick and Earle Smith discovered old popcorn dating back 4000 years in the New Mexico Bat Cave. For the Aztec Indians who called the caves home, popcorn (or *momochitl*) played an important role in society, both as a food staple and in ceremonies. The Aztecs cooked popcorn by heating sand in a fire; when it was heated, kernels were added and would pop when exposed to the heat of the sand.

The American love affair with popcorn began in 1912, when popcorn was first sold in theaters. The popcorn industry flourished during the Great Depression by advertising popcorn as a wholesome and economical food. Selling for five to ten cents a bag, it was a luxury that the downtrodden could afford. With the introduction of mobile popcorn machines at the World's Columbian Exposition, popcorn moved from the theater into fairs and parks. Popcorn continued to rule the snack food kingdom until the rise in popularity of home televisions during the 1950s.

The popcorn industry reacted to the decline in sales quickly by introducing pre-popped and un-popped popcorn for home consumption. However, it wasn't until microwave popcorn became commercially available in 1981 that at-home popcorn consumption began to grow exponentially. With the wide availability of microwaves in the United States, popcorn also began popping up in offices and hotel rooms. However, the home still remains the most popular popcorn eating spot: today, 70 percent of the 16 billion quarts of popcorn consumed annually in the United States are eaten at home.

36. What can the reader conclude from the passage above?

A) People ate less popcorn in the 1950s than in previous decades because they went to the movies less.

B) Without mobile popcorn machines, people would not have been able to eat popcorn during the Great Depression.

C) People enjoyed popcorn during the Great Depression because it was a luxury food.

D) During the 1800s, people began abandoning theaters to go to fairs and festivals.

37. What is the meaning of the word *staple* in the second paragraph?

A) something produced only for special occasions

B) something produced regularly in large quantities

C) something produced by cooking

D) something fastened together securely

38. What is the author's primary purpose in writing this essay?

A) to explain how microwaves affected the popcorn industry

B) to show that popcorn is older than many people realize

C) to illustrate the history of popcorn from ancient cultures to modern times

D) to demonstrate the importance of popcorn in various cultures

39. Which factor does the author of the passage credit for the growth of the popcorn industry in the United States?

A) the use of popcorn in ancient Aztec ceremonies

B) the growth of the home television industry

C) the marketing of popcorn during the Great Depression

D) the nutritional value of popcorn

40. What is the best summary of this passage?

    A) Popcorn is a popular snack food that dates back thousands of years. Its popularity in the United States has been tied to the growth of theaters and microwaves.

    B) Popcorn has been a popular snack food for thousands of years. Archaeologists have found evidence that many ancient cultures used popcorn as a food staple and in ceremonies.

    C) Popcorn was first introduced to America in 1912, and its popularity has grown exponentially since then. Today, over 16 billion quarts of popcorn are consumed in the United States annually.

    D) Popcorn is a versatile snack food that can be eaten with butter or other toppings. It can also be cooked in a number of different ways, including in microwaves.

41. Which of the following is not a fact stated in the passage?

    A) Archaeologists have found popcorn dating back 4000 years.

    B) Popcorn was first sold in theaters in 1912.

    C) Consumption of popcorn dropped in 1981 with the growing popularity of home televisions.

    D) 70 percent of the popcorn consumed in the United States is eaten in homes.

Symbiotic Relationships

The bacteria, fungi, insects, plants, and animals that live together in a habitat have evolved to share a pool of limited resources. They've competed for water, minerals, nutrients, sunlight, and space—sometimes for thousands or even millions of years. As these communities have evolved, the species in them have developed complex, long-term interspecies interactions known as symbiotic relationships. Ecologists characterize these interactions based on whether each party benefits. In mutualism, both individuals benefit, while in synnecrosis, both organisms are harmed. A relationship where one individual benefits and the other is harmed is known as parasitism. Examples of these relationships can easily be seen in any ecosystem. Pollination, for example, is mutualistic—pollinators get nutrients from the flower, and the plant is able to reproduce—while tapeworms, which steal nutrients from their host, are parasitic.

There's yet another class of symbiosis that is controversial among scientists. As it's long been defined, commensalism is a relationship where one species benefits and the other is unaffected. But is it possible for two species to interact and for one to remain completely unaffected? Often, relationships described as commensal include one species that feeds on another species' leftovers; remoras, for instance, will attach themselves to sharks and eat the food particles they leave behind. It might seem like the shark gets nothing from the relationship, but a closer look will show that sharks in fact benefit from remoras, which clean the sharks' skin and remove parasites. In fact, many scientists claim that relationships currently described as commensal are just mutualistic or parasitic in ways that haven't been discovered yet.

42. What is the meaning of the word *controversial* in the last paragraph?

    A) debatable

    B) objectionable

    C) confusing

    D) upsetting

CONTINUE

43. What is the author's primary purpose in writing this essay?

A) to argue that commensalism isn't actually found in nature

B) to describe the many types of symbiotic relationships

C) to explain how competition for resources results in long-term interspecies relationships

D) to provide examples of the many different ways individual organisms interact

44. Which of the following is not a fact stated in the passage?

A) Mutualism is an interspecies relationship where both species benefit.

B) Synnecrosis is an interspecies relationship where both species are harmed.

C) The relationship between plants and pollinators is mutualistic.

D) The relationship between remoras and sharks is parasitic.

45. Epiphytes are plants that attach themselves to trees and derive nutrients from the air and surrounding debris. Sometimes, the weight of epiphytes can damage the trees on which they're growing. The relationship between epiphytes and their hosts would be described as _____.

A) mutualism

B) commensalism

C) parasitism

D) synnecrosis

46. Why is commensalism controversial among scientists?

A) Many scientists believe that an interspecies interaction where one species is unaffected does not exist.

B) Some scientists believe that relationships where one species feeds on the leftovers of another should be classified as parasitism.

C) Because remoras and sharks have a mutualistic relationship, no interactions should be classified as commensalism.

D) Only relationships among animal species should be classified as commensalism.

47. What can the reader conclude from this passage about symbiotic relationships?

A) Scientists cannot decide how to classify symbiotic relationships among species.

B) The majority of interspecies interactions are parasitic because most species do not get along.

C) If two species are involved in a parasitic relationship, one of the species will eventually become extinct.

D) Symbiotic relationships evolve as the species that live in a community adapt to their environments and each other.

The Civil War

It could be said that the great battle between the North and South we call the Civil War was a battle for individual identity. The states of the South had their own culture, one based on farming, independence, and the rights of both man and state to determine their own paths. Similarly, the North had forged its own identity as a center of centralized commerce and manufacturing. This clash of lifestyles was bound to create tension, and this tension was bound to lead to war. But people who try to sell you this narrative are wrong. The Civil War was not a battle of cultural identities—it was a battle about slavery. All other explanations for the war are either a direct consequence of the South's desire for wealth at the expense of her fellow man or a fanciful invention to cover up this sad portion of our nation's history. And it cannot be denied that this time in our past was very sad indeed.

48. What is the meaning of the word *fanciful* in the passage?

A) complicated

B) imaginative

C) successful

D) unfortunate

49. What is the author's primary purpose in writing this essay?

A) To convince readers that slavery was the main cause of the Civil War.

B) To illustrate the cultural differences between the North and the South before the Civil War.

C) To persuade readers that the North deserved to win the Civil War.

D) To demonstrate that the history of the Civil War is too complicated to be understood clearly.

50. What is the main idea of the passage?

A) The Civil War was the result of cultural differences between the North and South.

B) The Civil War was caused by the South's reliance on slave labor.

C) The North's use of commerce and manufacturing allowed it to win the war.

D) The South's belief in the rights of man and state cost the war.

Patient Nutrition

Providing adequate nutrition is one of the most important responsibilities of acute and long-term care facilities. Patients enter these facilities with a wide range of health issues from fractures and infections to dementia or cancer. Because the needs of every patient will be different, it's the task of every health care facility to ensure that patients receive the proper nutrition.

Patients, like all people, have two basic nutritional needs: they require macronutrients, the carbohydrates, fats, and proteins that provide energy; and micronutrients, which are the vitamins and elements the body needs to function properly. A good diet will provide the appropriate amount of macronutrients, or calories, to keep the patients energized and satiated without leading to weight gain while also providing necessary amounts of micronutrients. Such a diet will help patients remain comfortable and heal properly. A poor diet, on the other hand, can make recovery significantly more difficult.

The energy needs of patients can vary widely. Generally, energy needs are directly related to a person's weight and inversely related to age; it's also generally true that men require more calories than women. Thus, a thirty-five-year-old woman who weighs 135 pounds will require around 1800 calories a day, while an older woman would require fewer, and a heavier woman would require more. A man of the same age and weight would require 2000 calories a day.

Activity level also has a significant impact on a patient's energy needs. A bedridden patient will obviously expend fewer calories and thus will need to eat fewer. An elderly, bedridden women can need as little as 8.5 calories per pound of body weight: if such a patient weighed 135 pounds, she would need only 1150 calories a day. However, many patients, bedridden or otherwise, have hidden energy needs. The process of healing can be extremely energy intensive—even an immobile patient can use up vast reserves of calories as her body fights infection, knits a fracture, or heals bed sores. Patients on a low-energy diet may also develop deficiencies in micronutrients if the quality of their meals is not monitored closely.

→

CONTINUE

51. What is the main idea of the passage?

    A) Patients' diets should include a balance of macro- and micronutrients.

    B) Health care workers can determine how many calories patients need by looking at their weight, age, and activity level.

    C) Meeting the nutritional needs of patients is a complicated but vital responsibility of health care workers.

    D) Activity level of patients should be monitored closely to ensure that each patient receives the amount of macronutrients he or she requires to heal properly.

52. Which of the following is not a fact stated in the passage?

    A) Patients require energy from carbohydrates, fats, and proteins as well as essential vitamins and elements to heal properly.

    B) A bedridden patient may require extra calories to provide the body with energy to fuel the healing process.

    C) A poor diet can delay healing in patients.

    D) Female patients should receive fewer calories than male patients so they don't gain weight.

53. According to the passage, which of the patients described below would likely need to consume the most calories per day?

    A) an elderly man on bed rest

    B) a young, overweight man undergoing physical therapy for a broken leg

    C) an elderly man with chronic bed sores

    D) a young, underweight man recovering from a respiratory infection

54. Which of the following is not a detail stated in the passage?

    A) A thirty-five-year-old woman who weighs 135 pounds would require at least 2000 calories a day.

    B) Patients' energy needs vary directly with weight and inversely with age.

    C) Carbohydrates, fats, and proteins are macronutrients.

    D) An elderly, bedridden female patient can require as little as 8.5 calories per pound of body weight.

55. What is the meaning of the word *hidden* in the last paragraph?

    A) intentionally kept out of sight

    B) not obvious to the casual observer

    C) easily forgotten

    D) masked by outside complications

Vocabulary

1. Which of the following statements uses a euphemism?

   A) He passed away last week.

   B) He died yesterday.

   C) The baby was born last month.

   D) The dog ran away but was found after two days.

2. Saving money may be smart, but she thought he was too <u>frugal</u>. Select the meaning of the underlined word.

   A) wealthy

   B) poor

   C) thrifty

   D) lavish

3. Which word means *happiness*?

   A) exemplary

   B) exuberance

   C) excitement

   D) expansion

4. Their divorce was especially <u>acrimonious</u>. Select the meaning of the underlined word.

   A) easy

   B) lengthy

   C) pleasant

   D) bitter

5. Which of the following words is a synonym of *sad*?

   A) morose

   B) acerbic

   C) irate

   D) jovial

6. Which of these words is not spelled correctly?

   A) affect

   B) loose

   C) definately

   D) irritable

7. What is the best description of *they're*?

   A) contraction

   B) conjunction

   C) preposition

   D) subject

8. What is the best description of *quickly*?

   A) adjective

   B) interjection

   C) adverb

   D) verb

9. Which word that means *hurried* best fits? She didn't want to be late, so she _____ to work.

   A) scurried

   B) accelerated

   C) expedited

   D) rushed

10. Select the word or phrase that will be grammatically correct.

    They completed _____ homework on time.

    A) there

    B) they're

    C) their

    D) them

11. What is the best description of *upon*?

    A) noun

    B) preposition

    C) adjective

    D) subject

12. Which word means *lethargic*?

    A) tired

    B) confused

    C) angry

    D) rushed

13. Select the correct order of words.

    A) The old car was in the shop for repairs.

    B) For repairs, the old car was in the shop.

    C) The car old was for repairs in the shop.

    D) In the shop, the old car was for repairs.

14. The lecture was <u>ponderous,</u> and many of the students found themselves dozing off during class. Select the meaning of the underlined word.

    A) interesting

    B) boring

    C) exciting

    D) difficult

15. Which word that means *young* fits best in this sentence?

    The _____ animals learned to hunt alongside their mothers.

    A) immature

    B) naïve

    C) baby

    D) juvenile

16. Which word is not spelled correctly?

    A) alot

    B) allot

    C) allocate

    D) allotment

17. Select the meaning of the underlined word.

    The holiday bonuses were a <u>boon</u> for many families.

    A) loss

    B) challenge

    C) joy

    D) blessing

18. Which word that means angry best fits the sentence? He was _____ after being cut off in traffic.

    A) irate

    B) ecstatic

    C) forlorn

    D) cataclysmic

19. Select the word or phrase that will be grammatically correct. _____ best friend's birthday is tomorrow.

    A) your

    B) you are

    C) you're

    D) the

20. Which word means *learned*?

    A) absorbed

    B) taught

    C) remembered

    D) acquainted

21. Which word is not spelled correctly?

    A) argument

    B) arguement

    C) agreement

    D) aggravation

22. Which word is not spelled correctly?

    A) judgment

    B) jurisdictian

    C) judiciary

    D) judicial

23. Which word is not a synonym for *excited*?

    A) exhilarated

    B) enthusiastic

    C) thrilled

    D) exhausted

24. Select the meaning of the underlined word. He was <u>anxious</u> about the test results.

A) angry

B) sad

C) happy

D) worried

25. Select the word or phrase that will be grammatically correct in the sentence.

The child was _____ cold, so he asked his mother for his jacket.

A) very

B) not

C) too much

D) not much

26. Select the correct order of words.

A) She wanted him to read her a story.

B) She wanted to read a story by him.

C) She wanted her a story read by him.

D) She wanted a read story by him.

27. Which word is not spelled correctly?

A) pharmacy

B) medical

C) medecine

D) medication

28. Which word means *mistake*?

A) error

B) correction

C) accuracy

D) review

29. Select the word or phrase that is grammatically correct. I've been in nursing school _____ six months.

A) since

B) after

C) before

D) for

30. Which word is a synonym for *tired*?

A) energetic

B) driven

C) fatigued

D) melancholy

31. Select the correct order of words.

A) Into the hospital, checked the patient.

B) The patient checked into the hospital.

C) Checked into the hospital the patient.

D) The hospital checked into the patient.

32. Which word means *illness*?

A) injury

B) ailment

C) irritation

D) symptom

33. Which word is a synonym for *disease*?

A) unease

B) malady

C) seizure

D) hemorrhage

34. Select the word or phrase that will be grammatically correct. The doctor _____ the patient yesterday on rounds.

A) seen

B) saw

C) sees

D) will see

35. Select the meaning of the underlined word. <u>Tardiness</u> is not tolerated, and you will be counted absent.

A) illness

B) absence

C) lateness

D) attendance

36. Which of the following words is a synonym of *contagious*?

A) transmissible

B) poisonous

C) noncommunicable

D) venereal

37. Select the meaning of the underlined word.

The staff was concerned about a <u>rash</u> of flu cases at the hospital.

A) epidemic

B) irritation

C) disease

D) symptom

38. Select the meaning of the underlined word.

The patient complained of <u>bilateral</u> weakness.

A) right side

B) left side

C) both sides

D) upper body

39. Select the meaning of the underlined word. Since the two could not get along at the office, they were referred for <u>mediation</u>.

A) relaxation

B) medication

C) arbitration

D) arguments

40. Select the meaning of the underlined word. Careful hand washing is an essential <u>precaution</u> in the workplace.

A) measure

B) cause

C) prevarication

D) rule

41. Select the meaning of the underlined word.

The change in the patient's condition was <u>sudden</u>.

A) slow

B) insignificant

C) unexpected

D) consistent

42. Select the meaning of the underlined word.

Many medical tests should be scheduled <u>annually</u>.

A) every year

B) every month

C) every other year

D) every decade

43. Select the meaning of the underlined word.

Chest congestion may be <u>audible</u> when you examine the patient.

A) severe

B) able to be heard

C) mild

D) able to be seen

44. Select the meaning of the underlined word.

In many cases, the other senses can <u>compensate</u> for the loss of one sense.

A) worsen

B) improve

C) offset

D) acclimate

45. Select the meaning of the underlined word.

Bronchitis and ear infections are possible <u>complications</u> of the common cold.

A) developments

B) benefits

C) infections

D) panaceas

46. Select the meaning of the underlined word.

When you're cooking, it's important to get the <u>consistency</u> of the sauce correct.

A) color

B) shape

C) viscosity

D) fluidity

47. Select the meaning of the underlined word.

Allergies are a possible <u>contraindication</u> for some medications.

A) prescription

B) reason

C) reason not to take

D) medical need

48. Select the meaning of the underlined word.

Vitamin and mineral <u>deficiencies</u> can cause a number of symptoms.

A) insufficiencies

B) abundance

C) excess

D) tablets

49. Select the meaning of the underlined word.

The patient complains that his symptoms are <u>worsening</u>.

A) improving

B) gone

C) intensifying

D) changing

50. Select the meaning of the underlined word.

The pupils should <u>dilate</u> in low light.

A) expand

B) decrease

C) brighten

D) shine

51. Which word is a synonym for *slow*?

A) languid

B) fatigued

C) immobile

D) weary

52. Select the meaning of the underlined word.

Do not leave the door to the office <u>ajar</u>.

A) closed

B) locked

C) latched

D) open

53. Select the meaning of the underlined word.

<u>Terrified</u> of heights, he tried not to look down as he crossed the narrow bridge.

A) wary

B) fond

C) full

D) scared

54. What is the best description of the underlined word?

She <u>goes</u> to class on Saturdays.

A) subject

B) verb

C) noun

D) adverb

55. Select the meaning of the underlined word.

It was her turn to <u>supervise</u> the children on the playground.

A) teach

B) watch

C) play with

D) release

CONTINUE

1. Which word from the following sentence is a conjunction?

   We went to the grocery store, stopped for coffee, and picked up our dry cleaning.

   A) our

   B) for

   C) and

   D) to

2. Select the best word for the blank in the following sentence.

   You need to get up now in order ___ make it to class on time.

   A) for

   B) to

   C) when

   D) of

3. Which of the following sentences is grammatically incorrect?

   A) Who goes to school on South Street.

   B) The boy goes to school on South Street.

   C) The girl attends the South Street School.

   D) Which of the children go to school on South Street?

4. Which of the following sentences is grammatically correct?

   A) The boy started school yesterday.

   B) The boy starts school yesterday.

   C) The boy started school tomorrow.

   D) The boy did start school tomorrow.

5. Select the best word for the blank in the following sentence.

   Please _____ your mom today.

   A) calling

   B) calls

   C) called

   D) call

6. Which word from the following sentence is a conjunction?

   Did you go to class, or did you stay home sick today?

   A) Did

   B) stay

   C) today

   D) or

7. Select the best word for the blank in the following sentence.

   The flight _____, so we will have to wait at the airport.

   A) delays

   B) delayed

   C) is delayed

   D) will delay

8. Which of the following sentences is grammatically incorrect?

   A) Monitors track the patient's heart rate and oxygen levels.

   B) Monitor track the patient's heart rate and oxygen levels.

   C) You should carefully monitor the patient's vital signs.

   D) Watch the monitors from the nurses' station.

9. Which of the following sentences is grammatically correct?

   A) I need to do my homework now, so I can go to the movie now.

   B) I need to do my homework now, so I cannot go to the movie now.

   C) I need to doing my homework now, so I cannot go to the movie now.

   D) I need to do my homework now, so I cannot going to the movie now.

10. Which word from the following sentence is a noun?

The puppy's favorite toy is pink and fuzzy.

A) pink

B) fuzzy

C) favorite

D) toy

11. Which word from the following sentence is the subject?

The bell will ring in five minutes.

A) bell

B) five

C) will

D) ring

12. Which of the following sentences is grammatically correct?

A) You can have either the cake nor the cookie.

B) You can't have neither the cake or the cookie.

C) You can have either the cake or the cookie.

D) You can having either the cake or the cookie.

13. Which word from the following sentence is a noun?

Put the groceries on the table, please.

A) table

B) Put

C) please

D) on

14. Which word from the following sentence is a preposition?

He checked into the hospital early that morning for his surgery.

A) checked

B) He

C) into

D) hospital

15. Which of the following sentences is grammatically correct?

A) Who is going to class on Saturday.

B) Who is goes to class on Saturday?

C) Whose going to class on Saturday?

D) Who is going to class on Saturday?

16. Which word from the following sentence is a subject?

After the children finished painting, they had to clean up their mess.

A) mess

B) painting

C) finished

D) they

17. Which word from the following sentence is a subject?

She popped popcorn, grabbed a drink, and sat down to watch her favorite show.

A) She

B) popcorn

C) drink

D) show

18. Select the best word for the blank in the following sentence.

_____ you want to work in home health care after graduation?

A) Does

B) Do

C) Was

D) Doing

19. Which word in the following sentence is incorrect?

The members of the team, all of whom played good in the game last night, are having a celebratory dinner.

A) team

B) whom

C) good

D) are

20. Select the best word or phrase for the blank in the following sentence.

She _____ a doctor's appointment in the morning, so she was late to work that day.

A) has

B) had

C) will have

D) was

21. Which of the following sentences is grammatically correct?

A) The baby is due in December.

B) The baby dues in December.

C) The babies is due in December.

D) The baby are due in December.

22. Which word from the following sentence is a direct object?

She finished decorating the kitchen for the party early that morning.

A) morning

B) She

C) kitchen

D) early

23. Which word from the following sentence is a direct object?

He was scheduled to work a long shift.

A) shift

B) He

C) long

D) work

24. Which of the following sentences is grammatically correct?

A) I learned to write good working at the paper.

B) I learned to write well working at the paper.

C) I teached to write well working at the paper.

D) I learned to write well working to the paper.

25. Which of the following sentences is grammatically incorrect?

A) The librarian at the reference desk is very helpful.

B) The reference desk librarian is very helpful.

C) Is the reference desk librarian helpful?

D) Can the reference desk librarian helpful?

26. In the following sentence, which is the dependent clause?

The librarian who works on Saturday had to leave early because she wanted to see a play.

A) The librarian who works on Saturday

B) had to leave early

C) because she wanted to see a play

D) The librarian who works on Saturday had to leave early

27. In the following sentence, which is the dependent clause?

Although we left the baseball game early, we still got stuck in heavy traffic.

A) Although we left the baseball game early

B) we left

C) we still got stuck in heavy traffic

D) in heavy traffic

28. Which of the following sentences is grammatically correct?

A) The baseball game was canceled because of rain.

B) The baseball game will canceled because of rain.

C) The baseball game was cancel because of rain.

D) The baseball games was canceled because to rain.

29. Which word or phrase from the following sentence is the predicate?

The boy threw the ball across the field.

A) The boy

B) threw the ball across the field

C) across the field

D) The boy threw the ball

30. Which of the following sentences is grammatically incorrect?

A) The dance was scheduled for next Saturday night.

B) The dance is scheduled for next Saturday night.

C) Schedule the dance for next Saturday night.

D) Scheduling the dance for next Saturday night.

31. Which word or phrase from the following sentence is the predicate?

Michelle and her dog walk in the park every day.

A) Michelle

B) Michelle and her dog

C) walk in the park every day

D) in the park every day

32. Which of the following sentences is grammatically correct?

A) I heard about the plane crash on the news.

B) I read about the plane crash on the news.

C) I heard on the plane crash on the news.

D) I hear about the plane crash to the news.

33. Which of the following sentences contains a predicate adjective?

A) Dinner smells amazing.

B) We are going to dinner.

C) He ate a sandwich.

D) The car has a leak in the radiator.

34. Which of the following sentences contains a predicate adjective?

A) The doctor is concerned about her symptoms.

B) I scheduled an appointment.

C) I have to work on Tuesday.

D) He bought a new phone.

35. What word is best to substitute for the blank in the following sentence?

Although both girls enjoyed the movie, _____ decided not to see it again.

A) she

B) we

C) they

D) her

36. Which of the following sentences is grammatically incorrect?

A) Nurses may work in the home, doctor's office, or hospital.

B) Nurses works in the home, doctor's office, or hospital.

C) Nurses can work in the home, doctor's office, or hospital.

D) Nurses may work in either the home, doctor's office, or hospital.

37. What word is best to substitute for the underlined word in the following sentence?

The ambulance took the patient to the hospital after he called 911.

A) brought

B) accompanied

C) assisted

D) went

38. Select the word in the sentence that is not used correctly.

He swimmed across the lake last summer.

A) across

B) lake

C) swimmed

D) summer

39. Select the word in the sentence that is not used correctly.

Neither the dog or the cat like going to the vet.

A) Neither

B) like

C) going

D) or

40. Select the best word or phrase for the blank in the following sentence.

I _____ never going to work there.

A) am not

B) will

C) will not

D) am

41. Which of the following sentences is grammatically incorrect?

A) Take the patient into the examining room.

B) Takes the patient into the examining room.

C) You should take the patient into the examining room.

D) He takes the patient into the examining room.

42. The following sentence contains which part of speech or can be described in which way?

The butcher, who has his own shop, is known for the quality of his meat.

A) prepositional phrase

B) adverb

C) compound sentence

D) conjunction

43. Select the best word for the blank in the following sentence.

_____ you planning to attend the meeting?

A) Is

B) Are

C) Will

D) Was

44. Which of the following sentences is grammatically incorrect?

A) I checked the patient's vital signs and entered them into the computer.

B) I changed into scrubs at the beginning of my shift.

C) The patient, who had surgery that day, was nervous.

D) The patients was prepped for surgery that morning.

45. The following sentence contains which type of phrase or clause?

We are baking cookies to take to the school bake sale.

A) dependent clause

B) prepositional phrase

C) predicate adjective

D) adverbial phrase

46. Select the best word for the blank in the following sentence.

Can you _____ on the patient in room 302?

A) watch

B) check

C) talk

D) care

47. Select the best word for the blank in the following sentence.

She was scared ___ spiders, so she avoided the basement.

A) to

B) for

C) of

D) from

48. Select the best word for the blank in the following sentence.

They were _____ for a new car to purchase.

A) looks

B) looking

C) wanting

D) shops

49. Select the best word for the blank in the following sentence.

I am waiting _____ the bus.

A) for

B) to

C) catch

D) catching

50. Select the best word or phrase for the blank in the following sentence.

I _____ overtime later this week, so I cannot go out tonight.

A) will work

B) am work

C) working

D) works

51. Select the best word for the blank in the following sentence.

_____ to school and study hard to do well in life.

A) Go

B) Goes

C) Going

D) Gone

52. Which of the following sentences is grammatically correct?

A) Take the dog of the vet.

B) You need to take the dog to the vet.

C) The dog need to go to the vet.

D) The dogs need to going to the vet.

53. Which of the following is grammatically incorrect?

A) Take the garbage to the curb.

B) You should take the garbage to the curb.

C) The garbage needs to go to the curb.

D) You takes the garbage to the curb.

54. Select the best word for the blank in the following sentence.

The hospital cafeteria opens _____ 8:00 a.m.

A) for

B) at

C) when

D) to

55. Which of the following sentences is grammatically correct?

A) My best friend and I has tickets to a concert on Friday.

B) My best friend and I have tickets to a concert on Friday.

C) Me and my best friend has tickets to a concert on Friday.

D) Me and my best friend have tickets to a concert on Friday.

CONTINUE

Biology

1. Which type of nutrient is broken down by trypsin?

    A) proteins

    B) fats

    C) sugars

    D) none of the above

2. Enzymes are created from amino acid chains. As such, what might prevent the action of an enzyme?

    A) a pH close to 7

    B) a high temperature

    C) the lack of hydrogen ions in solution

    D) a lack of ATP in the cell

3. If a scientist wants to determine the rate at which an enzyme works, what could he or she measure?

    A) the rate at which the enzyme is degraded

    B) the rate at which the product disappears

    C) the rate at which the reactants disappear

    D) the rate at which the products appear

4. Which of the following is true regarding deoxyribonucleic acid (DNA) in the human body?

    A) DNA is used as an energy source.

    B) DNA is used as a template for creation of proteins.

    C) DNA is only found in the brain.

    D) DNA is made of sugar.

5. How many kingdoms of life are there?

    A) 3

    B) 6

    C) 7

    D) 9

6. Plants absorb carbon dioxide (CO_2) to create sugar for energy. What is the primary by-product of this process?

    A) oxygen

    B) nitrogen

    C) carbon monoxide

    D) carbon

7. What prevents ultraviolet radiation produced by the sun from damaging life on earth?

    A) the ozone layer

    B) greenhouse gases

    C) the vacuum between earth and the sun

    D) the water layer

8. Which of the following is not present in an animal cell?

    A) nucleus

    B) mitochondria

    C) cytoplasm

    D) cell wall

9. Mitosis is the process of cell division to create new cells. What is the process of cell division required to create new sex cells, or gametes?

    A) telosis

    B) meiosis

    C) kinesis

    D) phoresis

10. Humans can turn glucose into ATP, the basic energy molecule in the body. What is a by-product of this process?

    A) carbon dioxide

    B) oxygen

    C) nitrogen

    D) phosphorus

11. Which of the following is not in the Kingdom Plantae?

    A) cactus

    B) algae

    C) oak tree

    D) sunflower

12. What is the primary difference between a cell membrane and a cell wall?

    A) A cell membrane is flexible, whereas a cell wall is rigid.

    B) A cell membrane is not found in plants, whereas a cell wall is.

    C) A cell membrane is not found in animals, whereas a cell wall is.

    D) A cell membrane is composed of protein, whereas a cell wall is composed of sugar.

13. When determining the mass of an ant, you should use

    A) meters

    B) grams

    C) liters

    D) kilograms

14. Plants are autotrophs, meaning that:

    A) They consume organic material produced by animals.

    B) They produce their own food.

    C) They can move by themselves.

    D) They can automatically transform from a seed into a plant.

15. Which of the following is not true of a virus?

    A) Viruses have DNA.

    B) Viruses do not have a nucleus.

    C) Viruses cannot survive without water.

    D) Viruses can be infectious.

16. How many pairs of human chromosomes exist?

    A) 17

    B) 13

    C) 23

    D) 29

17. Which of the following can be found in abundance in a fatigued muscle?

    A) glucose

    B) lactic acid

    C) ATP

    D) none of the above

18. What organ system contains your skin?

    A) the respiratory system

    B) the integumentary system

    C) the lymphatic system

    D) the circulatory system

19. If a gene is expressed, then that means:

    A) It is influencing a phenotype trait.

    B) It is being copied into another set of DNA.

    C) It will be passed on from mother to son.

    D) The gene will produce some hormones.

20. Which of the following structures is found in eukaryotes but not in prokaryotes?

    A) a cell wall

    B) mitochondria

    C) proteins

    D) DNA

21. A mutation in DNA can be caused by which of the following:

    A) ultraviolet radiation

    B) chemical exposure

    C) DNA replication error

    D) all of the above

22. One of the primary differences between fungi and plants is that:

    A) Fungi can produce their own food and plants cannot.

    B) Plants have chlorophyll and fungi do not.

    C) Fungi can grow without water and plants cannot.

    D) Fungi and plants have no major differences.

23. Which of the following organisms is capable of asexual reproduction?

    A) squash plant

    B) amoeba

    C) salmon

    D) koala bear

24. Where are the cilia NOT found?

    A) in the bronchi

    B) in the alveoli

    C) in the upper airways

    D) fallopian tubes

25. Water is a unique molecule vital to life on earth. Which of the following properties is not a property of water that contributes to its usefulness?

    A) a high heat capacity

    B) a high surface tension

    C) its liquid state across a wide variety of temperatures

    D) its ability to degrade toxins

26. The Golgi body is responsible for

    A) protein synthesis

    B) packaging and transportation of proteins

    C) replication of DNA

    D) formation of ribosomes

27. A nucleosome is a structure of tightly packed DNA, allowing for eventual formation into chromatids. What are nucleosomes wrapped around?

    A) ribosomes

    B) DNA polymerase

    C) histones

    D) telomeres

28. If a recessive trait is linked to the X chromosome, where will it most likely be seen?

    A) males

    B) females

    C) both genders

    D) neither gender

29. Which of the following is not a carbohydrate?

    A) glycogen

    B) starch

    C) cellulose

    D) guanine

30. Although plant cells and animal cells are roughly the same size, the volume of cytosol inside an animal cell is significantly larger than that in a plant cell. What is responsible for this difference?

    A) the presence of chlorophyll in plant cells

    B) the presence of an endoplasmic reticulum in plant cells

    C) the presence of a large storage vacuole in plant cells

    D) the presence of a cell wall in plant cells

1. Which of the following is a true statement about the periodic table?

   A) The size of elements increases from right to left.

   B) The electron shell size increases from top to bottom.

   C) The electronegativity increases from top to bottom.

   D) The radioactivity of elements decreases from left to right.

2. A double bond between two atoms—for example, the double bond between oxygen in O_2—has how many electrons?

   A) 2

   B) 4

   C) 6

   D) 8

3. A 50 liter volume of water vapor is condensed into liquid. Approximately how much volume will the liquid be?

   A) less than 50 mL

   B) between 50 mL and 200 mL

   C) about 1 liter

   D) more than 1 liter

4. Which of the following is the process that produces a liquid from a gas?

   A) vaporization

   B) condensation

   C) sublimation

   D) denitrification

5. Chemical bonding

   A) uses electrons that are closest to the nucleus of the atoms bonding.

   B) always uses electrons from only one of the atoms involved.

   C) uses all the electrons in all atoms involved.

   D) uses the valence electrons of all the atoms involved.

6. Which of the following would have the most dramatic effect in changing the reaction rate?

   A) increasing the temperature twofold

   B) increasing the pressure twofold

   C) decreasing the activation energy threefold

   D) decreasing the concentration of reactants twofold

7. A student notices that a reaction has a reaction rate of 0. For this to be true, which of the following must be true?

   A) The activation energy must be lower than 0.

   B) The temperature is 0 Kelvin.

   C) The Arrhenius constant is 0.

   D) The reactants must be lower than 1 M in concentration.

8. In the graph below, showing reaction rate of the enzyme over time, what is the rate at 2 hours?

   A) 1

   B) 2.5

   C) 3

   D) 4.5

CONTINUE

9. What is true of elements found in the same group (column) in the periodic table?

   A) They have the same atomic mass.

   B) They have the same level of reactivity.

   C) They have the same number of protons.

   D) The have the same number of valence electrons.

10. Compounds that are acidic will be able to lower the pH of a solution by doing which of the following?

    A) accepting H+ ions

    B) releasing H+ ions

    C) binding with acidic species in solution

    D) reducing oxidative species in solution

11. Which of the following elements is the most electronegative?

    A) chlorine

    B) iron

    C) magnesium

    D) silicon

12. A scientist has isolated Fe (III), a variant of iron that has a charge of 3+. Which of the following compounds could be created from this element?

    A) FeO_2

    B) FeCl

    C) $FeCa_3$

    D) Fe_2O_3

13. What is the VSEPR structure of a PO4 (phosphate) molecule?

    A) tetrahedral

    B) octahedral

    C) linear

    D) trigonal biplanar

14. What type of reaction is the following?

    $CaCl_2 + 2NaOH \rightarrow Ca(OH)_2 + 2NaCl$

    A) single replacement

    B) double replacement

    C) synthesis

    D) acid base

15. What are the products of the following reaction?

    $NaOH + HCl \rightarrow$

    A) dihydrogen monoxide and sodium chloride

    B) sodium hydride and chlorohydroxide

    C) hydrochloride and sodium monohydroxide

    D) sodium chloride and sodium hydroxide

16. In the following chemical reaction, what is the correct stoichiometric coefficient for silicon dioxide?

    $4Si + 2O_2 \rightarrow Si + SiO_2$

    A) 1

    B) 2

    C) 3

    D) 4

17. When you notice that a chemical reaction equation is not balanced, which of the following can be performed to balance the equation?

    A) change the formula of the products

    B) change the subscripts of the molecular formulas

    C) change the coefficients of the reactants or products

    D) change the reaction type

18. A scientist places mercury oxide (HgO) into a sealed chamber and heats it to 400°C, causing a reaction to occur. When she opens the chamber, she notices liquid mercury has formed as well as oxygen gas. This reaction is a

A) endothermic synthesis reaction.

B) exothermic combustion reaction.

C) endothermic decomposition reaction.

D) exothermic replacement reaction.

19. Which of the following produces a gas from a solid?

A) melting

B) plasmification

C) condensation

D) sublimation

20. A student isolates a substance and succeeds in purifying it. She then puts it into the lab refrigerator at 4°C. When she comes back the next day, she notices that it has solidified. Which of the following statements should be true about the substance?

A) It has a melting point below 4°C.

B) It has a boiling point less than that of water.

C) It has a freezing point higher than that of water.

D) It has a vaporization point at around 90°C.

21. The specific heat of ethanol is about 2.3 J/g × K. If you want to heat 100g of ethanol from 25°C until its boiling point, and have it all be vaporized, how much energy do you need?

A) 5.45 kJ

B) 97.7 kJ

C) 12.2 kJ

D) 822 kJ

22. In our atmosphere, nitrogen is the most common element and makes up approximately what percentage?

A) 25%

B) 51%

C) 65%

D) 78%

23. Which of the following is correct regarding an aqueous substance?

A) It is soluble in water.

B) It is very reactive.

C) It is soluble in hydrocarbon.

D) It can dissolve most other compounds.

24. According to electron theory, what is the maximum number of bonds a carbon atom can have?

A) 2

B) 3

C) 4

D) 5

25. The temperature at which all molecular motion stops is

A) −460°C

B) −273 K

C) 0 K

D) 0°C

26. In a redox reaction, which of the following describes oxidation?

A) It is the loss of protons.

B) It is the gain of protons.

C) It is the loss of electrons.

D) It is the gain of electrons.

27. Which of the following transformations would have an energy change equal in magnitude but opposite in sign?

A) melting and vaporization

B) sublimation and vaporization

C) condensation and vaporization

D) condensation and sublimation

28. What is the charge on sodium in the compound NaOH?

A) −1

B) 0

C) 1

D) 2

29. What is a pH of 10?

A) acidic

B) basic

C) neutral

D) negative

30. What is $AgNO_3 + HCl \rightarrow HNO_3 + AgCl$ an example of?

A) combustion

B) single replacement

C) double replacement

D) synthesis

1. Blood is prevented from changing direction in the veins by:
   A) pressure from the heart
   B) valves
   C) suction from the heart
   D) none of the above

2. The liquid part of the blood is called:
   A) plasma
   B) blood fluid
   C) serous fluid
   D) none of the above

3. Blood cells that are responsible for transportation of oxygen are called:
   A) leukocytes
   B) thrombocytes
   C) erythrocytes
   D) none of the above

4. What is the thyroid cartilage commonly known as?
   A) vocal box
   B) Adam's apple
   C) vocal cords
   D) none of the above

5. When exhaling, the diaphragm:
   A) relaxes
   B) contracts
   C) does nothing
   D) none of the above

6. Which bone forms the rib cage of the thoracic region with the ribs?
   A) sternum
   B) fibula
   C) occipital bone
   D) none of the above

7. The humerus and ulna form the:
   A) shoulder joint
   B) elbow joint
   C) wrist joint
   D) none of the above

8. The patella is also called:
   A) breastbone
   B) kneecap
   C) finger bone
   D) none of the above

9. The bone that is stationary during the movement is called the:
   A) insertion
   B) agonist
   C) origin
   D) none of the above

10. How many origins does a quadriceps have?
    A) 4
    B) 5
    C) 3
    D) none of the above

11. Which part of the brain is responsible for higher brain functions?
    A) the pons
    B) the cerebral cortex
    C) the cerebellar cortex
    D) none of the above

12. How many thoracic spinal nerves are in the human body?
    A) 8
    B) 9
    C) 12
    D) none of the above

13. In which region of the small intestine are most of the nutrients absorbed?

   A) the jejunum

   B) the ileum

   C) the duodenum

   D) none of the above

14. Testes are an organ found in:

   A) females

   B) plants

   C) males

   D) amoebas

15. What are the two main parts of the human body's central nervous system?

   A) the heart and the spinal cord

   B) the brain and the spinal cord

   C) the peripheral nerves and the brain

   D) the spinal cord and the peripheral nerves

16. When measuring blood pressure, the numbers represent:

   A) the systolic and diastolic pressures, respectively

   B) the diastolic and systolic pressures, respectively

   C) the pressure in the arteries and the veins, respectively

   D) none of the above

17. The superior vena cava:

   A) ascends from the right atrium

   B) ascends from the left atrium

   C) descends from the right atrium

   D) none of the above

18. The rectum is a part of:

   A) the anus

   B) the large intestine

   C) the small intestine

   D) none of the above

19. Where does digestion start?

   A) the stomach

   B) the small intestine

   C) the mouth

   D) none of the above

20. The large intestine mainly:

   A) absorbs water

   B) digests food

   C) moves the food from the esophagus to the small intestine

   D) none of the above

21. What is the name of the process that happens in the red bone marrow?

   A) hematopoiesis

   B) bone fusing

   C) calcification

   D) none of the above

22. The vertebral column protects the:

   A) brain

   B) heart

   C) spinal column

   D) none of the above

23. In the digestive system, the majority of nutrients are absorbed in the:

   A) esophagus

   B) stomach

   C) small intestine

   D) large intestine

24. What are the motor units made of?

   A) motor neurons

   B) muscle cells

   C) tendons

   D) none of the above

25. What is the name of a state of constant muscle contraction caused by rapid successive nerve signals?

    A) tetanus

    B) muscle tone

    C) temporal summation

    D) none of the above

26. Where does integration happen?

    A) ANS

    B) CNS

    C) PNS

    D) none of the above

27. Which part of the PNS is accountable for the fight or flight reaction?

    A) the parasympathetic

    B) the sympathetic

    C) the ENS

    D) none of the above

28. People who suffer from Type I diabetes are lacking function in which organ?

    A) liver

    B) pancreas

    C) stomach

    D) heart

29. In the human body, which of the following is responsible for clotting blood?

    A) platelets

    B) white blood cells

    C) red blood cells

    D) osteoplasts

30. The tidal volume is the amount of air moved during:

    A) deep breathing

    B) shallow breathing

    C) coughing

    D) none of the above

Physics

1. Which of the following quantities is a vector?

   A) 37 seconds

   B) 23 kilometers; east

   C) 178°F

   D) 1500 calories

2. A car travels with a constant speed of 40 mph for 15 minutes. How far does the car travel in this time?

   A) 10 miles

   B) 2.7 miles

   C) 0.375 miles

   D) 40 miles

3. A car has an initial velocity of 13.4 m/s. The car then slows to a speed of 2.8 m/s over 30 seconds. What was the car's acceleration during this period?

   A) 0.35 m/s^2

   B) 0.54 m/s^2

   C) 318 m/s^2

   D) 486 m/s^2

4. A 10 kg person travels to the moon, which has a smaller acceleration than the Earth due to gravity. What will happen to the person's mass?

   A) The person's mass will decrease.

   B) The person's mass will stay the same.

   C) The person's mass will increase.

   D) It cannot be determined from this information.

5. What force is required to accelerate a 10 kg object from rest to 10 m/s in 5 seconds?

   A) 15 N

   B) 20 N

   C) 100 N

   D) 500 N

6. If an object is launched from the roof of a building at an angle of 30°, which of the following statements is true? (Assume there is no air resistance.)

   A) The horizontal acceleration of the object is positive.

   B) The vertical acceleration of the object is positive while the object moves up and negative while the object moves down.

   C) The vertical acceleration of the object is always negative.

   D) The vertical acceleration of the object in the horizontal direction is zero.

7. The velocity of a projectile shot straight up at its maximum height is:

   A) greater than the initial speed of projection.

   B) the maximum velocity for the entire trajectory.

   C) the minimum velocity for the entire trajectory.

   D) between its maximum and minimum velocities.

8. A ball is thrown in a horizontal direction with a velocity of 40 m/s. If it was thrown from a height of 4.8 m, how far from its starting point will it strike the ground?

   A) 10 m

   B) 20 m

   C) 40 m

   D) 80 m

9. Which of the following would have the greatest momentum if they were all moving at the same velocity?

   A) a fly

   B) an elephant

   C) an airplane

   D) a car

10. An object is experiencing an upward force of 45 N and a downward force of 12 N. What is the net force on the object?

A) 3.75 N

B) 12 N

C) 33 N

D) 57 N

11. What is the momentum of an object with a mass of 15 kg moving with a velocity of magnitude 10 m/s in the −y direction?

A) 15 kg m/s

B) 150 kg m/s

C) −15 kg m/s

D) −150 kg m/s

12. What is the kinetic energy of a bullet with as mass of 0.5 g traveling with a velocity of 215 m/s?

A) 54 J

B) 108 J

C) 11, 556 J

D) 23,112 J

13. What is the potential energy of a 50 kg boulder that rests on a cliff 250 m high?

A) 12,500 J

B) 61,250 J

C) 122,500 J

D) 30,625,000 J

14. The ratio of the momentum of two particles with the same kinetic energy is

A) 1 : 4

B) 1 : 3

C) 1 : 2

D) 1 : 5

15. Which of the following statement is true concerning an object undergoing simple harmonic motion, such as a mass on the end of a spring?

A) The kinetic energy of the system is zero at the midpoint of the motion.

B) The potential energy of the system is always zero.

C) The velocity of the mass is constant during the motion.

D) The kinetic energy of the system reaches its maximum at the midpoint of the motion.

16. Which of the following statements is true about a negative point charge and the electric field it produces?

A) The magnitude of the electric field does not depend on the magnitude of the point charge, and the field is directed radially outward.

B) An electric field is not produced by a negative point charge.

C) The magnitude of the electric field depends on the magnitude of the point charge and increases as the distance from the point charge increases.

D) The magnitude of the electric field depends on the magnitude of the point charge, and the field is directed radially inward.

17. Which of the following statements about ideal conductors is not true?

A) The potential at every position on or within an ideal conductor is the same.

B) The potential at every position within an ideal conductor must be zero.

C) Any excess charge that an ideal conductor contains resides on its surface when in equilibrium.

D) The electric field within an ideal conductor is zero.

18. Which of the following is an example of a longitudinal wave?

   A) a wave on a string

   B) a light wave

   C) a sound wave

   D) ripples in a pond

19. A 1 kΩ resistor is attached to a 1.5 V battery. What will be the current through the resistor?

   A) 0.0015 A

   B) 0.15 A

   C) 15 A

   D) 150 A

20. Three 15 ohm resistors are wired in series. What voltage is required to produce a current of 2.5 amp in the wire?

   A) 18.0 V

   B) 37.5 V

   C) 112.5 V

   D) 8437.5 V

21. A wave with a frequency of 44 Hz is traveling at a speed of 10 m/s. What is the wave's wavelength?

   A) 0.23 m

   B) 4.4 m

   C) 54 m

   D) 440 m

22. Which of the following requires a medium to travel?

   A) visible light

   B) microwaves

   C) radio waves

   D) sound

23. Two waves with amplitudes of 9.2 m and 2.1 m experience constructive interference. What will be the amplitude of the resulting wave?

   A) 4.4 m

   B) 7.1 m

   C) 11.3 m

   D) 19.3 mD

24. According to Newton's first law, F = M × A, how fast will a 10 kilogram object accelerate when pushed with 50 newtons of force?

   A) 2.5 m/s^2

   B) 5.0 m/s^2

   C) 8.0 m/s^2

   D) 15.0 m/s^2

25. Upon touching a chair cushion and then a metal plate, John notices that the metal plate feels much colder than the cushion, although the surrounding air temperature is the same. What is an explanation for this?

   A) The chair cushion has a higher heat capacity than the metal plate.

   B) The metal plate has a higher heat transfer rate than the chair cushion.

   C) The metal plate can absorb more heat from the air than the cushion.

   D) The chair cushion produces some internal heat.

26. If a pitcher throws a baseball into the air and notices that it takes 5 seconds to reach its peak, how long will the baseball need to fall back to the ground? Neglect air resistance.

   A) 2.5 seconds

   B) 9.8 seconds

   C) 5.0 seconds

   D) 10.0 seconds

27. Which unit of measurement is not used in the International System of Units?

    A) centimeters

    B) milliliters

    C) grams

    D) inches

28. In order for work to be performed, a force has to be:

    A) applied to an object

    B) applied to a surface

    C) applied to a moving object

    D) applied over a distance to an object

29. If a rowboat weighs 50 kilograms, how much water needs to be displaced for the boat to float?

    A) 25 liters

    B) 50 liters

    C) 100 liters

    D) 500 liters

30. A ball with a mass of 0.5 kg is moving at 10 m/s. How much kinetic energy does it have?

    A) 15 Joules

    B) 25 Joules

    C) 50 Joules

    D) 55.5 Joules

ANSWER KEY

Mathematics

1. B)

Remember the order of operations (PEMDAS) to solve this question. First of all, solve the parenthesis and then the exponents. In this particular question, 43 + 2 comes first, which equals 45. Now, the expression becomes (45 − 1). Then, subtract 1 from 45. As there is no exponent in this equations, this results in 44.

2. C)

Remember the order of operations (PEMDAS) to solve this question. First of all, solve the parenthesis and then the exponents. In this particular question, 72 − 23 comes first, which equals 49. Now, the expression becomes (49 − 6). Then, subtract 6 from 49. As there is no exponent in this equations, this results in 43.

3. D)

Adding 20% is equivalent to paying 120% of the bill:

$$\$48.30 \times \frac{120}{100} = \$57.96$$

4. D)

A rational number is the one which can be written in the form of a simple fraction. Observing cly, only option (D) gives a number which cannot be written in the form of a fraction.

5. C)

You are asked to round this given number to the nearest hundredth. Considering the numbers on the right of the decimal, the answer is 1230.93.

6. B)

The absolute value of any negative number gives the positive of that same number, i.e., absolute value of −9 is +9.

7. C)

There are two ways to solve this question. First, you can add all the given numbers and find the exact answer. This method is time consuming and is less efficient.

Second, you can add only the numbers on the left of the decimal and then compare your answer with the answer choices that you are given. We add 45, 32, and 31 to get 45 + 32 + 31 = 108. Now, we can easily interpret that our answer must be very close to 108 when we also add the decimal points for each given number. In the answer choices, only option (C) is a number that is close to 108. (Note that this method of approximation saves time, but it is not very accurate if all the answer choices are very close to each other.)

8. B)

This is a very simple question. All you need to know is the PEMDAS rule. First of all, solve what is within the parenthesis and then multiply the answers of each parenthesis.

9 divided by 3 equals 3.

8 divided by 4 equals 2.

Multiply 3 and 2 to get the final answer:
$3 \times 2 = 6$.

9. B)

It's a simple division question. When you divide 7.95 by 1.5, you get 5.3.

To confirm your answer, you can cross-check by multiplying 5.3 by 1.5, producing 7.95.

10. C)

Use the area to find the length of a side of the square:

$A = l \times w = l^2$

$5,625 \text{ ft}^2 = l^2$

$l = \sqrt{5,625 \text{ ft}^2} = 75 \text{ ft}$

Now, multiply the side length by 4 to find the perimeter:

$P = 4l$

$P = 4(75 \text{ ft}) = 300 \text{ ft}$

11. C)

From the given information in the question, you know that 25% of the actual price of the desk is $45. Writing this in the form of an equation, it becomes:

$\left(\frac{25}{100}\right) \times x = \$45$ (25% of x equals $45)

$x = \frac{45}{0.25} \rightarrow \$180$

Therefore, the actual price of the desk equals $180.

12. B)

To find 5% of 2000, multiply 2000 by $\frac{5}{100}$,
i.e., $2000 \times 0.05 = 100$

13. B)

First, take the additional 30% off the clearance price:

$\$65.00 \times \frac{70}{100} = \$45.50$

Next, find what percentage of $85.00 is $45.50:

$\frac{\$45.50}{\$85.00} = \frac{x}{100}$

$(\$45.50)(100) = (\$85.00)(x)$

$x = \frac{(\$45.50)(100)}{\$85.00} = 53.5$

Angie is paying 53.5% of the original price, which means she received a $100\% - 53.5\% = 46.5\%$ discount.

14. D)

From the statement of the question, it is clear that a ribbon that is at least 26 inches long (i.e., 22 inch head and 4 inches for knot) but not longer than 28 inches is needed.

Examine the length of strings available in the answer options.

Option A) = 2 feet = 24 inches Incorrect

Option B) = $2\frac{3}{4}$ feet = 33 inches Incorrect

Option C) = $3\frac{5}{8}$ feet = 31.5 inches Incorrect

Option D) = $2\frac{1}{3}$ feet = 28 inches Correct

15. D)

The money Jane earns is equal to $15 times the number of hours she babysits:

$15h$

The total money in Jane's bank account is equal to the money she started with plus the money she earns:

$275 + 15h$

Set this expression equal to $400:

$400 = 275 + 15h$

16. D)

First, convert everything to kilograms:

$800 \text{ g} \times \frac{1 \text{ kg}}{1000 \text{ g}} = 0.8 \text{ kg}$

$300 \text{ g} \times \frac{1 \text{ kg}}{1000 \text{ g}} = 0.3 \text{ kg}$

Next, find the total weight:

$1.2 \text{ kg} + 0.8 \text{ kg} + 0.3 \text{ kg} = 2.3 \text{ kg}$

Now, find the total cost by multiplying by $4/kg:

$2.3 \text{ kg} \times \frac{\$4}{1 \text{ kg}} = \$9.20$

17. C)

The pie requires $\frac{3}{8} = 0.375$ cup of sugar, whereas cupcakes require $\frac{3}{5} = 0.6$ cup of sugar. This makes a total of $0.375 + 0.6 = 0.975$ cup of sugar.

Leslie has $\frac{15}{16} = 0.9375$ cup of sugar.

Therefore, it is clear that Leslie needs more sugar than she already has. The exact amount of sugar the pie required can be calculated by subtracting total sugar from required sugar, i.e.:

$0.975 - 0.9375 = 0.0375$

18. A)

Rewrite the given equation as:

$|3x + 2| = 5$

$+ (3x + 2) = 5$ or $-(3x + 2) = 5$

$3x = 5 - 2$ or $-3x - 2 = 5$

$x = 1$ or $x = -\frac{7}{3}$

Therefore, $(1, -\frac{7}{3})$.

19. D)

The given equation can be rewritten as:

$\frac{|2k + 4|}{8} = 2 \rightarrow |2k + 4| = 16$

$+ (2k + 4) = 16 \rightarrow 2k = 12 \rightarrow k = 6$

Or, $-(2k + 4) = 16 \rightarrow -2k - 4 = 16 \rightarrow -2k = 20 \rightarrow k = -10$

Therefore, $k = -10, 6$.

20. C)

Consider the given inequality:

$\frac{2x + 7}{9} < 2$

Multiply by 9 on both sides:

$2x + 7 < 18$

Subtract 7 on both sides:

$2x < 18 - 7$

$2x < 11$

Divide by 2 on both sides:

$x < \frac{11}{2}$

21. A)

This question looks like a lengthy multiplication question, but actually it's not. You know that $25 \times 5 = 125$. Similarly, $7 \times 2 = 14$. This means that the denominators of all the fractions are canceled out by numerators of second and third fractions, and you are left with only $4 \times 4 = 16$.

22. B)

A simple trick in solving these complex fraction-multiplication questions is to look for the numbers that can cancel each other. For example, in this given question, we see that $3 \times 3 = 9$, which cancels the 9 of the denominator.

Similarly, $\frac{125}{25} = \frac{5}{1} = 5$.

The net result of this multiplication after cancelation of numerators and denominators becomes:

$\frac{2}{6} \times 5 \times \frac{1}{10} = \frac{1}{6}$ or $\frac{5}{30}$

23. C)

Adding the given fractions, we get:

$\frac{1(5) + 4}{25} \rightarrow \frac{5 + 4}{25} \rightarrow \frac{9}{25}$

24. D)

There were a total of 8 slices of pizza, which means that each slice was $\frac{1}{8}$ of the total pizza. Alan ate 3 slices, i.e., $\frac{1}{8} + \frac{1}{8} + \frac{1}{8} = \frac{3}{8}$.

Remaining pizza $= 1 - \frac{3}{8} \rightarrow \frac{8 - 3}{8} \rightarrow \frac{5}{8}$

25. B)

Finding the sum of the expressions in the parenthesis first, you get:

$\left(\frac{3}{4} + \frac{1}{5}\right) \rightarrow \frac{15 + 4}{20} = \frac{19}{20}$

$\left(\frac{2}{3} + \frac{3}{2}\right) \rightarrow \frac{4 + 9}{6} \rightarrow \frac{13}{6}$

Now, $\frac{19}{20} - \frac{13}{6} = \frac{19(6) - 13(20)}{120} \rightarrow \frac{-146}{120} \rightarrow \frac{-73}{60}$

26. C)

Finding the difference of fractions given in the parenthesis first, you get:

$\frac{5}{6} - \frac{1}{2} = \frac{5 - (3)}{6} = \frac{2}{6} = \frac{1}{3}$

Now, $\frac{2}{9} + \frac{1}{3} \rightarrow \frac{2 + 3}{9} \rightarrow \frac{5}{9}$

27. C)

Considering the given inequality:

$3x > 5 - 2$

$3x > 3$

$x > 1$

28. B)

157 (correct: C = 100, L = 50, V = 5, I = 1)

29. D)

Simplify the following expression:

$5\frac{1}{3} - 21/3$

$5.33 - 2.33 = 3$

30. C)

Answer is $6\frac{3}{4}$

$5\frac{1}{4} + 1\frac{1}{2} = 6 + \frac{1}{4} + \frac{2}{4} = 6\frac{3}{4}$

31. C)

$0.28 = \frac{28}{100}$

The lowest common denominator is 4.

$\frac{28}{4} = 7$

$\frac{100}{4} = 25$

$= \frac{7}{25}$

32. D)

5 divided by 20 equals .25.

33. A)

The question is straightforward, but the exact dollar amounts are a little more difficult to interpret. Since the question asks for *approximately* how much, you know we have a little wiggle room, and the answer choices will not be very similar. So if you see one that is possibly right, you have your answer.

In 2003, the profit was just a little bit under $4 million, so we know it is about 3.8 or 3.9. In 2004, the profit jumps to just over $6 million, so we know it is probably about 6.1 or 6.2.

In either case, 6.1 − 3.8 = 2.3, as does 6.2 − 3.9 = 2.3, so you know answer choice (A) is correct. Even if you arrived at an estimate of 6.2 − 3.8 = 2.4, that is certainly *approximate* for this exam.

34. B)

The question asks for the difference in profit between 2001 and 2000. In 2001, approximately $2.2 million was earned, and in 2000, approximately $1.2 million was earned.

2.2 − 1.2 = 1 million

35. D)

Remember the order of operations (PEMDAS) to solve this question. First of all, solve the parenthesis and then the exponents. In this particular question, 43 is within the parenthesis, so solve it first: 43 = 64.

Now, multiplying it by 2 to solve the parenthesis, it becomes 64 × 2 = 128.

So, the expression becomes 3 × 128 ÷ 4. Following PEMDAS, multiply 128 by 3, and then divide the answer by 4.

This results in 384 ÷ 4 = 96.

36. A)

This question also involves the order of operations (PEMDAS). To solve this question, solve the parenthesis first, and then multiply the answer by 1.

After that, add 5 to get our final answer. (5 × 3) = 15, so the expression becomes 15 × 1 + 5 = 15 + 5 = 20.

37. B)

First of all, we find the value of 53 to solve the parenthesis (remember the order of operations PEMDAS). You know that 53 = 5 × 5 × 5 = 125, so the expression becomes (125 + 7) × 2.

Solve the parenthesis first because it is given more preference in PEMDAS; it becomes 132 × 2.

Multiplying these two numbers, you get your final answer, which is 264.

38. C)

Substitute 5 for *x*:

$4(5) \div (5 - 1) = 20 \div 4 = 5$

39. C)

The 4 is in the tenths place. Because the number to the right of the 4 is 5 or greater, it will be rounded up to give 707.5.

40. A)

When you subtract 45.548 and 67.8807 from 134.679, you get 21.2503. Applying the rounding rules, you get 21.3 (note that you were asked to round up to the nearest tenth only).

41. D)

To find the median of any given list, first check if the numbers are arranged in ascending order. In this case, these given numbers are already arranged in order. Then, check if the total number of entries in the list is even or odd. Since the total number of entries in this list is 6, and 6 is an even number, the median of this list equals the average of two entries that are in the middle of this list, i.e.:

Median $\rightarrow \frac{(7 + 9)}{2 = 8}$

42. C)

Any number divided by 1 gives the same number as a result.

Therefore, $\frac{0.12}{1} = 0.12$.

43. D)

Anything multiplied by zero results in zero as the answer. You are multiplying 0 by 5 and 6, so the answer is still 0.

44. A)

Please note that it's a tricky question. The perimeter of the rectangular field is given as 44 yards, and the length of the field is given as 36 feet (units are different).

1 yard = 3 feet

44 yards = 132 feet

The perimeter of the rectangular field equals:

Perimeter = 2 × (length) + 2 × (width)

132 = 2(36) + 2 × width

Width = (132 − 72)/2 = 30 feet

45. A)

Find the area of all the sides of the shed. Two walls measure 5 feet by 7 feet; the other two walls measure 4 feet by 7 feet:

$A = 2l_1w_1 + 2l_2w_2$

$A = 2(5\text{ ft})(7\text{ ft}) + 2(4\text{ ft})(7\text{ ft})$

$A = 70\text{ ft}^2 + 56\text{ ft}^2 = 126\text{ ft}^2$

46. D)

Let's suppose that the unknown number is x. So, 35% of x is equal to 70. Write this in the form of an equation:

$(35 \div 100) \times x = 70$

$x = \frac{70}{0.35}$

$x = 200$

47. B)

First of all, you should know that 25% profit on the actual price means that we have multiplied the original price by 1.25: (1 + 0.25).

So, to find the actual price of the SUV, we divide it by 1.25:

$39,000 \div 1.25 = 31,200$, which is the original price of the SUV.

48. D)

Build an equation. Use m for muffins and c for cookies. The money earned for muffins is equal to the number of muffins times $1.50:

$1.5m$

The money earned for cookies is equal to the number of cookies divided by two times $1:

$\frac{c}{2}$

The total money earned is the sum:

$t = 1.5m + \frac{c}{2}$

Set the total equal to $29.50, and plug in the number of muffins to solve for c:

$29.5 = 1.5(11) + \frac{c}{2}$

$13 = \frac{c}{2}$

$c = 26$

49. A)

The number of people on Tuesday is 345. Every day, the number of people triples. On Wednesday, it becomes 3 × 345 = 1035.

On Thursday, the number of people who came to this convention became 3 × 1035 = 3105.

On Friday, the number of people who came to this convention became 3 × 3105 = 9315.

50. C)

Line up terms by their decimal points; add trailing zeros where appropriate:

```
  59.090
   5.007
 − 6.210
  47.873
```

51. D)

His new hourly salary would become $15.50 + $0.75 = $16.25

Percentage change $= \frac{Final\ Value - Original\ Value}{Original\ Value} \times 100$

$\frac{16.25 - 15.50}{15.50} \times 100$

$\frac{0.75}{15.50} \times 100 = 4.8\%$

52. B)

Find all the prime numbers that multiply to give the numbers.

For 2, prime factor is 2; for 3, prime factor is 3; for 4, prime factors are 2; for 5, prime factor is 5. Note the maximum times of occurrence of each prime, and multiply these to find the least common multiple.

The LCM is $2 \times 2 \times 3 \times 5 = 60$.

53. B)

Rearranging the given equation, we get:

$3|4n| = 26 - 2$

$3|4n| = 24$

$|4n| = 8$

$n = 2$ or

$4n = -8$

$n = -2$

54. D)

The given equation can be rewritten as:

$|2r + 1| - 10 = 13 \rightarrow |2r+1| = 23$

$+(2r+1) = 23 \rightarrow r = 11$

$-(2r+1) = 23 \rightarrow -2r - 1 = 23 \rightarrow -2r = 24 \rightarrow r = -12$

Therefore, $r = 11, -12$.

55. A)

Observing closely, note that for every number in the numerator, there is an equivalent denominator that cancels the numerator. Therefore, the net result of this multiplication comes out to be 1.

Answer Key – Reading

1.	A)	15.	B)	29.	A)	43.	B)
2.	D)	16.	A)	30.	A)	44.	D)
3.	C)	17.	A)	31.	B)	45.	C)
4.	A)	18.	A)	32.	A)	46.	A)
5.	C)	19.	D)	33.	C)	47.	D)
6.	A)	20.	C)	34.	B)	48.	B)
7.	A)	21.	D)	35.	C)	49.	A)
8.	B)	22.	C)	36.	A)	50.	B)
9.	D)	23.	C)	37.	B)	51.	C)
10.	C)	24.	A)	38.	C)	52.	D)
11.	A)	25.	D)	39.	C)	53.	B)
12.	C)	26.	B)	40.	A)	54.	A)
13.	A)	27.	C)	41.	C)	55.	B)
14.	B)	28.	B)	42.	A)		

Answer Key – Vocabulary

1.	A)	15.	D)	29.	D)	43.	B)
2.	C)	16.	A)	30.	C)	44.	C)
3.	B)	17.	D)	31.	B)	45.	A)
4.	D)	18.	A)	32.	B)	46.	C)
5.	A)	19.	A)	33.	B)	47.	C)
6.	C)	20.	A)	34.	B)	48.	A)
7.	A)	21.	B)	35.	C)	49.	C)
8.	C)	22.	B)	36.	A)	50.	A)
9.	D)	23.	D)	37.	A)	51.	A)
10.	C)	24.	D)	38.	C)	52.	D)
11.	B)	25.	A)	39.	C)	53.	D)
12.	A)	26.	A)	40.	A)	54.	B)
13.	A)	27.	C)	41.	C)	55.	B)
14.	B)	28.	A)	42.	A)		

1. C)

And is a conjunction, joining two things.

2. B)

To is the correct choice.

3. A)

Option A is a question but has no question mark.

4. A)

Yesterday implies past tense, so *started* is the correct verb choice.

5. D)

The implied subject is *you*, tense is present, so *call* is correct.

6. D)

Or, joining two parts of the sentence, is a conjunction.

7. C)

Present passive is the best choice here, so the correct choice is *delayed*.

8. B)

Subject and verb do not match.

9. B)

A is incorrect because you cannot attend a movie and do your homework at the same time. C and D both have verb errors.

10. D)

Toy, as a noun, is a person, place, or thing.

11. A)

The bell is carrying out the action *(ringing)*.

12. C)

Either has to go with *or*. Option D has a verb error.

13. A)

Table is a noun.

14. C)

Into is a preposition.

15. D)

Option A does not have a question mark; B has a verb error; and C uses the possessive *whose*.

16. D)

The first part of the sentence is a dependent clause; *they*, referring to the children, is the subject.

17. A)

She is the one who did everything and is therefore the subject.

18. B)

Do is correct because it's in the second person, present tense.

19. C)

Good, describing how the team played, must be replaced by an adverb, *well*.

20. B)

The appointment has already happened, so *had*, or the past tense, is correct. *Was* does not make sense in this context.

21. A)

Subject and verb agree.

22. C)

Kitchen is the direct object, or the thing being decorated.

23. A)

Shift is the direct object.

24. B)

I learned to write well working at the paper is the only correct option. A has an incorrect adjective, C has an incorrect verb, and D has an incorrect preposition.

25. D)

D is incorrect since *can* requires a verb, not *helpful*, an adjective.

26. C)

Because she wanted to see a play is the dependent clause: it starts with a subordinating conjunction (because) and cannot stand alone.

27. A)

Although we left the baseball game early is a dependent clause; therefore it can't stand on its own in a statement.

28. A)

B and C have verb errors, while D has a preposition error.

29. B)

The predicate is the verb, plus anything following.

30. D)

D is a sentence fragment because it's lacking a subject.

31. C)

The predicate is the verb, plus anything following.

32. A)

C and D use incorrect prepositions. B is technically correct; however, *on the news* implies something heard, rather than something read.

33. A)

A predicate adjective directly describes the subject of the sentence.

34. A)

A predicate adjective directly describes the subject of the sentence.

35. C)

The two girls are the subject of the clause; therefore, the pronoun must be third person plural.

36. B)

The subject and verb do not agree.

37. A)

Brought is the best substitute.

38. C)

Swam is the past tense of *swim*.

39. D)

Neither goes with *nor*, not *or*. The verb agrees with the subject or noun it's closest to.

40. D)

Am is correct. *Will* does not agree with the verb tense, and the others produce a double negative.

41. B)

The verb does not agree with the implied subject, *you*.

42. C)

Who has his own shop is a dependent clause.

43. B)

Are is the only verb that agrees with the subject *you*.

44. D)

Subject and verb disagree.

45. B)

To take to the school bake sale is a prepositional phrase.

46. B)

Only *check* can be paired with the word *on*.

47. C)

Of is the only correct response when paired with *scared*.

48. B)

Looking is the only choice that works with both *were* and *for*.

49. A)

For is correct. *Catch* would require the addition of *to*.

50. A)

Will work is correct, because it is in the future tense.

51. A)

Go agrees with the implied subject, *you*.

52. B)

A has a preposition error; C and D have verb errors.

53. D)

Subject and verb do not agree.

54. B)

At refers to time or place.

55. B)

The pronoun is the subject of the sentence, so it should be *I*, not *me*. Also, the subject is plural, so the verb should be *have*, not *has*.

Answer Key – Biology

1. A)	9. B)	17. B)	25. A)
2. B)	10. A)	18. B)	26. B)
3. D)	11. B)	19. A)	27. C)
4. B)	12. A)	20. B)	28. A)
5. B)	13. B)	21. D)	29. D)
6. A)	14. B)	22. B)	30. C)
7. A)	15. C)	23. B)	
8. D)	16. C)	24. B)	

Answer Key – Chemistry

1. B)	9. D)	17. C)	25. C)
2. B)	10. B)	18. C)	26. C)
3. A)	11. A)	19. D)	27. C)
4. B)	12. D)	20. C)	28. C)
5. D)	13. A)	21. C)	29. B)
6. C)	14. B)	22. D)	30. C)
7. C)	15. A)	23. A)	
8. B)	16. B)	24. C)	

Answer Key – Anatomy and Physiology

1. B)	9. C)	17. A)	25. A)
2. A)	10. A)	18. B)	26. B)
3. C)	11. B)	19. C)	27. B)
4. B)	12. C)	20. A)	28. B)
5. A)	13. A)	21. A)	29. A)
6. A)	14. C)	22. C)	30. B)
7. B)	15. B)	23. C)	
8. B)	16. A)	24. B)	

Answer Key – Physics

1.	B)	9.	C)	17.	B)	25.	B)
2.	A)	10.	C)	18.	C)	26.	C)
3.	A)	11.	D)	19.	A)	27.	D)
4.	B)	12.	C)	20.	C)	28.	D)
5.	B)	13.	C)	21.	A)	29.	B)
6.	C)	14.	C)	22.	D)	30.	B)
7.	C)	15.	D)	23.	C)		
8.	C)	16.	D)	24.	B)		

FREE DVD FREE FREE DVD

From Stress to Success DVD from Trivium Test Prep

Dear Customer,

Thank you for purchasing from Trivium Test Prep! Whether you're looking to join the military, get into college, or advance your career, we're honored to be a part of your journey.

To show our appreciation (and to help you relieve a little of that test-prep stress), we're offering a **FREE *From Stress to Success* DVD*** by Trivium Test Prep. Our DVD includes 35 test preparation strategies that will help keep you calm and collected before and during your big exam. All we ask is that you email us your feedback and describe your experience with our product. Amazing, awful, or just so-so: we want to hear what you have to say!

To receive your **FREE *From Stress to Success* DVD***, please email us at 5star@triviumtestprep. com. Include "Free 5 Star" in the subject line and the following information in your email:

1. The title of the product you purchased.

2. Your rating from 1 – 5 (with 5 being the best).

3. Your feedback about the product, including how our materials helped you meet your goals and ways in which we can improve our products.

4. Your full name and shipping address so we can send your **FREE *From Stress to Success* DVD***.

If you have any questions or concerns please feel free to contact us directly at 5star@triviumtestprep.com.

Thank you, and good luck with your studies!

* Please note that the free DVD is <u>not included</u> with this book. To receive the free DVD, please follow the instructions above.

EXCLUSIVE TEST TIPS

Here at Trivium Test Prep, we strive to offer you the exemplary test tools that help you pass your exam the first time. This book includes an overview of important concepts, example questions throughout the text, and practice test questions. But we know that learning how to successfully take a test can be just as important as learning the content being tested. In addition to excelling on the HESI A^2, we want to give you the solutions you need to be successful every time you take a test. Our study strategies, preparation pointers, and test tips will help you succeed as you take the HESI A^2 and any test in the future!

STUDY STRATEGIES

These are some of the best ways to get the most out of your studying! Whether you're studying with our guides or studying for a class in school with notes you took in class, these strategies will put you on the path to success.

1. Spread out your studying. By taking the time to study a little bit every day, you strengthen your understanding of the testing material, so it's easier to recall that information on the day of the test. Our study guides make this easy by breaking up the concepts into sections with example practice questions, so you can test your knowledge as you read.

2. Create a study calendar. The sections of our book make it easy to review and practice with example questions on a schedule. Decide to read a specific number of pages or complete a number of practice questions every day. Breaking up all of the information in this way can make studying less overwhelming and more manageable.

3.   Set measurable goals and motivational rewards. Follow your study calendar and reward yourself for completing reading, example questions, and practice problems and tests. You could take yourself out after a productive week of studying or watch a favorite show after reading a chapter. Treating yourself to rewards is a great way to stay motivated.

4.   Use your current knowledge to understand new, unfamiliar concepts. When you learn something new, think about how it relates to something you know really well. Making connections between new ideas and your existing understanding can simplify the learning process and make the new information easier to remember.

5.   Make learning interesting! If one aspect of a topic is interesting to you, it can make an entire concept easier to remember. Stay engaged and think about how concepts covered on the exam can affect the things you're interested in. The sidebars throughout the text offer additional information that could make ideas easier to recall.

6.   Find a study environment that works for you. For some people, absolute silence in a library results in the most effective study session, while others need the background noise of a coffee shop to fuel productive studying. There are many websites that generate white noise and recreate the sounds of different environments for studying. Figure out what distracts you and what engages you and plan accordingly.

7.   Take practice tests in an environment that reflects the exam setting. While it's important to be as comfortable as possible when you study, practicing taking the test exactly as you'll take it on test day will make you more prepared for the actual exam. If your test starts on a Saturday morning, take your practice test on a Saturday morning. If you have access, try to find an empty classroom that has desks like the desks at testing center. The more closely you can mimic the testing center, the more prepared you'll feel on test day.

8.   Study hard for the test in the days before the exam, but take it easy the night before and do something relaxing rather than studying and cramming. This will help decrease anxiety, allow you to get a better night's sleep, and be more mentally fresh during the big exam. Watch a light-hearted movie, read a favorite book, or take a walk, for example.

PREPARATION POINTERS

Studying isn't the only way to get ready for a test. Some of the biggest hurdles can be the prep work that you do before walking into the testing room. Feel cool, calm, and collected by preparing for your tests the right way.

1. Preparation is key! Don't wait until the day of your exam to gather your pencils, calculator, identification materials, or admission tickets. Check the requirements of the exam as soon as possible. Some tests require materials that may take more time to obtain, such as a passport-style photo, so be sure that you have plenty of time to collect everything. The night before the exam, lay out everything you'll need, so it's all ready to go on test day! We recommend at least two forms of ID, your admission ticket or confirmation, pencils, a high protein, compact snack, bottled water, and any necessary medications. Some testing centers will require you to put all of your supplies in a clear plastic bag. If you're prepared, you will be less stressed the morning of, and less likely to forget anything important.

2. If you're taking a pencil-and-paper exam, test your erasers on paper. Some erasers leave big, dark stains on paper instead of rubbing out pencil marks. Make sure your erasers work for you and the pencils you plan to use.

3. Make sure you give yourself your usual amount of sleep, preferably at least 7 – 8 hours. You may find you need even more sleep. Pay attention to how much you sleep in the days before the exam, and how many hours it takes for you to feel refreshed. This will allow you to be as sharp as possible during the test and make fewer simple mistakes.

4. Make sure to make transportation arrangements ahead of time, and have a backup plan in case your ride falls through. You don't want to be stressing about how you're going to get to the testing center the morning of the exam.

5. Many testing locations keep their air conditioners on high. You want to remember to bring a sweater or jacket in case the test center is too cold, as you never know how hot or cold the testing location could be. Remember, while you can always adjust for heat by removing layers.

TEST TIPS

You've made it to the testing room! It's almost time to put all of your hard work to the test, literally. Good luck!

1. Go with your gut when choosing an answer. Statistically, the answer that comes to mind first is often the right one. This is assuming you studied the material, of course, which we hope you have done if you've read through one of our books!

2. For true or false questions: if you genuinely don't know the answer, mark it true. In most tests, there are typically more true answers than false answers.

3. For multiple-choice questions, read ALL the answer choices before marking an answer, even if you think you know the answer when you come across it. You may find your original "right" answer isn't necessarily the best option.

4. Look for key words: in multiple choice exams, particularly those that require you to read through a text, the questions typically contain key words. These key words can help the test taker choose the correct answer or confuse you if you don't recognize them. Common keywords are: *most, during, after, initially,* and *first.* Be sure you identify them before you read the available answers. Identifying the key words makes a huge difference in your chances of passing the test.

5. Narrow answers down by using the process of elimination: after you understand the question, read each answer. If you don't know the answer right away, use the process of elimination to narrow down the answer choices. It is easy to identify at least one answer that isn't correct. Continue to narrow down the choices before choosing the answer you believe best fits the question. By following this process, you increase your chances of selecting the correct answer.

6. Don't worry if others finish before or after you. Go at your own pace, and focus on the test in front of you.

7. Finally, Relax. With our help, we know you'll be ready to conquer the HESI A^2. You've studied and worked hard!

Keep in mind that every individual takes tests differently, so strategies that might work for you may not work for someone else. You know yourself best and are the best person to determine which of these tips and strategies will benefit your studying and test taking. Best of luck as you study, test, and work toward your future!

Made in the USA
Middletown, DE
12 February 2020